89 398

Art in Action

Credits

Cover Photo: Lee L. Waldman.

Illustrations: 30, 31, Sylver Kinsella.

Publisher's Photos: All photos by Rodney Jones Studios except as credited below. Key: (t) top, (c) center, (b) bottom, (l) left, (r) right.

UNIT 1: Page 12, Kenneth C. Poertner; 14, Camerique Stock Photography; 24(l), Joseph A. DiChello, Jr.; 24(r), Daniel D'Agostini; 39(t), Zoological Society of San Diego.

UNIT 2: Page 42, Robert E. Mates; 46, Peter Balestrero; 48, CIDEM—City of Montréal; 53(l), 53(r), Four By Five, Inc.; 55(l), Imagery; 62, Geoffrey Clements; 67(r), Summer Productions/Taurus Photos; 69(r), DRK Photo.

UNIT 3: Page 113(l), Four By Five, Inc. N.Y.; 114, Rick Stewart/Focus West.

UNIT 4: Page 129(r), Alec Duncan; 142, Scala/Art Resource, NY; 146, Lee Boltin; 147(l), Scala/Art Resource, NY; 150, 151(r), Michael Cavanagh, Kevin Montague; 154, TASS from Sovfoto; 155(l), Walt Disney Productions; 156(t), 156(b), Rob Wellington Quigley, AIA, Architect; 157(t), 157(c), Robert A.M. Stern, Architect; 157(b), RNP Architecture & Planning, Photo by Myles E. Baker; 158(t), 158(b), Rob Wellington Quigley, AIA, Architect; 159, David G. Krauss, Inc.

UNIT 5: Page 160, David G. Krauss, Inc.; 164(l), Michael Cavanagh, Kevin Montague; 168(l), NASA; 169(r), 170(tl), 170(tr), 170(b), Lee Boltin; 176(t), Bruce Hazelton/Focus West; 178(l), 178(r), Myles E. Baker; 186(t), Michael Cavanagh, Kevin Montague; 186(b), Robert Wallace.

UNIT 6: Page 192(l), Lee Boltin; 194(l), 194(r), W.H. Muller/Peter Arnold, Inc.; 195(l), Julius Shulman; 212(l), 212(r), 215(t), Lee Boltin.

Coronado Staff

Program Development and
  Project Editor: Alba Mingst
  Assistant Editors: DeLynn Decker, Patricia McCambridge

Project Designer: Janis Heppell
  Assistant Designer: Lisa Peters
  Photo Research: Debra Saleny

Art in Action

Guy Hubbard
Indiana University

CORONADO PUBLISHERS
San Diego Orlando Dallas Chicago

ACKNOWLEDGMENTS

For permission to reprint copyrighted material, grateful acknowledgment is made to the following:

W. S. BENSON & COMPANY, INC.: Epigraph by Mort Baranoff from *The Creative Eye, Volume I* by Kelly Fearing, Evelyn Beard, and Clyde Inez Martin, copyright © 1969, 1979 by W . S. Benson and Company.

LITTLE, BROWN AND COMPANY: Epigraph by Nelly Munthe from *Meet Matisse* by Nelly Munthe, copyright © 1983 by Nelly Munthe.

XEROX EDUCATION PUBLICATIONS: "Foul Shot" by Edwin A. Hoey from *Read* magazine, copyright © 1962 by Xerox Corporation.

Printed in the United States of America   ISBN 0-15-770040-2(7)

8901 062 987654

Table of Contents

Unit III   Composing with Colors   93

Unit IV   Sculpting and Forming   127

Unit V Working with Ceramics, Crafts, and Textiles 161

Unit VI Expressing Feelings and Imagination 189

How to Use This Book

To the Students

As you open this book, you will step into the world of art. Some of the finest artworks from all over the world have been reproduced within these pages. Art pieces by students like yourself are also included. Although art exists all around us, the following lessons offer an opportunity for you to discover, explore, and experience a variety of art forms that you may never have encountered before.

Even if you do not consider yourself an artist, or have no intention of pursuing the study of art in your future career, a knowledge of art forms and skills will broaden your experience, deepen your appreciation of the visual arts, and help you to develop skills that you can put to use in other areas of study. By experiencing various art activities, you will exercise your powers of observation, your problem-solving skills, and your creative imagination. As an added bonus, you will experience the delight of expressing yourself in ways that can be enjoyed by yourself and others. Perhaps most important of all, studying and creating artworks will enable you, as author Leo Tolstoy once remarked, to partake in "a human activity having for its purpose the transmission to others of the highest and best feelings to which men have risen."

This book is divided into six units which organize art learning into categories such as design, drawing, painting, and sculpture. The sixth unit is different from the others in that it allows you a choice of techniques and materials for creating your artwork. These final lessons concentrate on creative expression and the use of your imagination through art. You are encouraged to be creative while doing the art lessons in other units, of course, but Units I through V concentrate on developing your skills and knowledge about art. The lessons in Unit VI, on the other hand, give you an opportunity to think more creatively, use your imagination, make more choices, and express your feelings in your artwork.

The format for following the lessons in this book is based on choices. There are several ways of selecting art lessons to complete. The most obvious method relies on the way the lessons are organized. Each lesson includes a lesson number and title, followed by a brief introduction entitled *Observing and Thinking Creatively.* Essential information which you will need to know in order to complete the lesson is included in the introduction. This section provides background information, defines art terms, describes what you are to do, offers suggestions and ideas, and encourages you to use your own observations, creativity, and imagination to complete the lesson.

Following the introduction are selections of artworks by famous, experienced artists as well as art by students from different parts of the United States and throughout the world. These reproductions offer you visual examples and models that show how various artists work. Observing the artwork produced by other people can help you in improving your own. Spend some time studying these pictures, observing how the artists have used lines, shapes. colors, textures, and so on to produce effective designs. Also read the captions that appear next to well-known artworks. They provide basic information about media and techniques, as well as details about the artist or art piece.

The *Instructions for Creating Art* appear toward the end of each lesson. They clearly explain each step for completing the art activity. The suggested *Art Materials* you are to use are identified in a box following the instructions.

Art Strands

As you look through the book, you will discover that the lessons include diagrams, called *strands*. Each strand is a group of related lessons organized around a particular kind of art learning. The strands offer alternative selections for choosing which art lessons to do, depending upon your personal preferences and the art program your teacher decides to offer. There are two different kinds of strands included in this book, which are explained on the following page.

Unit Strands

Each of the six units includes two or three different strands. These strands organize related lessons within each unit in a sequential order. Instead of completing every lesson in the book, you will choose only those lessons in the unit strand that interest you most. Your teacher, however, may request that you do certain lessons and not others. The following step-by-step instructions and diagram for Strand E explain how to follow unit strands.

Strand E: Drawing Methods and Media

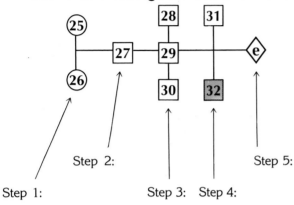

Step 1:   Step 2:   Step 3:   Step 4:   Step 5:

Step 1: In this strand, you must begin at Step 1 by completing either Lesson 25 *or* 26.

Step 2: At Step 2, you must complete Lesson 27 since this is the only lesson offered.

Step 3: Now you will choose Lesson 28, 29, *or* 30 to complete, but you will not do all three of them.

Step 4: Next, you will choose either Lesson 31 or 32.

Step 5: At the end of each strand, a diamond shape with an *e* inside signifies *evaluation* of your artwork. At this step, you should review the lessons you have completed in connection with the **Learning Outcomes** listed at the back of this book. (See the explanation of **Learning Outcomes** that follows for further directions on how to use them.)

Learning Outcomes

The **Learning Outcomes** for each lesson are listed in a section of that title at the back of the book. They are to be used to determine whether or not you have met the objectives for each lesson and to evaluate your work. The **Learning Outcomes** are divided into three categories: *Understanding Art*, *Creating Art*, and *Appreciating Art*. The items listed for *Understanding Art* require you to explain and define specific art terms, materials, techniques, and basic information about art presented in each lesson. For *Creating Art*, you are to

consider how you actually produced your artwork and whether you used the art materials and tools effectively. For example, if you were asked to make a drawing using contour lines, does your artwork reflect this objective? The category of *Appreciating Art* focuses on making judgments about your own artwork as well as that of other artists. You are to respond to art by deciding whether or not the art is effective, what you like or dislike about it, what qualities make it effective, and what you think an artist is expressing in a particular piece of art. In other words, you are to express your personal preferences and judgments about art and give your reasons for them.

You should refer to the **Learning Outcomes** both before and after you complete each lesson. In this way, you will know what is expected of you and whether you have met the objectives for each lesson. When you complete a strand, the diamond shape with an *e* inside (◇) signifies *evaluation*. At this point, your teacher may direct you to complete a formal evaluation of your work based on the **Learning Outcomes**. You may be asked to review the lessons you have completed for a particular strand in connection with the **Learning Outcomes**. Or you may be asked to select for evaluation one or more examples of your artwork and evaluate them either orally with your teacher or in written form. Use the directions and questions in the **Learning Outcomes** to complete your evaluation.

The How to Do It Section

This section appears at the back of the book. It includes specific directions for how to do certain activities referred to in the lessons, such as mixing colors, preparing clay, or making papier-mâché. The art skills explained in this section are shown in italics and marked with an asterisk in each lesson.

The Glossary

As you read the information in the lessons, you will be introduced to new art terms. These words are identified in heavy type and are defined in the **Glossary** at the end of this book. They are also defined in the text the first time they are used. You may be asked to define these terms in the **Learning Outcomes** and when your work is evaluated.

Artists' Reference

This section precedes the **Index** and lists all the well-known artists and their works that appear throughout the book.

Color Reference

Many lessons in *Art in Action* require the use of color. Basic information about color is presented here so that you may refer to it at different times as you proceed through the book. (See Lesson 41 for further information on **analogous** and **complementary colors**.)

Characteristics of color

Hue: another word for color, identified by a common name, such as green, red, or yellow-orange.

Value: the lightness or darkness of a color. Adding black, white, or gray to a hue changes its color value. Darker colors are said to be lower in value than brighter colors. The addition of black to a color produces a **shade**. White added to a hue produces a **tint**. A **tone** is made when gray is added to a color.

Intensity: the brightness or purity of a color. A pure hue is in its brightest form and is most intense. The addition of a **complementary** color (a hue that is opposite another hue on the color wheel) dulls a color's intensity.

Classifying colors

Primary colors: red, yellow, and blue. These colors cannot be produced by combining other hues. (See the colors in the center triangle in the color wheel.)

Secondary colors: orange, green, and violet. These hues are produced by mixing two primary colors. (See the colors between the circle and the triangle in the color wheel.)

Intermediate colors: red-orange, yellow-orange, yellow-green, blue-green, blue-violet, and red-violet. As each name indicates, an intermediate color is produced by combining a primary and a secondary color. (See the colors between the primary and secondary hues on the outer circle of the color wheel.)

COLOR WHEEL

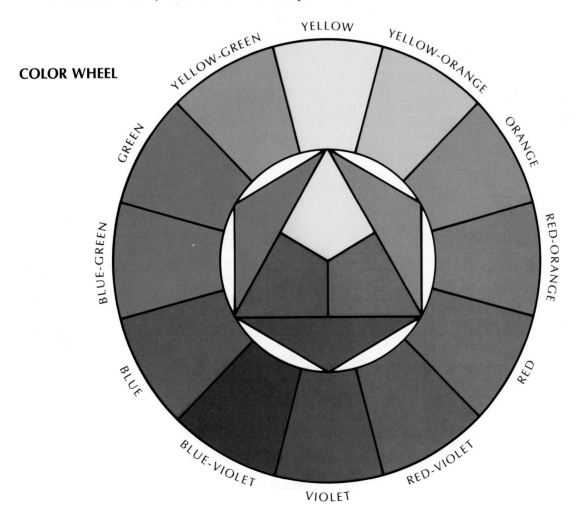

les bêtes de la mer...
H. matisse 50

Beasts of the Sea; *Henri Matisse; National Gallery of Art, Washington; Ailsa Mellon Bruce Fund 1973; Date: (19)50; Paper on canvas; 2.955 × 1.540 (116⅜ × 60⅝ in.)*

Unit I

Exploring Creative Design

An avalanche of colors has no strength. It is only when they are organized that they can express the emotion of the artist.

Henri Matisse

Art is all around us—in a bridge spanning a rushing river, in barren trees weaving designs against the horizon, in a golden dandelion bursting from a crack in the sidewalk. Artists are sensitive observers of their world. They study fascinating designs in their environment. They observe shapes, colors, and textures, and then express what they see in the visual language of art.

The lessons in this unit and throughout this book will introduce you to the basic **elements of design—line, shape, space, form, texture, color,** and **value.** As you observe your environment, you will discover these elements in nature and in man-made forms. In this unit, you will learn to incorporate these elements in your designs.

In addition to these visual elements, there are also **principles of design** that will guide you in arranging and composing your designs effectively. These principles include ways of bringing **balance, variety, rhythm** or **movement, emphasis, proportion,** and **unity** to your artwork.

Throughout this unit, as you explore different ways of using the elements and principles of design, you will discover that, to be creative, you must bring your own ideas and imagination to your work. In this way, each design will become your special creation —representing and expressing what you like, how you feel, and who you are.

As you work through the following unit, you may choose to complete each lesson in order. Or you can select those lessons that are most interesting to you by following the art strand at the end of each lesson. Further instructions for using the strands appear at the beginning of this book.

1 Collage from Unusual Materials

Observing and Thinking Creatively

Have you ever thrown things away that you thought you might use for something, but you didn't know what? Every day we throw many things away—food wrappers, worn-out clothing, newspapers, old letters, and school papers. Yet, some artists use materials like these in their art. A work of art that is created from various materials glued to a surface is called a **collage**. Instead of using a single art **medium** or material such as paint, charcoal, or clay, this type of art combines different materials to create a **design**. Simple shapes and forms are arranged to express a mood, feeling, or subject the artist has in mind. It is the combination of materials and the arrangement of shapes, colors, and **textures** that produce a pleasing collage.

Collages were made in France over 60 years ago by the famous artists Pablo Picasso and Georges Braque. They created their collages from pieces of newspaper, package labels, theater tickets, old envelopes, and pieces of torn cloth. A collage by Pablo Picasso is shown below. Today, artists use these same materials along with many new ones, like plastic, aluminum foil, wood, metal, and new kinds of paper.

In this lesson, you will experiment with different art materials by arranging colors, shapes, textures, and spaces to create a collage. When all parts of your artwork reflect what you have learned about arranging , you will have achieved **unity** of design.

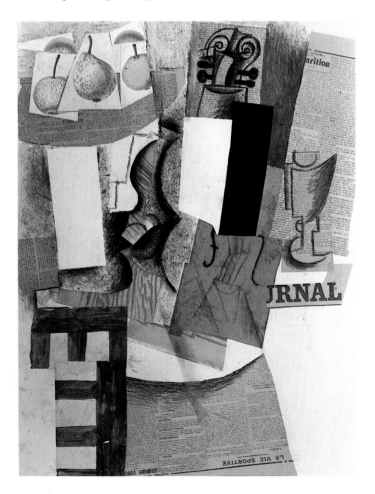

Cubist artists divide images of objects into shapes which are arranged so that your eyes move around the composition. They often use a variety of materials, such as pieces of fabric, metal, foil, and paper glued to the picture surface. Can you tell what kinds of materials Pablo Picasso used to create *The Violin?*

Pablo Ruiz Picasso. The Violin and Compote of Fruit. *1913. Pasted paper, charcoal and gouache on paperboard. H. 25⅜" W. 19½". Philadelphia Museum of Art: The A.E. Gallatin Collection.*

Children's Saturday Art Class. Indiana University, Indiana

Instructions for Creating Art

1. Collect some flat materials from around your home, neighborhood, or school. Select materials having different colors and textures. Study the art materials list below for ideas about things to collect. You may get additional ideas from the pictures in this lesson.

2. Pick out a few interesting things from your collection that look good together. Cut or *tear** the things you have chosen into a variety of shapes and sizes. Arrange them into a design. Experiment by overlapping some shapes and moving others around to create a **balanced** arrangement. Use the empty spaces in the background as part of your design.

   As you arrange your materials, decide which part of the design you want to emphasize; this part will function as a **center of interest** and focus attention on your design. You can create a center of interest by adding a splash of color, unusual shapes, or more intricate lines and details.

   It is important to tie in other areas of a design with the center of interest so that the eye moves from one part to another. Colors can be repeated, shapes can relate, and textures can add interest. Even the unused space is important. The arrangement of colors, shapes, textures, and spaces should work together to produce a **unified** design.

3. When your arrangement looks unified, glue*

the pieces in place. Write your name and the title of the piece at the bottom of the finished collage. The title should reflect the idea or message you want to convey.

For an explanation, turn to the How to Do It section at the back of this book.

Art Materials

A collection of flat materials such as foil, plastic wrap, labels from cans, corrugated paper, tissue, plastic foam food trays, buttons, scraps of cloth, etc. Sheet of thick paper or cardboard 12″ × 18″ or bigger	Rubber cement or strong glue Scissors Pencil and eraser Newspaper (to cover work area)

Strand A: The Art of Designing

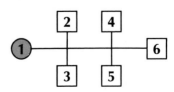

To evaluate your artwork, turn to the Learning Outcomes section at the back of this book.

2 Artistic Messages from Music

Observing and Thinking Creatively

Colors add brilliance to our world. They also suggest certain moods or feelings. How does the color blue make you feel? Think of one or two words that describe this feeling. What image or object comes to mind when you think of blue? Now think about the color red. What mood, feeling, or emotion does this color express for you? What image do you see?

Blue is the color of night, shadows, water, and sky. It is a color that can make you feel cool, peaceful, and sometimes sad. Bright yellows and reds will make you think of very different things, such as fast racing cars speeding around a track. Red, purple, and orange are colors for fire, war, and anger, but they can also be the colors of sunsets and leaves in the fall.

Patterns and textures also suggest special effects in art. **Patterns** are created by the arrangement and **repetition** of shapes or forms. **Texture** refers to the way a surface looks and feels—rough, smooth, soft, or bumpy.

Artists use colors, patterns, and textures to express feelings in their work. Observe the pictures in this lesson. Note how each artist has created a design that represents a feeling, message, or mood.

Music also conveys messages and feelings. In this lesson, you will discover how to use colors, patterns, and textures to express the **rhythm** and **movement** you hear in a musical selection.

Henri Matisse is famous for his use of very bright colors and simplified forms. Overlapping shapes in *Mimosa* give this picture a feeling of depth and movement. Matisse often cut paper into abstract forms which he arranged to create unique designs.

Mimosa, Henri Matisse. McDougal, Littell & Company (Illinois).

8

Azalea Middle School. St. Petersburg, Florida

Instructions for Creating Art

1. Choose a piece of music you like, or respond to a musical selection your teacher may play. It can be any kind of music—jazz, country, rock, classical, or a theme tune from a movie. Listen to the rhythm and mood of the music.

2. Collect pieces of paper with different colors, patterns, and textures, such as pieces of foil, newspaper, magazines, wallpaper, or product wrappers. Select colors that reflect the rhythm and mood of your music. For example, you might use bright, bold colors to express jazz or rock, soft colors for mellow tunes, and dark, somber shades for sad songs.

3. As you listen to the music, make a picture out of pieces of colored paper *glued** to a large sheet of paper. Try to capture the rhythm and movement of the music as you create. The picture may show real objects, or the shapes can be **abstract.** Cut or tear the paper into a variety of sizes and shapes. You can show rhythm and movement by forming shapes with curves, slants, spirals, diagonals, zigzags, or by repeating some shapes to create **repetition** of patterns. You can also use these same techniques to express feelings and moods in your artwork. Experiment by arranging the shapes in different ways. You can fill all the space on your paper, or you can leave spaces

where the background shows through. Some pieces can be placed side by side, while others might overlap. This kind of picture-making is called a **collage.**

4. When you have created a **unified** design in which the colors, patterns, and textures express the rhythm and mood of the music, glue the pieces in place.

*For an explanation, turn to the How to Do It *section at the back of this book.*

Art Materials

Colored paper from magazines, wallpaper, wrapping paper, tissue paper, etc.	Rubber cement, glue, or paste
Scissors	Sheets of heavy paper 12″ × 18″ or bigger

Strand A: The Art of Designing

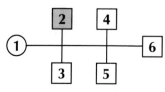

To evaluate your artwork, turn to the Learning Outcomes *section at the back of this book.*

9

3 The Glow of Tissue Paper

Observing and Thinking Creatively

Artists often work like scientists—they experiment with their materials to discover certain effects. They sometimes practice for a long time to learn how to use a particular art material, or **medium**, such as paints or clay. In this lesson, you will experiment with the medium of colored tissue paper.

Tissue paper comes in many bright colors. It is **transparent**, so that it glows when light shines through it. You can use tissue paper in many different ways to achieve unusual and striking effects. You can actually "paint" with tissue paper by brushing white glue mixed with water over it. If you gently tear and overlap different colors of tissue paper, the colors will blend or bleed together to produce new shades of color. If you crumple or wrinkle tissue paper before gluing it down, it will add a different surface **texture** to your art. Another effect can be created by overlapping several layers of tissue paper on top of each other. Some artists like to add outlines and details using black pen or ink on top of the tissue paper. These dark lines add interest and **contrast** to the artwork. Contrast can also be achieved by placing light colors of tissue paper beside dark-colored construction paper.

In this lesson, you will discover how to use a variety of colors and textures to make a design.

Holy Ghost School. Rochester, New York

Children's Saturday Art Class. Indiana University, Indiana

Holy Ghost School. Rochester, New York

Instructions for Creating Art

1. Fill a sheet of white paper with a **collage** showing a view of a city or the countryside. Experiment by "painting" over various colors and shapes of tissue paper with a mixture of *water and white glue.** Try overlapping pieces of tissue in different ways or crumpling them to achieve different textures. Avoid getting the paper so wet that it tears.

2. Try adding darker pieces of tissue paper or construction paper to parts of your design to create a strong contrast with the bright tissue paper. Stop occasionally as you work and check to see if your design includes a variety of shapes and colors. Repeating certain colors will help to **unify** your design. When the glue is dry, you can add interesting patterns and details by drawing on the collage with black waterproof ink.

3. The pictures in this lesson may give you some ideas, but be sure to use your own creativity to make your picture original. If you like, display your finished piece on a wall or window where all can enjoy the glow of tissue paper in your artwork.

For an explanation, turn to the How to Do It section at the back of this book.

Art Materials

White drawing paper	Dark-colored construction paper
Colored tissue paper	
White glue (mixed with water)	Black waterproof ink and pen
Glue brush	Newspapers (to cover work area)

Strand A: The Art of Designing

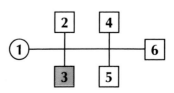

To evaluate your artwork, turn to the Learning Outcomes section at the back of this book.

4 *Stained Glass Windows*

Observing and Thinking Creatively

Do you know that sunlight is made up of many different colors? We see this when sunlight passes through droplets of water in the air, producing a rainbow. Sunlight also makes colors appear brighter. Perhaps you have noticed how the rays of the sun shining through trees make the leaves gleam with color. Or you may have admired the way a **stained glass** window glows when sunlight passes through it. Stained glass windows, such as the one pictured below, are made with pieces of colored glass. They have been used to create beautiful lighting effects in many churches and cathedrals throughout Europe and America.

Artists observe how sunlight affects colors, and they use these observations in their artwork. They also experiment with colors using different art materials or **media**. In this lesson, you will experiment with light and color by making a stained glass window using cardboard and colored cellophane or tissue paper.

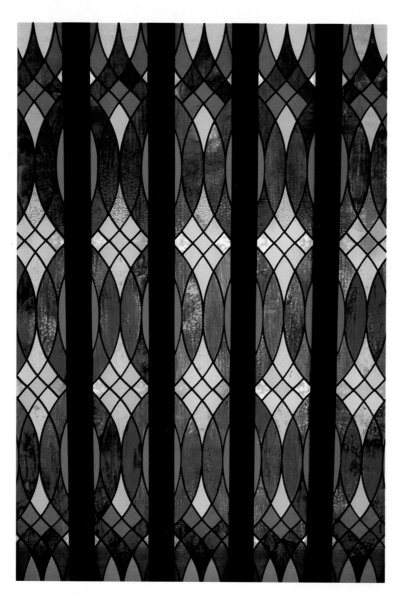

Maple Dale School. Milwaukee, Wisconsin

Maple Dale School. Milwaukee, Wisconsin

Instructions for Creating Art

1. Think about some of the interesting windows you have seen. Observe the examples in this lesson. Make a preliminary sketch of a window shape on a fairly small piece of paper.

2. Draw a design or picture for the inside of your window, showing a variety of shapes and colors. Limit your choice of colors to no more than five, and repeat them to unify your design. Outline each shape with thick, dark lines, using crayons, pastels, or colored markers. Then color the inside shapes. This will be your model.

3. Using your model as a guide, draw the lines of your window onto a large piece of thin black cardboard or construction paper. Using pointed scissors, carefully cut out the spaces that will be colored, leaving an outline of black construction paper around each shape. Also leave a border around the edges of your window. Cut pieces of cellophane or tissue paper to fit the cut-out spaces of your window design. **Balance** your bright and dark colors.

4. Looking at your colored drawing, *glue** or tape the colored cellophane or tissue paper onto the back of your cardboard window.

5. When your stained glass design is finished, put it up against a classroom window to see how it looks. Does the arrangement of shapes and colors produce a balanced design?

*For an explanation, turn to the How to Do It section at the back of this book.

*For an explanation, turn to the How to Do It section at the back of this book.

Art Materials

Drawing paper	Pencil and eraser
Your choice: crayons, colored markers, or oil pastels	Pointed scissors
	Cardboard or newspaper padding
Black construction paper or cardboard	Glue or tape
Colored cellophane or tissue paper	

Strand A: The Art of Designing

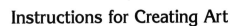

To evaluate your artwork, turn to the Learning Outcomes section at the back of this book.

To evaluate your artwork, turn to the Learning Outcomes section at the back of this book.

13

5 Shadow Pictures

Observing and Thinking Creatively

Have you ever watched someone's shadow? Have you noticed how the shadow changes as a person moves into different positions? Your shadow is an image of your shape. It shows the outlines of your body, but does not show details.

The ancient Greeks used to give plays using shadows. The actors performed in front of a strong light so their shadows fell on a white wall or curtain. The audience could see only the shadows of the actors, although they would also hear their voices. These dramas were called *shadow plays*.

Artists sometimes make shadow images in their art with **silhouettes**. A silhouette is an outline of a solid shape. Like a shadow, it is usually done in solid black, with no details showing inside. The important part of a silhouette is the exact outline shape—not the details. Perhaps you have seen a silhouette of someone's face in which just the side view, or **profile**, of the face was drawn and then cut from black paper.

In this lesson, you will make a picture using solid black shapes, or silhouettes. The most important part of your picture will be the **composition**, or arrangement of shapes in the most pleasing positions. The outlines of your shapes will also be important, because they give the only clues to what the shapes represent. You will not draw details inside the shapes. They will be solid black, like shadows.

San Diego High School. San Diego, California

San Diego High School. San Diego, California

Instructions for Creating Art

1. Think of an interesting design or picture for a silhouette. Most silhouettes are done with black on white; these colors create a dramatic **contrast** and make the shapes stand out sharply. Begin by lightly sketching the outline shapes with white chalk on the dark paper.

2. Carefully cut out the silhouette shapes so that they can be easily recognized. Arrange them on your background paper until you have achieved a balance of light and dark areas. Use the empty spaces in the background as an essential part of the design.

3. When you have arranged your silhouette shapes as you want them, glue them onto the background paper. Apply the glue very sparingly near the edges of the cut shapes, press them firmly in place, and carefully wipe away any excess glue.

Art Materials

Pencil and eraser, or white chalk	Glue
	Scissors
Dark paper (for silhouette)	Newspaper (to protect work area)
Drawing paper or light-colored paper (for background)	Water, paper towels

Strand A: The Art of Designing

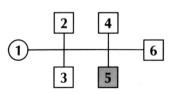

To evaluate your artwork, turn to the Learning Outcomes section at the back of this book.

15

6 *Art from Nature*

Observing and Thinking Creatively

Have you ever walked on the beach and picked up interesting pebbles or seashells left by the waves? Perhaps you have found interesting seed pods or pinecones on a hike in the woods. Nature is full of fascinating objects. Like scientists, artists observe, study, and collect objects from nature to use in their artwork. Some artists draw, paint, or take photographs of objects from nature. Others use the objects as part of their pictures or designs. In this lesson, you will make a **collage** using objects from nature.

Part of the fun of this lesson is gathering and collecting natural objects. Take some time to walk through areas where you live and collect objects like nuts, cones, seed pods, pieces of bark, leaves, pebbles, feathers, etc. Closely observe the shape, color, and texture of these objects and learn all you can about them. Then experiment by arranging them in different ways to make a collage.

South African Student

16

Standley Junior High School. San Diego, California

San Diego High School. San Diego, California

Instructions for Creating Art

1. Make a collection of objects that are natural and not man-made. You can also collect parts of natural objects that look interesting. Take care not to damage or destroy anything that is alive and growing.

2. Arrange some of the things from your collection to make a design or picture of an animal or plant. Use a piece of cardboard or plywood as a sturdy background. Your picture should fill most of the background area. Some of the pieces will lie flat, and some will stick out. Experiment to discover the most interesting way of arranging your collection.

3. When you have achieved a pleasing arrangement, *glue** the pieces down firmly. Your original picture will be a **collage** made up of objects from nature.

For an explanation, turn to the How to Do It section at the back of this book.

Art Materials

A collection of small natural objects: nuts, cones, seed pods, pieces of bark, leaves, dried flowers, pebbles, feathers, shells, seaweed, fossils, driftwood, etc.

Glue

Sheet of cardboard (12″ × 18″ or larger)

Scissors

Newspaper (to cover work area)

Water, paper towels

Strand A: The Art of Designing

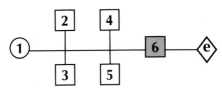

To evaluate your artwork, turn to the Learning Outcomes *section at the back of this book.*

7 Printing with Natural Objects

Observing and Thinking Creatively

Have you ever walked along the beach and left your footprints in the sand? Perhaps you have seen the prints an animal left behind in the ground. Prints often form patterns and designs that are fascinating to observe.

Nature is full of objects with interesting shapes and **textures** that can be used to make prints. A corncob, for example, can be used as a roller to make a long, textured print. Other natural objects like leaves, weeds, bark, nuts, and pinecones can also make delicate, beautiful prints.

In this lesson, you will rediscover the shapes and textures of natural objects by using them to create a nature print design.

Montgomery Junior High School. San Diego, California

Montgomery Junior High School. San Diego, California

Lewis Junior High School. San Diego, California

Instructions for Creating Art

1. Look around the area where you live, and see what natural objects you can find. Collect a variety of objects from nature, choosing ones with different shapes and textures.

2. Brush some thick paint onto one of your objects and press it onto white paper. If the print is smeared and runny, use less paint. If it is faint and dry, use more. Select several colors that look good together. Experiment by using different parts of your objects to make prints. Try overlapping and repeating some shapes to create interesting patterns and textures and **unify** your design.

3. Select the practice prints that you like, and combine them to make a new design. Print your final design on another sheet of paper.

Art Materials

Objects found in nature: leaves, pinecones, seashells, tree bark, feathers, etc.

Tempera paint and brushes

White paper

Mixing tray

Pencil and eraser

Newspapers (as a pad to print on)

Water, paper towels

Strand B: Printmaking

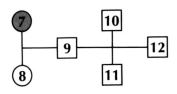

To evaluate your artwork, turn to the Learning Outcomes section at the back of this book.

19

8 Printing with Man-made Objects

Observing and Thinking Creatively

One of the greatest inventions of all time happened when people learned to make prints, or copies, of things. **Printing** was first done in China about fifteen hundred years ago. Up until about five hundred years ago, an entire page of a book had to be cut out of a single piece of wood in order for the page to be printed. Then, in 1456, a new process was developed using individual letters that could be clamped together and printed. The same letters could be rearranged on the printing press and used for other pages. Using this process, many more books could be printed, and learning flourished. Printmakers also developed methods for printing original pictures. In addition to books, what are some other things that are printed today?

The best way to learn about printmaking is to make prints of your own. Prints can be made from almost anything that is fairly flat on one side. Artists have used erasers, blocks of wood, nuts and bolts, bottlecaps, paper clips, and bottles to make prints.

In this lesson, you will explore printmaking with man-made objects found around your home, school, or community.

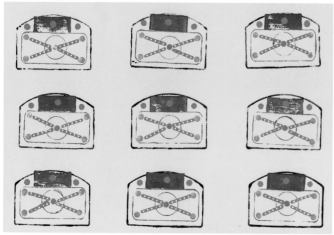

Montgomery Junior High School. San Diego, California

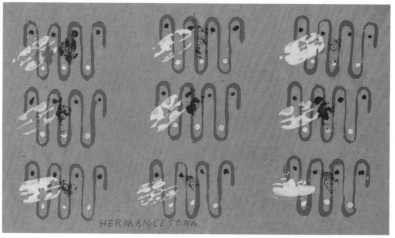

Montgomery Junior High School. San Diego, California

Instructions for Creating Art

1. Collect objects that have different shapes and at least one fairly flat side. Choose things that have been made in factories or workshops.

2. Practice making clear prints with the things you have collected. First, apply paint to the surface of an object and press the object firmly on a piece of paper. A good print has a solid, even color. If it is watery and splotchy, you have put too much paint on your object. If the print looks dry and faint, you need more paint on your object. A smooth pad of newspaper under your printing paper may help you get better prints. Experiment by printing with your objects in different ways.

3. Make a design using your favorite printing objects. Repeat the prints throughout the design. When you repeat lines, shapes, and colors to form patterns, you are using the principle of **repetition.**

Art Materials

A collection of small printing objects: paper clips, erasers, fabric, lids, jewelry, etc.

Water soluble printing ink or tempera paint

Brushes

White paper

Newspaper

Water, paper towels

Strand B: Printmaking

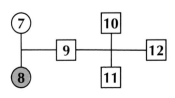

To evaluate your artwork, turn to the Learning Outcomes *section at the back of this book.*

21

9 *One-Time Printmaking*

Observing and Thinking Creatively

Do you realize that most things you read—newspapers, magazines, books, even pictures—are printed in thousands of copies? One way of printing is very different from all others in that it makes only one single print, or **monoprint**. It is somewhat like making a print from a drawing.

One-time printing is easy and quick to do. After one print has been made, the artist must draw a new design or picture to make another print. This method allows artists to test out new ideas by making many original prints. Then they may select the best ones to keep.

In this lesson, you will experiment by making one-time prints from your own designs. This method of printmaking will provide an opportunity for you to use lines, shapes, and textures in new, interesting ways.

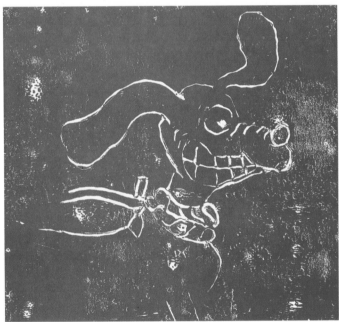

Tuba City Jr. High School. Tuba City, Arizona

Children's Saturday Art Class. Indiana University, Indiana

Steps in making a monoprint:
1) spread ink with brayer; 2) scratch design into ink; 3) press paper onto design, then gently peel away.

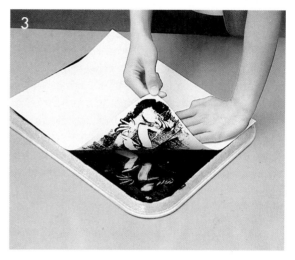

Instructions for Creating Art

1. Spread an even layer of tempera paint or printer's ink on a flat surface, such as a sheet of glass, a plastic or metal tray, or shiny pages from a magazine. Spread the ink out with a brush, or use a **brayer**,* or printer's roller. Make sure the layer of ink is thin and smooth.

2. Now scratch a design or picture into the wet color, using your fingers, scissors, a stick, or anything else that will remove the paint or ink. Show rhythm in your design by using free-flowing curves and swirls. Experiment with different tools to create a variety of lines, shapes, and **textures**.

3. Place a piece of thin white paper on top of the drawing. Gently rub the paper with the flat of your hand, and then carefully peel away the paper. Pin your **monoprint** to the wall to dry. Make several prints, and then choose your best one. Explain why it is your favorite.

*For an explanation, turn to the How to Do It section at the back of this book.

Art Materials

Printing ink (water-based) or tempera paint

Flat, nonabsorbent surface—glass, a plastic or metal tray, or shiny mag-azine paper

Brush or brayer

Scissors, sticks, etc., for drawing in the ink

Newspapers to cover work area

White paper

Water, paper towels

Strand B: Printmaking

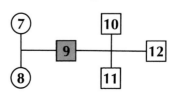

To evaluate your artwork, turn to the Learning Outcomes section at the back of this book.

10 Relief Prints and Patterns

Observing and Thinking Creatively

Designs exist all around you, both in nature and in the man-made environment. Some designs consist of repeated lines, shapes, and colors that combine to make **patterns**. Designs and patterns can be seen in the intricate lines of a spider's web, the trail left by an insect in the sand, and the colors and shapes on a butterfly's wing. If you look around your community, you will also see designs and patterns formed by fences, freeways, buildings, and on rooftops, floors, walls, and fabrics.

In this lesson, you will use string to create a design made with simple lines, shapes, and colors. To do this, you will glue your string design onto a piece of cardboard to form a **block relief**, or raised surface. Then you will use this block to print your design in a repeated pattern.

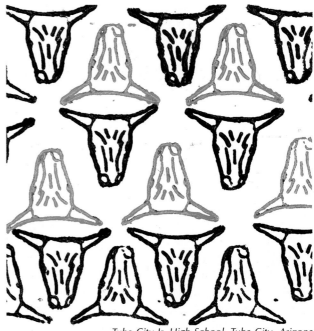

Tuba City Jr. High School. Tuba City, Arizona

Printing with string: Press inked string block on paper. Repeat design in various patterns.

Instructions for Creating Art

1. Experiment with making interesting designs using a piece of string. When you have one you like, make a line drawing of your design on a piece of cardboard. Then place a bead of white glue on the lines and lay the string on top. After the glue dries, paint the string with a brush, or roll color over it with a **brayer**.* The paint should be fairly thick and sticky.

2. Now turn the cardboard over and press your string design onto white paper. When you lift up the cardboard block, you will see a print of your design. Placing a pad of newspaper under the white paper will give you better prints. Practice making prints until they are clear and clean.

3. Next, practice repeating your design in various arrangements. If you decide to use different colors, make all the prints you want of one color first, before changing to another color. This will keep your colors from running together. You might make a row of prints right next to each other. Or you might make one print and then leave some space before making the next one. Make at least three arrangements that are pleasing to look at. Then choose your favorite and use it to print a big sheet of white paper. Your decorated paper can be used to wrap a gift or cover a book.

For an explanation, turn to the How to Do It section at the back of this book.

Art Materials

Thick string	Plastic tray for rolling out printing ink
Scissors	
Pieces of thick cardboard about 3″ × 4″	Practice paper
	Large sheets of thin white paper
White glue	
Water soluble printing ink or tempera paint	Newspaper padding
	Water, paper towels
Brush or brayer	

Strand B: Printmaking

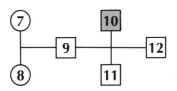

To evaluate your artwork, turn to the Learning Outcomes section at the back of this book.

11 *Block Prints with Vegetables*

Observing and Thinking Creatively

Many patterns you see on cloth or paper are printed using **blocks**. Some blocks are made by gluing designs of cardboard or string onto a larger piece of cardboard or wood. Other blocks are made by carving designs in a flat surface. For hundreds of years designs have been cut into blocks of wood or metal, and because these blocks are very hard, they can be used for many years without breaking. In some Asian countries, really good printing blocks have been passed down from one generation to the next because they are so valuable.

If you look around, you will probably see many designs that have been printed with blocks. Block-printed patterns can be seen on shirts, ties, dresses, furniture fabric, and draperies.

In this lesson, you will learn how to make a block print with a root vegetable such as a potato, carrot, or turnip.

Madison High School. San Diego, California

San Diego High School. San Diego, California

26

Designing a vegetable printer: 1) Cut away parts you do not wish to print; 2) apply paint to raised design; 3) arrange prints to form a pattern.

Instructions for Creating Art

1. Cut across a root vegetable, making the cut perfectly flat. Root vegetables are firm enough to produce good prints.

2. Dig out small parts of the vegetable with a knife or nail file to make a simple design. Remember, the cut-out areas should not show on your print, so make your cuts fairly deep. Be sure to use your carving tool carefully so that you are cutting away from your body.

3. Now place a sheet of practice paper on a smooth pad of newspaper. Apply paint to the parts of your design that stick out. Then stamp your block onto the paper, and practice making good prints. Notice that your block design comes out backwards on the paper. Wipe off the paint and try another color. Experiment by overlapping colors.

4. Try arranging your prints into a repeating pattern. Look at the pictures on these pages for possible ideas. When you have a pattern that you like, repeat it to fill a large piece of paper. You may want to draw guidelines in pencil to help you place your designs evenly.

5. Next, fill another sheet of paper with a different arrangement of your prints.

Art Materials

Root vegetables, such as potatoes, carrots, or turnips	Brushes
	Newsprint paper
	Newspaper
Knives, nail files, etc. (to cut the printing block)	Pencil and eraser
	Ruler
Tempera paint	Water, paper towels

Strand B: Printmaking

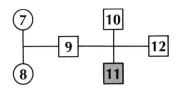

To evaluate your artwork, turn to the Learning Outcomes *section at the back of this book.*

12 *Printed Lettering*

Observing and Thinking Creatively

Printing gives us a way of repeating shapes over and over. Printed letters in books or newspapers are done in one color. To print more than one color, a page must be run through the **printing press** again to pick up the new color. A full-color picture printed in a book is made of four colors and must be run through a press four times. The yellow in the picture is printed first, then red, then blue, and, finally, black.

Did you know that the printed words you are reading right now were made by letters that were formed backwards? Words and letters are always arranged in reverse for printing, but they do not always have to be printed in a book for reading. Printed words can be repeated to create a design. In this lesson, you will design letters and make a linoleum block that will print your name.

Steps in printmaking: 1) creating the design; 2) transferring the design onto the linoleum block; 3) cutting away background space; 4) printing the design

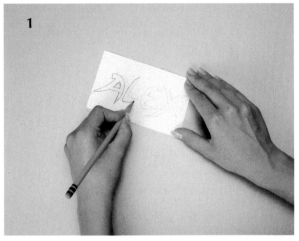

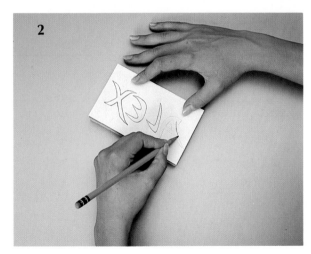

Instructions for Creating Art

1. Make practice sketches of designs for your initials or first name. Use thin paper cut to a size that is the same size as your linoleum block. Make your letters big and thick, using interesting shapes, points, or curves.

2. Choose the letter design that most reflects your personality to use in making a linoleum print. Draw over the lines of your sketch with a dark pencil.

3. Place the paper, sketch down on the linoleum block. Pressing firmly, follow the lines of the sketch on the back of the paper. Lift the paper. Your name should show in reverse on the linoleum block. Filling in the letters with a dark marker will make the letters show clearly.

4. Using a *cutting tool** carefully cut away all the linoleum except your darkened letters. Be sure to push the cutting tool away from you as you work. Remember to cut away the insides of o's and other closed letters. Do not cut through the block.

5. Next, spread some printing ink on a thick sheet of glass or other non-absorbent smooth surface. Spread the ink evenly with a **brayer.** Then use the brayer to transfer the ink to the letters on the linoleum block. Press your inked block firmly onto a sheet of paper. When you lift the block, you will see your name printed just the way you originally designed it.

6. Design a piece of artwork with your name or initials using the linoleum block. By changing colors, overlapping letters, or repeating prints, you can create a complex design from a simple linoleum block.

For an explanation, turn to the How to Do It section at the back of this book.

Art Materials

Drawing paper and printing paper	Printing ink (water-soluble)
Dark marker	Sheet of glass or dinner tray made of metal or plastic
Pencil and eraser	
Linoleum cutting tools	Newspapers (to make a pad under the printing)
1 linoleum block 3″ × 5″	Water, paper towels
Brayer	

Strand B: Printmaking

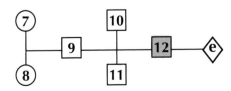

To evaluate your artwork, turn to the Learning Outcomes section at the back of this book.

13 Calligraphy and Fine Handwriting

Observing and Thinking Creatively

Did you know that lettering is a kind of drawing? Instead of drawing with pencils, artists often use brushes or pens for lettering. These artists draw beautiful letter shapes using thin and thick flowing lines. This kind of elegant handwriting is called **calligraphy**.

Beautiful books were lettered by hand before the invention of printing. Hand lettering is still used today for special kinds of work and for personalized messages. Lettering was originally done with a turkey quill cut into the shape of a pen. Today most artists letter with manufactured pens, which are easier to use and last longer.

In this lesson, you will create an artwork using calligraphy. Keep in mind that good lettering is always easy to read. Also, be very careful when using permanent black ink—it will stain clothing and furniture.

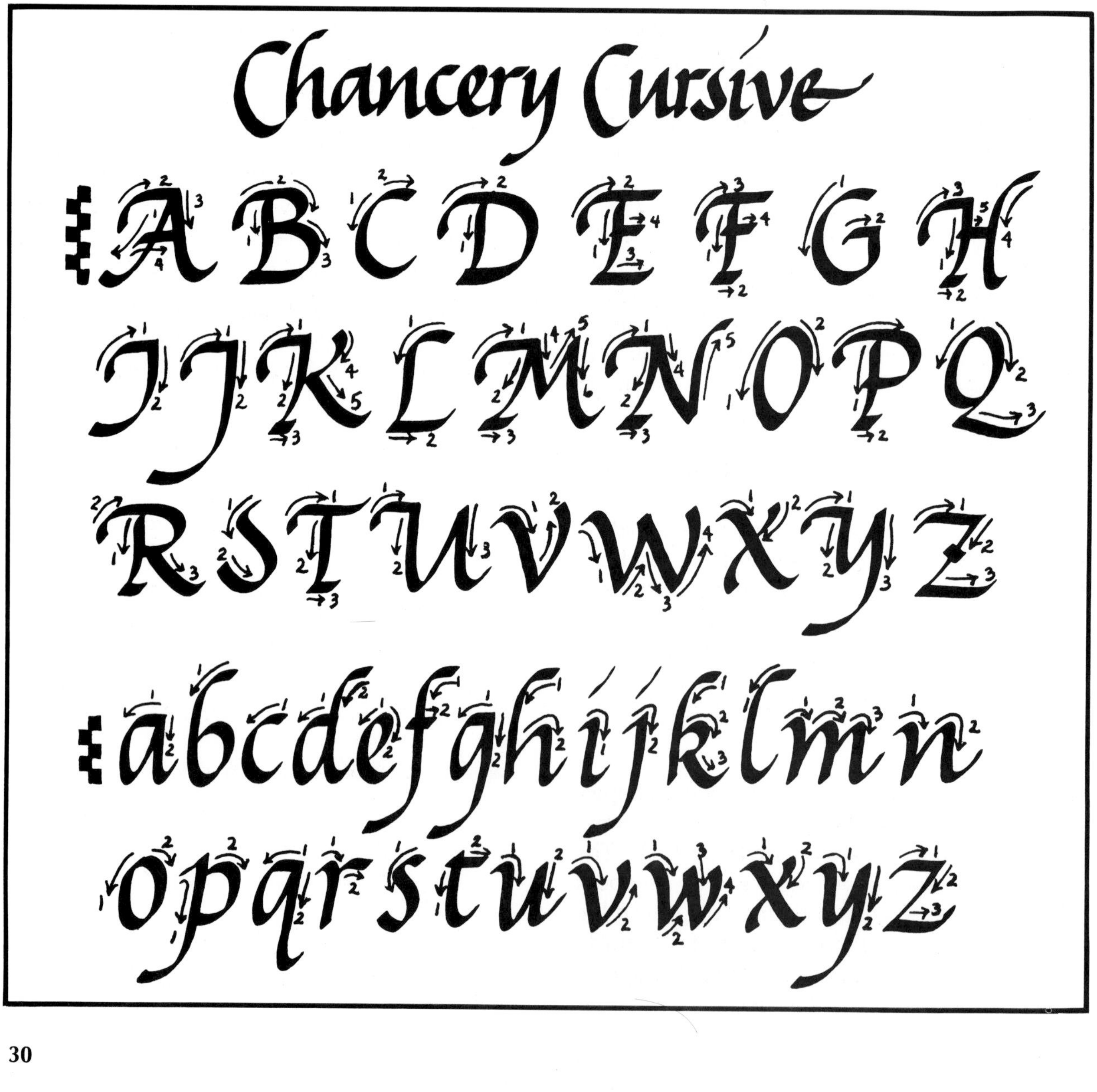

Chancery Cursive

ABCDEFGH
IJKLMNOPQ
RSTUVWXYZ

abcdefghijklmn
opqrstuvwxyz

*When you're good to others,
you are best to yourself.*

*Benjamin
Franklin*

Instructions for Creating Art

1. Lettering is best done with a calligraphy pen, which uses a variety of metal points, or **nibs**, that fit into the end. The nibs vary from extremely broad and flat to narrow and pointed. For this lesson, use a medium nib with a square **chisel** end.

2. Firmly insert the nib into the pen holder. To fill the nib with ink, dip it into the ink bottle until ink covers the entire nib, and you can see the inside of the nib filled up. Then gently tap it against the bottle to get rid of excess ink, and make a practice line on a piece of scratch paper to get rid of any ink blobs.

3. Practice making lines of varied lengths and thicknesses on a sheet of paper. Never press down too hard with the pen nib. Just slide it smoothly over the paper's surface. Hold the pen at a constant angle so the thick and thin lines will occur in the same places. Draw vertical lines from top to bottom, always pulling the pen toward you. If you push it away from you, it will dig into the paper and make a blot or scratchy line.

4. Now practice making different letter shapes. The height of capital letters should be about seven times the width of the pen nib. The height of lower case letters should be about five times the width of the pen nib. Using the nib, make short marks that are touching to determine the heights of letters. Draw light pencil guidelines at these heights.

5. Study examples of lettering shown on page 30. The numbers and arrows next to the letters indicate the order and direction of the lines. Practice lettering the alphabet. Then pick a short verse or quotation that you like. Using very light pencil lines, write the words on your paper. Leave plenty of space between the lines—your finished lettering will take up more space than your pencil guide.

6. Now, carefully letter the words in ink. Practice lettering the verse until you have a copy that pleases you. When you are finished, wash the pen and nibs with water or pen cleaner.

Art Materials

Practice paper	Lettering pens and pen nibs
Fine quality drawing paper	
Pencil and eraser	Black waterproof ink
	Pen cleaner
Ruler	Water, paper towels

Strand C: Letters and Words

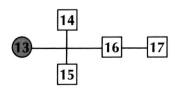

To evaluate your artwork, turn to the Learning Outcomes section at the back of this book.

14 *Letter Designs*

Observing and Thinking Creatively

Have you ever noticed all the different letter shapes used in advertising? These letters have been specially designed to emphasize the messages in the advertisements. For example, flowing, curved letters give a different feeling from solid, square ones. What types of products would you use curved letters to advertise? Think of products that might be advertised in bold, square letters.

Just as people have favorite colors, they often like some lettering designs better than others.

What kinds of letters do you prefer? Whatever their shape, letters should always be easy to read, and the **proportion** of their height and width need to be balanced. Beautiful letters also have white space around them; they are spaced evenly and not crowded together.

In this lesson, you will design special letters for your name that reflect your personality. Because there are hundreds of ways of making letters, you can be as creative as you like.

Ed Ruscha has created a lettering style for *Annie,* based on the popular musical of the same name which was derived from the comic strip *Little Orphan Annie.* The bright, bold colors and curved letters outlined in black reflect Annie's outgoing personality. What other character traits has the artist captured in his design?

Ed Ruscha, Annie, 1965, Oil on Canvas, 22" × 20", collection of Newport Harbor Art Museum, purchased by the Acquisition Council with a Matching Grant from the National Endowment for the Arts.

Boone Jr./Sr. High School. Boone, Iowa

C.W. Long Middle School. Atlanta, Georgia

Instructions for Creating Art

1. Look through books, magazines, newspapers, and pamphlets that use various kinds of lettering. Notice the many different letter shapes used in advertisements. After you have gathered some ideas for lettering, experiment with different designs of your own. Invent letter designs that suit the kind of person you are. Draw all the letters in your name, using various designs. Be as creative as you can. Then decide on one kind of lettering and create a design for your name.

2. Make a name card for your desk or bedroom door. The letters should be at least one and one-half inches high. Color them and create designs around them if you want.

Art Materials

Practice paper	Pen and ink
Pencil and eraser	Drawing paper or poster board
Colored markers, crayons, or colored pencils	Ruler

Strand C: Letters and Words

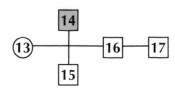

To evaluate your artwork, turn to the Learning Outcomes *section at the back of this book.*

15 *Monograms and Trademarks*

Observing and Thinking Creatively

Everyone knows what the initials U.S.A. stand for. Can you think of people or companies who are known just by their initials? Many people put their initials on clothes, cars, wallets, luggage, towels, and handkerchiefs to personalize them. When initials are put together to make a design, it is called a **monogram**.

The job of creating advertising for companies and businesses is done by artists who specialize in **graphic design**. One of the many kinds of art

graphic designers do is to design lettering for the business name and initials of their clients. Companies often use their initials as a monogram design on their products, stationery, and business cards. When a company uses its initials in this way, it is called a **trademark** or **logo**. Perhaps you can think of cars or food products with initials used in this way.

In this lesson, you will design a monogram for your own initials.

Courtesy of Communicating Arts Group of San Diego

Courtesy of International Business Machines Corporation

Children's Saturday Art Class. Indiana University, Indiana

Correia Special Education Department. San Diego, California

Instructions for Creating Art

1. Experiment with the style of lettering you want to use in your design. Make it as creative and unusual as you like, choosing a style that fits your personality. When you are pleased with your lettering, try putting your initials together in different ways.

2. Choose the monogram design you like best and draw it very large on a sheet of paper. Make your letters with black ink or use colors.

3. The monograms in this lesson may give you ideas, but create your own original design for your monogram.

Art Materials	
White paper	Colored markers or pen and ink
Pencil and eraser	

Strand C: Letters and Words

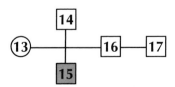

To evaluate your artwork, turn to the Learning Outcomes section at the back of this book.

16 *Word Pictures*

Observing and Thinking Creatively

Do you remember when you first learned to write the letters of the alphabet? Did your teacher insist that you write each letter in a certain way? Even though the basic letter shapes of our alphabet are fixed, artists often create many alphabet designs to describe different messages and products. For example, letter shapes used on a sack of dog food will be very different from those on a bottle of expensive perfume or on a poster advertising a vacation in Hawaii.

Study the lettering used on posters, billboards, record albums, and magazines that you see every day. The letter shapes are often designed to show a feeling that fits the meaning of the words. A word like *weak* might be drawn to look limp and tired. Words like *scared* or *wicked* would look jagged and sharp. In this lesson, you will discover how to design your own letter shapes and create word pictures.

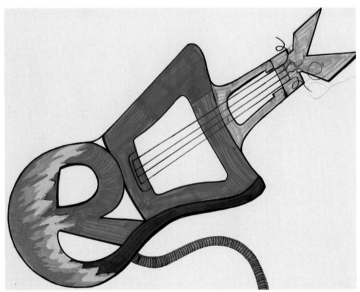

Martin Luther King Jr. High School. Jersey City, New Jersey

Martin Luther King Jr. High School. Jersey City, New Jersey

Note how Mary Ellen Solt arranged separate letters from the word *forsythia* to form the forsythia bush, pictured above. Each letter represents a flower or leaf cluster. Artists sometimes use colors and shapes in unexpected ways to express what they see.

Permission granted by Mary Ellen Solt. "Forsythia" from Flowers in Concrete, *Fine Arts Department, Indiana University, 1966.*

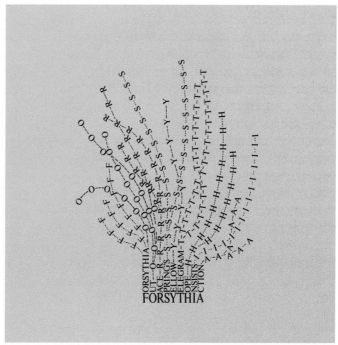

Instructions for Creating Art

1. Choose four words that express different emotions or feelings. Write one word in small letters in each corner of a sheet of paper.

2. Near each word you wrote, draw the word again so that it fills one quarter of the paper. Draw it to look like its meaning.

3. Select colors that also reflect the meanings, and color in each picture word. The letters in each word should look as though they belong together to form a single design. This is called **unity**, and is a principle of good design.

4. The pictures in this lesson may give you ideas for designing words, but use your own imagination to create your word pictures.

Art Materials

White paper

Pencil and eraser

Your choice: colored markers, crayons, or paints and brushes

Mixing tray (for paints)

Water, paper towels

Strand C: Letters and Words

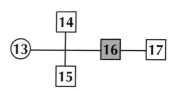

To evaluate your artwork, turn to the Learning Outcomes *section at the back of this book.*

17 Art for Advertising

Observing and Thinking Creatively

Suppose your school is planning a special event like a band concert, award ceremony, soccer game, graduation dance, or school play. How would you publicize the event?

There are many ways to advertise an event. You might announce it at a special assembly or over a microphone. You might distribute printed materials or design a poster advertising the event. **Visual** advertising has a more lasting effect, because people often remember what they see better than what they hear.

Visual art created for advertising purposes is one kind of **graphic design**. We see graphic design all around us—on posters, signs, buildings, buses, food packages, and in magazines, newspapers, books, and brochures. All of these designs have been created by graphic artists with the purpose of capturing people's attention and communicating messages.

You have surely noticed large billboards along the roadside. What techniques have the graphic designers used to catch your attention? Because people have only a few moments to read the words on a billboard as they go by, the message must be brief. Magazine and newspaper ads can contain more words, since people have more time to read them.

One popular form of advertising art is the poster. Posters are used at school and community locations to promote products, events, ideas, and services. You may have favorite posters displayed on the walls of your room.

In this lesson, you will use graphic art to create a poster of your own. But first, spend some time observing different kinds of advertising art. Notice how the pictures and lettering work together to create a unified design and communicate the message convincingly. Now, use your observations along with your own ideas to design a poster advertising an event or presenting a meaningful message.

Woodside Middle School. Fort Wayne, Indiana

38

The world's greatest zoo is right under your nose.

San Diego Zoo

Design is © of the Zoological Society of San Diego.

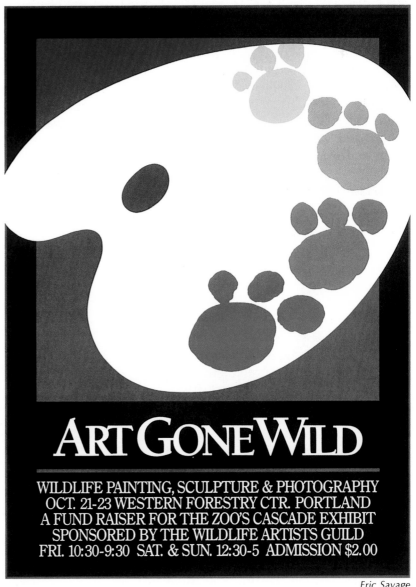

ART GONE WILD

WILDLIFE PAINTING, SCULPTURE & PHOTOGRAPHY
OCT. 21-23 WESTERN FORESTRY CTR. PORTLAND
A FUND RAISER FOR THE ZOO'S CASCADE EXHIBIT
SPONSORED BY THE WILDLIFE ARTISTS GUILD
FRI. 10:30-9:30 SAT. & SUN. 12:30-5 ADMISSION $2.00

Eric Savage

Standley Jr. High School. San Diego, California

Instructions for Creating Art

1. Think of an upcoming event you would like to advertise—perhaps a school play, concert, club meeting, dance, or athletic event. Perhaps you would like to promote a book sale, car wash, free kittens, or an election. You might also choose a special message or issue that concerns you, such as driving carefully, conserving our natural environment, or the harmful effects of smoking.

2. When you have decided on a subject for your poster, write your message or compose a slogan. A **slogan** is a short, catchy saying, like "Only you can prevent forest fires." Keep your message or slogan brief, clear, and direct, so people can read and understand it quickly. If you are advertising a school event, be sure to include the date, time, and place.

3. Decide how you will use your message or slogan in the design of your poster. Think about the best way to communicate the message to your intended audience. You may want to use pictures or illustrations, special lettering effects, or simple graphic designs that emphasize color. The lettering, message, and illustrations should all work together to create an effective, eye-catching design.

4. Make a preliminary sketch of your poster on a large sheet of paper. Keep in mind that a simple, bold design is usually most effective. Experiment with different color combinations, types of lettering, illustrations, and designs. Fit the style of lettering and design to the meaning of the poster. For example, if you are designing a poster promoting a school carnival, you would probably use bright colors and a lively message.

Before making your finished poster, read and complete the *Exploring Art* activity on the next page.

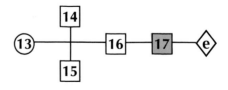

Art Materials

Drawing paper	Tempera paints
Pencil and eraser	Brushes
Ruler	Mixing tray
Poster paper	Water, paper towels

Strand C: Letters and Words

To evaluate your artwork, turn to the Learning Outcomes *section at the back of this book.*

40

Exploring Art

Designing a Poster

Before beginning this art activity, read and complete the instructions in Lesson 17 for sketching a poster design. Then consider the following elements in making your final design.

- **Create a focus of attention.**

  In order to catch someone's eye, it is important to create a focus, or **center of interest**, by emphasizing one part of your poster. You can create interest through the use of illustrations or by designing special lettering. You might make the illustration large and bright. Or you can emphasize words by using unusual lettering shapes and striking color combinations.

- **Work for unity of design.**

  All the parts—illustrations, lettering, and message—should work together to produce a unified design. The observer's eye should flow naturally from one part to another. There are several techniques for achieving unity of design: lettering and illustrations can be overlapped; one color might be used in the background; or symbols, lines, and shapes may join different elements.

  Space is also an important element in designing a poster. Be sure to leave enough open space so your poster is uncluttered and easy to read. A strong, simple design is usually most effective.

- **Select colors that suit your message.**

  As you design your poster, think about the message you want to convey. Use colors to create a mood or elicit a response. Bright, cheerful colors usually create excitement, while darker colors suggest a more serious mood. For example, red is used to show excitement, anger, or danger. Blue is a soothing, peaceful color. Shades of red, orange, and yellow are *warm* colors, while blues and greens are *cool*. If you want a very bright poster, choose colors that are opposite each other on the color wheel, such as orange and blue. If you want a softer, quieter look, choose colors that are close together.

- **Design attractive and easy-to-read letters.**

  If you observe the lettering on different kinds of posters and advertisements, you will note that the most effective lettering is usually simple, attractive, and easy to read. Lettering can be designed in many shapes and sizes to fit the mood of your poster—tall and thin, short and fat, straight or slanted, plain or fancy. Experiment with different lettering shapes, styles, and arrangements. Pencil in very light guidelines for your lettering.

  You may want to emphasize certain words by designing letters that fit their meaning. For example, the word *soft* could be designed to look soft, and the word *fire* might look like flames. Keep in mind, however, that the design should not prevent people from reading the message clearly.

- **Display your poster in an appropriate place.**

Original artwork by Tomie dePaola. Poster designed by Martin Williams Advertising, Minneapolis.

Vincent van Gogh, Detail from Fishing Boats at Saintes-Maries-de-la-Mer, *1888,*
Pencil, reed pen and brown ink, 9⅞ × 12⅝", The Solomon R. Guggenheim
Museum, New York. The Justin K. Thannhauser Collection.

Unit II

Drawing Objects and Figures

The painter draws with his eyes, not with his hands. Whatever he sees, if he sees it clear, *he can put down. The putting of it down requires, perhaps, much care and labor, but no more muscular agility than it takes for him to write his name. Seeing* clear *is the important thing.*

Maurice Grosser

Drawing is a way of rediscovering the world by *seeing* it clearly, and then expressing this vision through art. Learning to *see*—really see by observing the finest details—is as necessary to drawing as breathing is to life.

Look closely at your thumb. Observe every detail as if your eyes were a microscope. Do you notice lines and patterns that you may not have seen before? Do you see how the patterns in your thumbprint give it a

unique design? In the same way, each drawing you make is an expression of your own individuality.

The lessons in this section will help you develop your drawing skill by expressing what you see through lines, forms, and figures. You will experiment by drawing different subjects using a variety of art materials. By practicing these different ways of drawing, you will discover your own art style.

18 Doodles That Come Alive

Observing and Thinking Creatively

Just about everyone likes to doodle. Doodling happens when you just let your pencil wander over a sheet of paper. What kinds of doodles do you like to make? Do you sometimes make letters, shapes, or lines? Do your doodles usually have meaning, or are they just designs? At school, you may sometimes doodle in the margin of your notebook, or maybe you doodle when you talk on the telephone.

Artists also let their pencils and brushes wander over sheets of paper. Sometimes they discover ideas for art from the doodles they make. Ideas often appear when you least expect them.

Doodles start out by just happening. Then you begin to see an idea in the lines on your paper; you might add other lines to make a figure, shape, or design. In this lesson, you will discover an idea for a picture or design from doodling.

Jean Dubuffet created many doodle designs. Some of the outlines in *Genuflexion of the Bishop* are darker. Do you know why? In what other ways is your attention directed to certain shapes?

Jean Dubuffet, Genuflexion of the Bishop, 1901, Oil on Canvas, 86¾" × 118", Joseph Winterbotham Collection. © The Art Institute of Chicago. All Rights Reserved.

44

Mark Tobey's careful use of flowing, crisscrossing lines and spaces creates a sense of rhythm in this painting. Notice how some of the spaces are filled with color, which gives dimension to the space.

Mark Tobey, Threading Light, *1942. Tempera on cardboard. 29⅜ × 19½". Collection, The Museum of Modern Art, New York.*

Instructions for Creating Art

1. Start doodling on a sheet of paper. Make all kinds of lines and shapes. Fill in some spaces and leave others empty. Let your pencil wander over the paper. Do not think about making any particular shape; just let your pencil doodle. If you want, make several different doodles on separate sheets of paper.

2. Choose one of your doodles to develop into a picture or design. Do some of the lines and shapes remind you of objects? Do some patterns occur repeatedly? Explore these questions and use your imagination to turn your doodles into an original design in which you have used the lines, shapes, and patterns from doodling.

3. Arrange your doodles into a finished picture. Fill in any parts that need more lines. Erase lines that detract from the design. If you wish, color your doodle or shade it in with colored

pens or pencils. Your creation has come from combining ideas from your imagination and the logical, thinking part of your mind.

Art Materials

Your choice: crayons, colored markers, or pens	Paper
	Pencil and eraser

Strand D: Lines, Shapes, and Textures

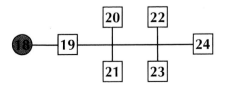

To evaluate your artwork, turn to the Learning Outcomes *section at the back of this book.*

19 *Contour Drawing*

Observing and Thinking Creatively

Look at a simple object, such as a clock, chair, vase, lamp, or cup. Closely observe the object by slowly following the edges or **contours** of the object with your eyes. This simple exercise demonstrates how artists observe their world and then translate their perceptions into drawings and pictures. Art is a way of seeing by first observing whole shapes and forms and then focusing on finer details.

In this lesson, you will observe an object and draw the edges or contours of the object as you look at it. To do this, your eyes and hand must work in concert, just as a musician's hand plays a melody on an instrument and his ears hear it in the same instant. Your drawing will consist of contour lines that form the edges of the object. The aim of this lesson is to draw an object's shape and form by using lines.

Henri Matisse uses simple, flowing lines to define the contours of the *Girl with Gold Necklace*. Note how he varies lines and patterns to create interest.

Henry Matisse, Girl with Gold Necklace, 1944, Ink on Paper, University of Arizona Museum of Art, gift of Edward J. Gallagher, Jr.

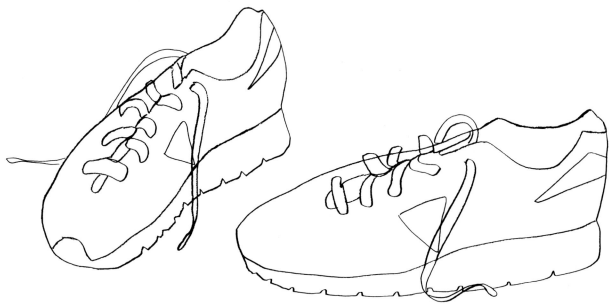

San Diego High School. San Diego, California

Instructions for Creating Art

1. Select a simple object to draw, such as a bottle, vase, cup, teapot, shoe, seashell, fruit, gourd, or piece of driftwood. First, follow the contours of the object by very slowly moving your eyes around its edges. Then, using your finger as a drawing tool, follow the contours of the object with your fingers.

2. Next, practice **blind contour drawing** by observing the object and drawing it *without* looking at your paper. First, tape your paper to the table so that it will not slip. Now place your pencil on the paper. Look at the object and very slowly move your eyes along the contours, carefully following every line and curve. As your eyes move, also move your pencil on the paper at the same slow speed. Press your pencil down fairly hard as you draw, and resist erasing any lines. Do not look at your paper. Trust that the nerves in your hand and mind are making connections. Remember that the objective of this lesson is to discover these connections and not to draw realistically. Keep moving your eyes in concert with your pencil. Draw both the inside and outside lines. You can also repeat the contours by overlapping lines. Look at your paper only when you have finished your drawing. Observe how the lines on your paper resemble the contours of the object.

3. Now you are ready to practice **modified contour drawing** by occasionally glancing at your paper as you draw. Take a clean sheet of paper and tape it to the table. Slowly move your eyes along the contours of the object while your pencil draws the lines at the same slow speed. Allow yourself to glance at your drawing only to note relationships of one part to another and to monitor lines and proportions. Ninety percent of your drawing time should be spent with your eyes focused on the object.

When you have completed this drawing, look at it and compare it to the first. How well did your eyes and hands communicate?

Art Materials

Object for drawing: bottle, vase, cup, teapot, shoe, seashell, fruit, gourd, piece of driftwood, etc.

Two sheets of drawing paper

Pencil

Tape

Strand D: Lines, Shapes, and Textures

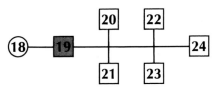

To evaluate your artwork, turn to the Learning Outcomes section at the back of this book.

20 *Light on Flat Objects*

Observing and Thinking Creatively

Many objects around us have flat surfaces. As you look around you, notice different flat surfaces, such as tabletops, desks, walls, doors, and window panes. In observing these objects, you will realize that almost all of them were designed and made by people. Very few things in nature are perfectly flat.

If you look closely at two adjoining walls, you will observe that the shading on one wall makes the color appear lighter or darker than it is on the other, even though both are the same color. The change occurs at the corners where one flat surface, or **plane**, meets the other. One wall is lighter because it faces the light; the other wall is darker because it faces away from the light.

In this lesson, you will learn how to use shading to show **value** differences, or the lightness or darkness of shapes and forms. Shading in various values of gray with a pencil can create a feeling of form and depth, thus making an object look solid.

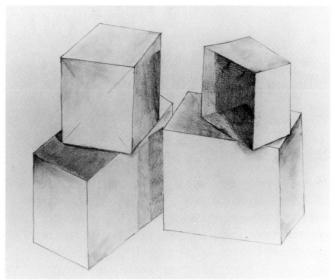

Instructions for Creating Art

1. Select a group of flat-sided objects of varying sizes, such as boxes, books, blocks, or chests. Arrange the objects so that some of them overlap for a good design. Now draw the outlines of the shapes. Make the drawing large enough to fill most of your paper.

2. Observe the surfaces of the objects and note value differences in light and dark areas. Carefully shade in the lightest side of each object first, then the darker surfaces. Very few sides will be completely white or black.

3. Pause to look at your drawing as you work. Does the shading make the object appear solid? Can you tell by looking at your picture from which direction the light is coming?

Art Materials

Flat-sided objects: large cardboard boxes, metal cabinets, suitcases, etc.

Drawing paper

Pencil and eraser

Strand D: Lines, Shapes, and Textures

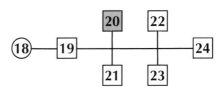

To evaluate your artwork, turn to the Learning Outcomes *section at the back of this book.*

21 Light on Rounded Objects

Observing and Thinking Creatively

Have you ever tried to draw rounded things, such as a ball, a tin can, or a vase? You probably discovered that it is more difficult to draw the shadows on curved surfaces than it is to shade flat surfaces. This is because the shading on flat-sided objects only changes where two flat surfaces meet; rounded objects, however, do not have sharp edges, so the shadows on them occur more gradually. Artists have to use different amounts of shading on curved surfaces to show gradual changes in light.

The easiest rounded shapes to begin drawing are **cylinders** and **spheres.** Cylinders include objects like pipes, cans, and bottles. Spheres are round objects, such as oranges or basketballs. The curves on these objects are even, causing the shadows to change from light to dark very evenly. If you begin by drawing shadows on simple objects, you will soon be able to draw the shadows on more complex surfaces.

Rembrandt especially enjoyed drawing and painting animals.
Study of an Elephant is a drawing made with heavy curving lines showing the deep shadows of the elephant's wrinkles. Notice how the varied use of curved lines gives the elephant a rounded form.

Rembrandt van Rijn, Study of an Elephant, *1637, Black chalk, 17.8 × 25.6 mm (7 × 10"), The Albertina Collection, Hofburg Esperanto Museum, Vienna, Austria.*

Shading curved surfaces: Note the different shading techniques used to sketch the potted plants. Find areas where the artist shaded with the side of the pencil using varying amounts of pressure, or made a variety of lines placed next to each other, or used cross-hatching.

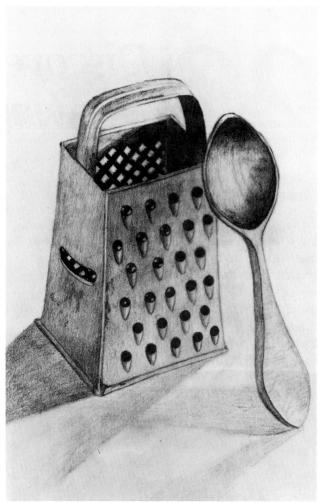

Instructions for Creating Art

1. Arrange a group of simple objects with rounded surfaces. For a good design, choose objects that are different in size, and place them so that some parts overlap. First, draw the outlines of these objects to fill your paper.

2. Look carefully at the shadows on the objects. Notice that the shading on round surfaces changes slowly and smoothly from light to dark. This kind of even shading is called **gradation**, and it helps make round objects look solid. You can achieve smooth, even shading by holding your pencil almost flat, applying varying amounts of pressure. You can also use fine light lines or dark, heavy lines placed close together. **Cross-hatching**, a method of drawing parallel lines in a crisscross manner, is another way of shading.

3. Shade the objects in your drawing. For darker areas, try pressing firmly with the flat side of your pencil, applying smooth, even strokes. Gradually decrease the pressure as you move to lighter areas. Leave parts white that are the lightest. Experiment by using different kinds of lines and pencil strokes until you achieve the shading effects you want. (Refer to page 219 for more information on shading.)

Art Materials

Round-surfaced objects: large pipe, coffee can, oil drum, basketball, round waste can, etc.

Drawing paper
Pencil and eraser

Strand D: Lines, Shapes, and Textures

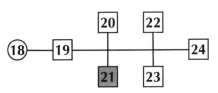

To evaluate your artwork, turn to the Learning Outcomes *section at the back of this book.*

22 Discovering and Drawing Textures

Observing and Thinking Creatively

If you have ever stepped on a hairbrush, you know what the spiky bristles feel like. When you press your hand hard against a rough surface, you can feel the texture and see the design it leaves on your skin. **Texture** refers to the way something looks and feels to the touch.

All surfaces have textures which make them look and feel rough, smooth, silky, glossy, and so on. How would you describe the different textures in the pictures shown in this lesson? Artists know that texture is an important element in making art interesting. For this reason, they experiment with various ways of showing texture in their artwork.

In this lesson, you will observe and draw the textures of several different objects.

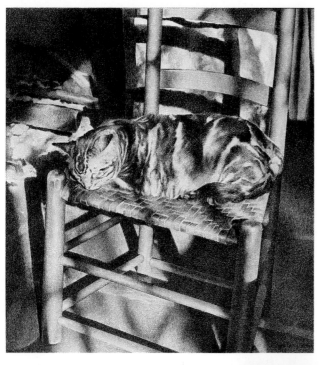

Charles Sheeler drew this picture of a sleeping cat in the sun with a chalklike crayon on rough paper to show all the different textures clearly. Notice how the cat's fur stands out against the smooth wooden chair. Observe the woven texture of the reed seat and the fuzziness of the shadows.

Charles Sheeler, Feline Felicity. *Conte crayon on white paper. Courtesy of the Fogg Art Museum, Harvard University. Purchase—Louise E. Bettens Fund.*

Post-Renaissance artists liked to portray precise details and textures. Note the ornamentation and the slight variations in color and shading to show the curvature of the hat and folds of the garment. How many different textures can you identify in this painting segment?

Jan Gossaert, Detail from L'Adoration des Mages (The Adoration of the Kings). *Reproduced by courtesy of the Trustees, The National Gallery, London.*

Instructions for Creating Art

1. Select three or four large, simple objects having different textures. Arrange these objects so that light-colored textures are placed next to darker surfaces. The **contrast** of objects will make each shape show up clearly. For example, your objects might consist of a straw hat and a wooden box placed up against a wall on a shaggy rug.

2. Before drawing, carefully observe each object and feel its texture. Is it rough, furry, silky, or gritty? Notice how each texture shows varying degrees of light and dark areas.

3. Take a sheet of drawing paper and divide it into as many sections as there are objects. Practice drawing and shading just the texture of each object. Do not draw the shapes yet. Continue to observe and draw until you are satisfied with each texture on your paper.

4. Use another sheet of drawing paper to make a simple outline drawing of the objects so that they fill your paper. Now shade in the different textures showing a contrast between light and

dark surfaces and between different textures. The drawing is finished when every space, including the background, is filled with a different texture.

Art Materials

Collection of textured objects: hairbrush, hat, box, log, basket, burlap, carpet, fur, velvet, etc.

Pencil and eraser

Two sheets of drawing paper

Strand D: Lines, Shapes, and Textures

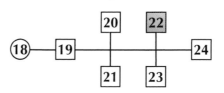

To evaluate your artwork, turn to the Learning Outcomes *section at the back of this book.*

23 Artists and Scientists as Observers

Observing and Thinking Creatively

Suppose you are fishing by yourself one day and you catch a very unusual fish—one that you have never seen before. Unfortunately, the fish slips off the hook and skitters away. Later, you describe this fish to your friends. Then you make a sketch of it to *show* them how it looked.

Describing what you have seen is a good way of telling people about your experience. Drawing what you have seen is an even better way of *showing* what something looks like. The cavemen of the Stone Age drew simple pictures on cave walls to record their experiences. For thousands of years artists, architects, engineers, doc-

tors, and soldiers have also learned to draw so they could show their ideas, plans, and observations to others.

Scientists learn about plants, animals, and rocks by observing and studying their every detail. They measure and weigh them and describe their shape, color, and **texture**. Artists also observe the subjects of their drawings closely and practice making sketches of them from different angles. Later, an artist may use a sketch as the basis for drawing a similar subject in a picture or design.

John James Audubon spent years observing the habits of birds and animals. His paintings are so clear and accurate that we can identify each creature even without knowing the title. In this reproduction of the *Black-Tailed Hare,* note how the artist drew the texture of the rabbit's fur.

Black-Tailed Hare, *John James Audubon, St. Louis Art Museum.*

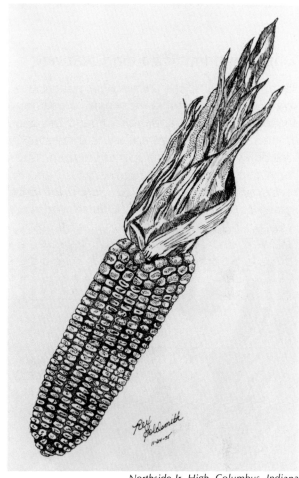

Instructions for Creating Art

1. Choose a fairly simple object from nature —a seashell, rock, starfish, fruit, or pinecone, such as the one pictured above. Run your fingers over the different parts of the object to feel its texture. Closely observe the object as if you are a scientific illustrator. Make several quick sketches of the object from different angles or positions.

2. Select one of your sketches and make a detailed drawing of the object. Beginning with the outlines, draw the object as well as you can. Try to put every detail you see into your drawing. Shade in the light and dark areas.

3. The pictures in this lesson may give you ideas for subjects to draw. Observe how the artists added details to their drawings. Then use your own way of drawing in detail.

Art Materials

A simple object from nature: a rock, leaf, branch, flower, seashell, starfish, seed pod, etc.	Pencil and eraser White paper

Strand D: Lines, Shapes, and Textures

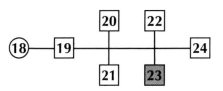

To evaluate your artwork, turn to the Learning Outcomes *section at the back of this book.*

24 Drawing Shapes and Spaces

Observing and Thinking Creatively

If you look around the place where you are now, you may observe objects, people, plants, and **spaces**. Usually, we don't think about the space around us because we are more interested in looking at things. Yet, the spaces between things have their own shapes. Unlike most people, artists are always studying the shapes of these spaces as they work. In artwork, these spaces are as important as the shapes of the main objects: the spaces help make the shapes stand out.

In this lesson, you will think about the spaces around objects. You will observe how these spaces make the main shapes of things appear more interesting. Instead of drawing just the objects, you will draw the spaces around them.

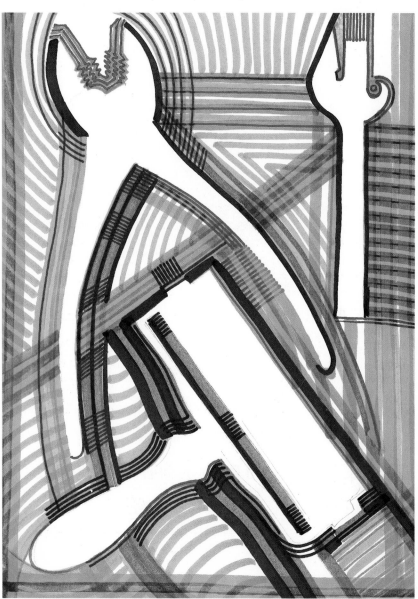

Children's Saturday Art Class. Indiana University, Indiana

Children's Saturday Art Class. Indiana University, Indiana

Instructions for Creating Art

1. Gather several objects that have interesting shapes. You might use things like vases, fruit, scissors, coins, and keys. Explore different ways of arranging a few of these objects. Consider both the placement of objects and the spaces between them. When you have discovered a pleasing arrangement, lightly sketch the outlines of the objects on a sheet of drawing paper.

2. Now decorate all of the background spaces with a design just using lines. Try using a pencil, pen, or colored marker. Make a design of your own invention. Be careful not to put any decoration inside the shapes.

3. When you have finished with your background design, the objects drawn on your paper will be the only blank areas left. This way of drawing is the opposite of what people usually do in their art. Ask yourself whether the parts you decorated make a good design by themselves. If they do, then you have successfully turned the spaces around objects into a work of art. If they don't make an attractive design, try another arrangement. As

you do this, think carefully about the spaces around the objects, as well as how pleasing the arrangement looks. Whenever you create any piece of art, think of the shapes and the spaces as essential parts of the design.

Art Materials

Miscellaneous objects for drawing: vases, fruit, scissors, coins, keys, etc.

White drawing paper

Pencil and eraser

Colored ballpoint pens or markers

Strand D: Lines, Shapes, and Textures

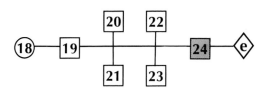

To evaluate your artwork, turn to the Learning Outcomes section at the back of this book.

25 Drawing Without a Pencil

Observing and Thinking Creatively

Can you remember what art materials you used to draw your first pictures when you were a young child? Perhaps you used crayons, paint, or colored markers. Most young children like to experiment by drawing large, simple shapes using color. They take delight in seeing how lines and shapes can represent real things.

When asked to do a drawing, many people will automatically reach for their pencils. However, good drawings are also done with charcoal, pen and ink, paintbrushes, pastels, and crayons. Artists sometimes use a combination of several drawing materials in one picture.

The drawing for this lesson may be done with anything you like—except a pencil. You will practice drawing the shapes, surfaces, and **textures** of objects.

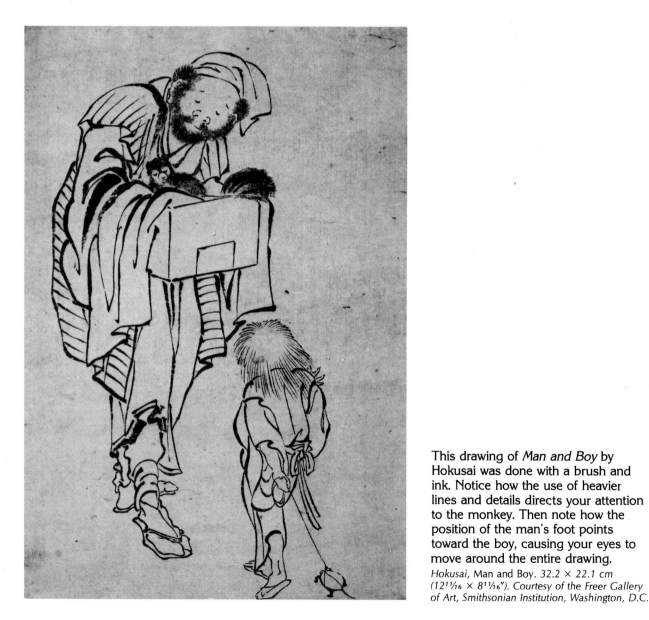

This drawing of *Man and Boy* by Hokusai was done with a brush and ink. Notice how the use of heavier lines and details directs your attention to the monkey. Then note how the position of the man's foot points toward the boy, causing your eyes to move around the entire drawing.

Hokusai, Man and Boy. 32.2 × 22.1 cm (12¹¹/₁₆ × 8¹¹/₁₆"). Courtesy of the Freer Gallery of Art, Smithsonian Institution, Washington, D.C.

Vincent van Gogh used the edge of a pen point to capture the effect of sharp blades of grass. Notice the variety of lines he used.

Vincent van Gogh, Tree in a Meadow, *1889, Reed pen and ink over traces of black chalk or charcoal, 493 × 613 mm, Gift of Tiffany and Margaret Blake, © The Art Institute of Chicago. All Rights Reserved.*

Meridian Middle School. Indianapolis, Indiana

Instructions for Creating Art

1. Find an object to draw that has a surface texture that is interesting to look at and nice to feel. It could be a hat, a boxing glove, a shoe, leaves from a tree—or anything else.

2. Draw the object you chose as big as possible on a sheet of paper. Practice making the surface textures look the way you see and feel them. Use anything you wish except a pencil to draw the object. Select a drawing material that will show the object and its texture best.

3. The pictures in this lesson may give you some ideas for drawing your picture, but experiment with your own ways of drawing without a pencil. Try drawing your object with two or three different materials, such as pen and ink, charcoal, pastels, or paints. Compare the effects you get with each.

Art Materials

Object with interesting texture: coat, drapery, basket, rough wood, etc.

Drawing paper

Pen and ink, crayons, charcoal, paints and brushes, etc.

Water, paper towels

Strand E: Drawing Methods and Media

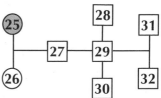

To evaluate your artwork, turn to the Learning Outcomes *section at the back of this book.*

26 Drawing with Color

Observing and Thinking Creatively

Think of the most colorful place you know. It might be a carnival or amusement park filled with brightly colored lights. It could be a shopping center with colorful window displays and decorations. Or perhaps it is someplace out-of-doors, like a boat harbor, a field full of flowers, or a tree-filled forest. If you were to draw and color this place, what art materials would you use? The choice of materials and tools an artist uses, such as pastels or paint and brushes, is called the **medium**. When artists think of an idea for a

picture, they try to use an art medium that best fits the subject matter of their artwork.

In this lesson, you will experiment with the medium of oil pastels to make a brilliantly colored picture. Because oil pastels are soft and rub off easily on paper, they are an excellent medium to use for brightly colored subjects. However, they are not as good for showing details. Your task will be to think of a subject that will fit in well with what oil pastels do best, and make a picture with this medium.

Bright slashes of pastels sweep your eyes to the center of interest in Toulouse-Lautrec's drawing. Note how he has used quick strokes on a strong diagonal line to emphasize the motion of the woman on the horse. How has the artist used colors to create an interesting effect?

Henri de Toulouse-Lautrec, Au Cirque Fernando, Ecuyere sur un Cheval Blanc (At the Circus Fernando, Rider on a White Horse), *1888, Pastel and gouache on board, 23⅝" × 31¼", Norton Simon Art Foundation.*

Audubon Jr. High School. Milwaukee, Wisconsin

Children's Saturday Art Class.
University of Indiana, Indiana

Instructions for Creating Art

1. Before making your picture, experiment with *oil pastels** by using them in different ways on a practice sheet of paper. The colors often show up best on medium and dark-colored paper. Apply the colors on your paper by rubbing or blending the shades, overlapping strokes, or using fine, closely spaced lines. Try using the sides of the colored sticks for bodies of solid color and the points for more detailed work. You may want to soften the pastels by dipping the ends in a bit of turpentine to make them more like paint. You can make interesting effects by scratching away some of the thick pastel with a pointed object, such as scissors or a pin.

2. While you are experimenting, think about ideas for your picture. If you have a parakeet or parrot, you might want to use pastels to draw its vibrant feathers. A vase of brightly colored flowers or a bowl of fruit is also a good subject for oil pastels. Choose a subject that interests you and one which will suit the medium of oil pastels.

3. When you have a good idea for a picture, make a preliminary sketch with chalk or light-colored pastel. Then draw the main outlines, and fill in solid areas of color. To create effective contrasts, place light objects next to

darker ones. Be sure to repeat colors to achieve **unity** of design. When the picture seems finished, study it carefully and ask yourself if it shows what you wanted it to. Do not be concerned if the picture turns out differently from what you expected. If your subject fits well with the medium of oil pastels, then you have completed your artwork successfully.

For an explanation, turn to the How to Do It *section at the back of this book.*

Art Materials

Drawing paper, colored construction paper	Oil pastels
	Turpentine
Chalk	Scissors or pins

Strand E: Drawing Methods and Media

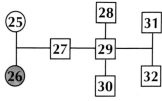

To evaluate your artwork, turn to the Learning Outcomes *section at the back of this book.*

27 *Joining Up Picture Ideas*

Observing and Thinking Creatively

Some artists can look at a piece of paper and **visualize**, or see in their minds, the finished picture before they even begin. Michelangelo, the great Italian artist who studied and worked at the same time as Leonardo da Vinci, could look at a block of stone and visualize a finished statue. He would then carve away parts of the stone and leave only the form he had pictured in his mind.

Everyone can learn to visualize. Being able to imagine how something might look will help you do many things in addition to art. In this lesson, you will use your imagination to visualize a finished artwork by filling in the empty space around parts of a photograph.

Romare Bearden makes collages from pieces of photographs and other pictures, fit together to make a totally new image. How many people are in *Eastern Barn?* How does the artist create a sense of depth around the very flat-looking figures?

Romare Bearden. Eastern Barn. 1968. Collage of glue, lacquer, oil and paper on composition board. 55½ × 44 inches. Collection of Whitney Museum of American Art. Purchase. Acq#69.14.

Eastwood Jr. High. Indianapolis, Indiana

Keystone Middle School. Indianapolis, Indiana

Instructions for Creating Art

1. Look through a few old picture magazines, and cut out some pieces of different photographs. You might find parts of houses, trees, or clouds.

2. Glue two of the photograph pieces onto a large sheet of paper. Leave plenty of blank space on the paper.

3. As you look at your paper, visualize a scene into which your photograph pieces fit naturally. Fill the blank space by drawing things you think belong in your picture. The photographs and your drawing should blend together to make one whole picture. This is called **unity**. The pictures in this lesson show examples of how to do this.

Art Materials

Old magazines	Pencil and eraser
Large sheet of	Glue
heavy white paper	Scissors

Strand E: Drawing Methods and Media

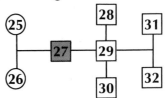

To evaluate your artwork, turn to the Learning Outcomes section at the back of this book.

63

28 Above and Below the Horizon

Observing and Thinking Creatively

If you live by the ocean, you know that you can look out over the water for a long way before the sea seems to end and the sky begins. If you live on flat land, you can also see far out to where the land seems to end and the sky begins. The meeting of sky and earth is called the **horizon**. It is the place where the curve of the earth stops you from seeing any farther.

Even though the horizon line is sometimes blocked from view, its height in relation to other objects can be determined by the eye level of the viewer. For example, if you sit on the floor of a room, you will see the underneath of tables and chairs; your eye level will be very low—an ant's point of view. When you sit on a chair or stand up, your eye level rises. If you climb to the top of a stepladder, you will get a bird's-eye view. Thus, the height of the horizon is determined by your eye level.

Next time you go outside, observe the horizon. Follow the earth until it meets the sky. Observe the horizon from different places, during different times of the day. Observing and understanding the horizon can help you in your artwork.

Impressionist Claude Monet used a high horizon line in *Cliff Walk (Etretat)* to emphasize the distance of the boats from land. Using dabs of bright color, Monet painted the reflections of sunlight bouncing off the windblown grass and waves.

Claude Monet, Cliff Walk (Etretat), 1882, Oil on canvas, 25¾ × 32¼ in. Mr. and Mrs. Lewis L. Coburn Memorial Collection. Courtesy of The Art Institute of Chicago.

The painter of this scene is looking up at the rooftops. Where is the horizon line of *Architectural Perspective?* The lines on the buildings and the ground lead directly to the center arch, through which we can see distant mountains.

Anon. Italian, Architectural Perspective: View of an Ideal City, *Walters Art Gallery, Baltimore.*

Instructions for Creating Art

1. Go to the chalkboard in your classroom. Sit close to one end of it. Make a chalk mark at exactly the same height as your eyes. Do the same at the other end of the chalkboard.

2. Join the two chalk marks together by drawing a straight line between them, as in the photograph above. If the chalkboard were a window, this line would be where you would see the horizon. The horizon line in your pictures is always at the same level as your eyes.

3. Now draw a level line across a piece of paper about halfway down representing the horizon.

4. Next, look in front of you. Decide where your eye level crosses through objects in your classroom. Which things are above eye level, and which are below? Use the line on the chalkboard as a guide.

5. When you are sure about the positions of the objects you can see in front of you, begin drawing. It doesn't matter if your drawing doesn't look real. Just be sure everything is in its right place—below, on, or above the eye level or horizon line.

Art Materials	
Drawing paper	Chalk and eraser
Pencil and eraser	Ruler

Strand E: Drawing Methods and Media

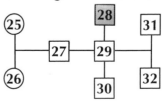

To evaluate your artwork, turn to the Learning Outcomes *section at the back of this book.*

29 *Two Ways of Showing Distance*

Observing and Thinking Creatively

When you look at a vase, you see it in three directions—from side to side, from top to bottom, and from front to back. Because the vase can be observed from three different directions, we say that it is three-dimensional. A **dimension** is a measurement in any one direction. Most things we see that are solid and fill space, like the vase, are three-dimensional. A line can be measured only in one direction, from one end to the other. A piece of paper can be measured from side to side (its width) and from top to bottom (its length). Thus, the surface of the paper has two dimensions.

Drawings and paintings are done on flat, two-dimensional surfaces. This means that artists have to find ways of showing the front-to-back dimension, or depth, if they want their pictures to look real. In this lesson, you will practice the following two methods of **perspective** drawing to show depth and distance in your pictures.

1. Objects of the same size appear larger when they are close to you and smaller when they are farther away.

2. Objects look closer to you if they overlap other objects.

Antonio Canaletto used size to create depth in the *Stonemason's Yard*. Notice the three-story building in the left foreground which is larger than the buildings across the river. What other objects show distance by their size in the picture?

Antonio Canaletto, Stonemason's Yard. *Reproduced by courtesy of the Trustees, The National Gallery, London.*

Maurice Utrillo painted many city scenes in older sections of Paris. What methods of perspective has the artist used to show distance in *Church of Le Sacre-Coeur, from Rue Saint-Rustique?*

Church of Le Sacre-Coeur, from Rue Saint-Rustique. Utrillo, Maurice. French, 1883-1955. Oil on Canvas, 19½ × 24 in. (50.0 × 61.0 cm.). Bequest of John T. Spaulding, 1948. 48.607. Courtesy, Museum of Fine Arts, Boston.

Instructions for Creating Art

1. Make separate drawings of six pieces of furniture of different sizes. You could draw a couch, TV set, table, bookcase, and different kinds of chairs. The furniture could be from your home, school, or anyplace else you choose. Make the drawings interesting, and show that you know what the pieces look like. It is important to draw all the objects in very different sizes.

2. Carefully cut out each of the drawings.

3. Arrange the cut-out drawings on a sheet of paper to show how close or far away they are. Make the bigger pieces look closer by overlapping them in front of the smaller pieces. When you have the pieces arranged the way you want them, glue the drawings down on the paper. Fill in the empty spaces to show other parts of your picture.

4. After you have experimented by arranging and overlapping different-sized objects in your picture, use the methods of perspective you have learned to make a drawing showing depth and distance. Choose a subject, such as trees, buildings, fruits, or flowers, that will

be appropriate for perspective drawing. The pictures in this lesson show how objects overlap, giving a sense of depth and perspective. Do larger shapes overlap others, so that they look the closest? Do smaller shapes in the distance look the farthest away?

Art Materials	
Furniture to draw	Glue
Pencil and eraser	Newspaper (to cover work area)
White paper	
Scissors	

Strand E: Drawing Methods and Media

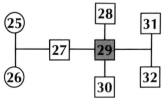

To evaluate your artwork, turn to the Learning Outcomes *section at the back of this book.*

30 Near, Far, and in Between

Observing and Thinking Creatively

By observing your surroundings, you may have noticed that objects look larger when they are closer, and smaller when they are farther away. Perhaps you have noted how such things as trees, telephone poles, buildings, and fences appear smaller in the distance. You may have also observed that when one shape overlaps another, it looks closer. These observations will help you in your artwork.

In this lesson, you will practice two more methods of **perspective** drawing to show depth and distance in a picture. The first is to draw finer details on objects that are closer to you. The second is to show differences in **value** by pressing heavily with a pencil when drawing objects that are nearer the front of a picture.

Louis Lozowick used three methods of perspective to show depth and distance in *Steel Valley*. Railroad tracks and the river trace strong parallel diagonal lines, and the distant buildings are lighter than objects in the foreground. Closer objects are larger; shapes overlap to suggest nearness.

Louis Lozowick, Steel Valley, 1942, Lithograph, 9½ in. × 13½ in., Memphis Brooks Museum of Art, Gift of Dr. Louis Levy. 47:507

Jacob van Ruisdael shows depth and distance in the drawing of *Sun Dappled Trees on a Stream* by using gradually fainter lines and decreasing the size of the trees in the distance. Observe how the leaves become less detailed as they get farther away.

Jacob van Ruisdael, Sun Dappled Trees on a Stream. *The Pierpont Morgan Library.*

Instructions for Creating Art

1. Look at the pictures in this lesson and note how different artists used perspective drawing to create a sense of depth and distance. Then decide on an outdoor scene or **landscape** you would like to draw. A landscape is a picture of natural land forms.

2. Draw outline shapes for all the parts of the landscape. In your picture, include some parts that are near to you, others that are far away, and some that are in-between. Your landscape picture could be from your imagination, or it may be an actual place where you have been. It might also be a drawing from a photograph in a book or magazine. Remember to draw just the outside lines of each shape. Do not add any details or shading yet. If you use a photograph, put it away after you have drawn the outlines.

3. After you have drawn all the outlines, begin adding details in the **foreground**, or parts of the picture that are nearest to you. These objects should show the most detail and shading. Draw and shade the nearest objects darker by pressing heavily with your pencil. The parts that are directly in the light should be left white for strong contrast.

4. Find the parts that represent the middle of your picture and fill in some details—but not as many as on the objects that are closest. The shading will not be as dark as it was in the foreground. This time, the light parts will be light gray instead of white.

5. Finally, the parts that are farthest away should appear faint and hazy and will not have any details. Their shading will also be different. The darker parts in the distance become lighter, while the lighter colors look grayer.

Art Materials

Pencil and eraser   Drawing paper

Strand E: Drawing Methods and Media

To evaluate your artwork, turn to the Learning Outcomes *section at the back of this book.*

31 Using Your Visual Memory

Observing and Thinking Creatively

In order to learn, you need to remember different kinds of information. For example, to learn music you must remember notes and scales; to learn language, you need to remember many different vocabulary words and sentence patterns. But how good are you at remembering what things look like?

Being able to recall from memory what something looks like is called **visual memory**. This ability to form in your mind an image or picture of what you have seen indicates how observant you are of your surroundings. Your visual memory is very important in art, because it enables you to draw what you have observed from memory.

Visual memory improves with practice. If you make a conscious effort to observe the world around you and store these observations in your mind, you will be able to include more images from your visual memory in your artwork.

Artists practice drawing from memory the things they have seen in order to refresh their visual memories. In this lesson, you will practice using your visual memory by making a drawing of a place you know well.

Edward Hopper painted this empty street as he remembered it in the early morning sunlight. He had a clear visual memory of the color of the buildings, window shades, barbershop pole, and fire hydrant. Why do you think he titled it *Early Sunday Morning?*

Edward Hopper. Early Sunday Morning. 1930. Oil. 35 × 60 inches. Collection of Whitney Museum of American Art. Acq #31.426.

Nigerian Student

Columbian Student

Instructions for Creating Art

1. Think of all the places in your neighborhood that you know. Then select one place to draw. Close your eyes and visualize this place in your mind. Imagine the colors, objects, and the people there. Visualize details, such as the clothes people are wearing, and the colors of cars, houses, or trees in the background. Think of your mind as a movie projector and your place as a scene in a movie. You are using your visual memory to do this.

2. When you have visualized the scene as you want to draw it, make a detailed list of all the things you remembered about it. Write the name of the place at the top of your list.

3. Now draw the place. First, remember what the largest shapes look like, and then recall as much detail as you can. As you draw, check the list you wrote. It will help you to include everything in your drawing.

4. If possible, go to the real place after school to see if you put everything in correctly. How good was your visual memory? Make any necessary changes in your drawing. Then complete your picture with paint, crayon, colored markers, or pen and ink.

Art Materials

Your choice: paints, crayons, colored markers, pastels, etc.

Pencil and eraser

Drawing paper

Strand E: Drawing Methods and Media

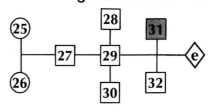

To evaluate your artwork, turn to the Learning Outcomes *section at the back of this book.*

32 Inside an Artist's World

Observing and Thinking Creatively

Think of all the indoor places you visit every day. Use your **visual memory** to recall one place you know well and picture it in your mind. First **visualize** the walls or sides. Note the objects and colors you see. Where are the doors and windows? Now picture the different parts of the room. What objects or pieces of furniture do you see in each part? Is the place light or dark? Are there people present?

It may not be easy for you to remember exactly what places look like—especially the insides of rooms, hallways, and gyms. Most people remember the walls and ceilings, some of the objects in the room, and perhaps how they are arranged. In drawing indoor pictures, artists also need to remember how a place is lit. Does the light come from the windows, or does it come from electric lights? Often, because of the lighting, many indoor pictures are darker than outdoor pictures and have more shadows in them. This lesson will help you use your visual memory to picture and draw an indoor place.

Vincent van Gogh remembered many details of the *Bedroom at Arles.* He also communicates memories of his feelings in that room by his choice of colors. Notice the mirror, pictures on the walls, the table, and the partially opened windows. Why would such details be important in a painting like this?

Vincent van Gogh, The Bedroom at Arles, 1888–1889, Oil on canvas, 29 × 36",
Helen Birch Memorial Collection, 26.417. Courtesy of The Art Institute of
Chicago.

Jonell Folsom, Nashville Shop. *Courtesy of the artist.*

St. Joseph Hill Academy. Staten Island, New York

Instructions for Creating Art

1. Think of an indoor place that you know well, like the inside of a local store, school bus, lunchroom, church, or room in your grandparents' house.

2. Visualize each part of the room—the walls, doors, ceiling, sides, corners, and center. Recall the lighting in the room. Is light streaming in from a window, or is the light source a lamp or overhead fixture? How does the light affect the objects in the room?

3. Draw what you visualize, using one of the materials in the Art Materials box. You may want to draw only a corner or section of the room. The important thing is to put in everything just as you remember it—from the world inside your mind.

Strand E: Drawing Methods and Media

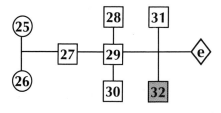

To evaluate your artwork, turn to the Learning Outcomes *section at the back of this book.*

33 Drawing Profiles

Observing and Thinking Creatively

In the days before cameras were invented, the only way to show what people looked like was to have artists draw or paint their **portraits**. Some artists liked showing side views. Side-view portraits are called **profiles**. Some very good ones were painted by Alesso Baldovinetti five hundred years ago in Italy. One of these is shown here. Although these pictures were painted and not drawn, they were done with such thin brushes that they look like drawings.

Profiles are not usually as hard to draw as other views of heads, because most of the important shapes are on the outside edges. Unique facial features, such as large eyes or a crooked nose, can be shown using lines and shading.

A good way of learning to draw portraits is to begin by drawing profiles. In this lesson, you will draw a profile by having someone model for you.

Alesso Baldovinetti painted *Profile of a Lady* with many details in the lady's dress, necklace, and elegant hair arrangement to distinguish her as an important person. Note the angle of the neck and position of the eyes, nose, and mouth. How does the use of wavy lines soften the profile?

Alesso Baldovinetti, Profile of a Lady, *(B & W) from the National Gallery, London. Alinari/Art Resource, New York. 18190.*

Compare the differences in features among the *Four Heads* drawn by Albrecht Dürer over 400 years ago. Note how the faces in the background are lighter.

Albrecht Dürer, Four Heads, 1513 or 1515, Pen and ink, 8¼" × 7⅞", The Nelson-Atkins Museum of Art, Kansas City, Missouri (Nelson Fund).

Azalea Middle School. St. Petersburg, Florida

Instructions for Creating Art

1. Look at the pictures of profiles in this lesson. Notice that the eyes are about halfway down the head. The end of the nose is about halfway between the eyes and the end of the chin. The mouth is about halfway from the end of the nose to the chin. Also notice how the back of the head sticks out. Finally, notice how the neck joins the head at an angle.

2. When you think you know where to draw all the parts of the head, you are ready to draw a profile. The best way to draw a profile is to have someone model for you.

3. Carefully observe the profile and facial features of your subject. Then begin drawing by lightly sketching an outline of the head. Your lines should be nearly invisible. Only after you have drawn the profile should you add the details and fill in the shading. When everything looks right, draw the ear in last. The top

of the ear is about level with the eyebrow, and the bottom of the ear is usually at the same level as the mouth. As you draw the profile, try to show individual features such as large eyes, an upturned nose, or high cheekbones.

Art Materials

Drawing paper   Pencil and eraser

Strand F: Faces and Figures

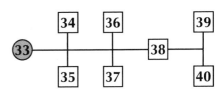

To evaluate your artwork, turn to the Learning Outcomes *section at the back of this book.*

75

34 Create a Face

Observing and Thinking Creatively

Faces are fascinating to observe. People have distinct facial features that give them expression and personality. Even though the arrangement of these features may be similar, sizes, colors, shapes, and proportions will vary from face to face. These differences make every face unique.

Study the various faces shown in this lesson. Notice how different artists have sketched faces and facial features. Can you identify the main shape of each head? Note the position and arrangement of facial features. Where do the eyes, nose, and mouth appear in relation to each other? Where are the ears in relation to the eyes?

In this lesson, you will sketch the facial features of someone you observe. As you draw the different parts, you will need to observe the proportions, the relationship of the parts to each other and to the whole. Then you will draw a portrait of the entire face.

Edward Hopper created this powerful *Self-Portrait* using charcoal. Observe how he drew a few basic lines to show the shape of the face and the proportions of certain facial features. For most of the portrait, however, the artist used shading to achieve a range of values, from light grey to black. Note how the far side of the face is hidden in shadow in contrast to the near side, which is drawn with greater detail and highlighted with light areas. These bold contrasts give the face solidity and create expression.

Edward Hopper, Self-portrait, 1903, charcoal on paper, 16½ × 12 inches, National Portrait Gallery, Smithsonian Institution, Washington, D.C.

San Diego City Schools. San Diego, California

San Diego City Schools. San Diego, California

San Diego City Schools. San Diego, California

Instructions for Creating Art

1. Observe the faces around you. Look at the full front view, the **profile**, and the three-quarter view of each face. How do the eyes, ears, nose, and mouth differ from face to face? How do they change when you observe the same face in different positions? What other similarities and differences do you see?

2. Choose someone's face to draw. Observe the facial features closely. Practice sketching just the eyes, nose, mouth, and ears on a large sheet of drawing paper. Try sketching them from different angles. Look carefully at all your sketches and select the ones that best capture the facial features of your model.

3. On a new sheet of drawing paper, draw a portrait of the person. You may want to draw either a full front view or a three-quarter view of the face. Closely observe the proportions of the head and the arrangement of facial features. Begin by drawing the main shape of the head. Then sketch in the facial features where you observe them.

4. Compare your sketch to the face of your model. Make any changes in the placement or proportion of facial features. Then add shading and final details to complete your portrait.

Art Materials

Two sheets of drawing paper

Charcoal (optional)

Pencil and eraser

Strand F: Faces and Figures

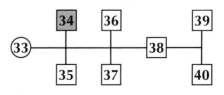

To evaluate your artwork, turn to the Learning Outcomes *section at the back of this book.*

35 Face Messages

Observing and Thinking Creatively

Faces are like mirrors that reflect our moods and feelings. Have you noticed the expressions on people's faces when they are feeling strong emotions, such as after winning a game or award, or after failing a big exam? Artists study these expressions and draw or paint them on people's faces in their artwork. For example, the faces painted by Rembrandt in *Belshazzar's Feast* show surprise and wonder. In contrast, the faces of the two tax gatherers, painted by Marinus, express heartlessness and greed.

When you look at artists' **portraits** of people, first ask yourself if they look real in the way they have been drawn or painted. Then notice what they show about the people and their feelings. When you have answered these questions, you will have a better understanding of what the artist was trying to portray. You will also be able to judge the quality of the art.

In this lesson, you will practice drawing a portrait of yourself showing your feelings, emotions, and expression.

The faces of *The Tax Gatherers* reflect different feelings about collecting taxes. To the man on the left, it is simply a job that pays well enough for his fur collared robe and fancy hat. What might the other man be thinking?

Marinus, The Tax Gatherers. *Reproduced by courtesy of the Trustees, The National Gallery, London.*

Rembrandt displays his great skill at portraying character in *Belshazzar's Feast*. Notice the expression on the guests' faces and their startled looks. What do you think might be happening?

Rembrandt van Rijn, Detail from Belshazzar's Feast, *Reproduced by courtesy of the Trustees, The National Gallery, London.*

Instructions for Creating Art

1. Look into a mirror. Imagine that different things have happened to you. For example, imagine that someone has just given you a thousand dollars, or that you have just hit your thumb with a hammer. What expressions does your face show? Do certain facial features change when your expressions change? How do the shapes of your eyes and mouth change when you smile? When you frown?

2. Decide on an expression you wish to show in a self-portrait. Begin by lightly sketching the main shape of your head. Before you draw eyes, nose and mouth, think about the emotion your face will reflect. This will help you to know how to arrange the facial features and how they will be shaped. Surprised eyes or a sad mouth may be drawn differently than sleepy eyes or a laughing mouth. Sketch the facial features to deliver a message or to show emotion. (Refer to Lesson 34 for more information on drawing faces.)

3. Complete your self-portrait showing the expression that tells how you feel. Add details, like laugh lines or a wrinkled nose, that help to show your expression.

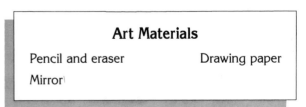

Art Materials

Pencil and eraser   Drawing paper
Mirror

Strand F: Faces and Figures

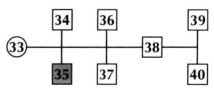

To evaluate your artwork, turn to the Learning Outcomes *section at the back of this book.*

36 *Drawing Close-ups*

Observing and Thinking Creatively

Do you recall a scene from a movie or television show in which a close-up view of the characters appeared on the screen? Perhaps the characters showed expressions of distress, joy, or surprise, and the camera close-up captured these emotions for the viewer.

People's faces often fill the entire space on a movie or television screen. Artists rarely showed this kind of close-up picture before photography was invented. Television and movie directors use close-ups when they want the audience to feel that they are observing something special. A director might use a close-up to show a strong emotion like fear. Close-ups are also used by poster designers and book illustrators.

In this lesson, you will draw a close-up. You can show any subject you like in the picture, as long as it is interesting to look at and fills the whole sheet of paper.

The narrow opening through which we see the terrified face of *Judith Harper* reveals a feeling of fear and suggests the possibility that she is being chased. Margaret Doogan chose this unusual way to give us an intimate glimpse of the woman as if we are peering through a keyhole.

Margaret Bailey Doogan, Judith Harper *(from the "Articulate" series). Oil and glitter on black paper, 44" × 30", 1983.*

Käthe Kollwitz created this lithograph of herself to emphasize her exhaustion. Observe her finger holding her eye open and the wrinkle lines. Can you feel the tiredness in this drawing?

Käthe Kollwitz, Self Portrait, 1934, Lithograph, 8¹/₁₆" × 7³/₁₆", Philadelphia Museum of Art: Given by Dr. and Mrs. William Wolgin.

Instructions for Creating Art

1. Think of a close-up picture you would like to draw. You may want to picture a scene in a spy story where two people are whispering. Or you might show a close-up of a girl's face as she makes the supreme effort to sprint toward the finish line in a race. To make a scary drawing, you might want to completely fill the picture with the head of a snarling tiger that seems about to leap out at you. You may find it is easier to sketch the whole shape as large as you can and then decide which part you want to use for your close-up picture.

2. When you have completed the outline sketch, add the details. Because everything in the picture will be so close, every little detail must be shown clearly. For example, if a person is wearing glasses, every detail of the hinges and the nosepiece should be carefully drawn. If you are drawing an animal, the fur, feathers,

or scales should be clearly defined. Add color with crayons, pastels, or colored markers to finish the picture.

Art Materials	
Your choice: crayons, oil pastels, or colored markers	White paper
	Pencil and eraser

Strand F: Faces and Figures

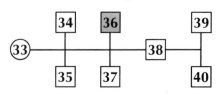

To evaluate your artwork, turn to the Learning Outcomes *section at the back of this book.*

37 Small into Large

Observing and Thinking Creatively

Can you recall seeing large pictures drawn or painted on walls or billboards? Perhaps you have wondered how artists are able to make such large pictures.

For hundreds of years painters have made small drawings on paper to plan pictures that will be enlarged to fit whole walls. The finished paintings are called **murals**. Because it is very difficult to enlarge all the parts of a design equally—to **scale**—artists use a **grid**. A grid can be made by dividing a piece of paper into equal squares. Then, instead of having to enlarge all the parts of a picture at once, the artist draws what is in each of the squares separately. In this way, the work of enlarging, reducing, or repeating a design is something that anyone can do, with a little practice.

In this lesson, you will learn one way to make drawings either larger or smaller.

Lenape Jr. High School. Doylestown, Pennsylvania

Instructions for Creating Art

1. Choose a drawing that you did for a previous lesson or create a new drawing of a face, figure, or animal.

2. Make the drawing into a **grid** of equal squares, each measuring one inch across. It is important to draw these squares accurately.

3. Take a much larger sheet of white paper and mark it into the same number of squares you made on your picture. The squares on the second sheet of paper will be much larger. First, count the number of squares across the top and down one side of your original picture. Then measure the length and width of your white drawing paper and divide it into the same number of squares.

4. On the large sheet of white paper, draw and shade all the parts you see in each square of the original drawing. Draw each part in the same position as it is on the picture. This is a **scale drawing.**

Art Materials	
Large drawing of a face, figure, or animal (about 9″ x 12″)	Pencil and eraser
	Ruler
Drawing paper (either 12″ × 18″ or 18″ × 24″)	Scissors

Strand F: Faces and Figures

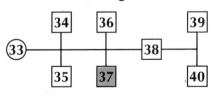

To evaluate your artwork, turn to the Learning Outcomes *section at the back of this book.*

38 *Human Measurements*

Observing and Thinking Creatively

If you are an observer of people, you will note that, except for identical twins, each person is unique in both face and **form**. Each human form is characterized by certain body **proportions**, the relationship of the body parts to each other and to the whole. You will observe that, when people stand up with their arms to their sides, their hands are positioned about halfway down their bodies, whether they are tall or short.

Anyone who studies art will need to observe body proportions in order to draw people. One of the most important things to learn about drawing people is to make the arms, legs, head, hands, feet, and body all look as though they belong together. Artists who draw the human form observe proportions and often practice drawing body parts before drawing the entire figure. Note how Michelangelo has drawn different parts of the body in his sketches shown below.

In this lesson, you will observe body proportions and sketch the human form.

Michelangelo drew *Studies for the Libyan Sibyl* in preparation for a painting. These sketches show changes he made as he practiced drawing different parts of the body.

Michelangelo, Studies for the Libyan Sibyl. *Red chalk on paper. H. 11⅜ in. W. 8⅜ in. Copyright © 1980 by The Metropolitan Museum of Art, Purchase, 1924, Joseph Pulitzer Bequest.*

In *Baseball Players Practicing*, Thomas Eakins has captured a moment in the sport by showing two players in different positions. The artist began the picture by first making sketches of the basic body proportions of the two players. Note the forms of each figure and the positions of the arms and legs. What adjustments in body proportions has the artist made?

Thomas Eakins, American 1844-1916, Baseball Players Practicing, *1875, Watercolor, Museum of Art, Rhode Island School of Design; Jesse Metcalf Fund and Walter H. Kimball Fund.*

Instructions for Creating Art

1. Study the artwork on page 84. Notice how Michelangelo has used lines and shading to make the body parts appear solid and **three-dimensional**. In the artwork shown above, observe the proportions of the baseball players in different positions.

2. Choose one person as a model to sketch. Observe the body proportions, noting sizes and relationships of hands, feet, arms, and legs. How does the size of the person's head relate to the height of the whole body? Is there a relationship between the size of your subject's hands and size of the face? How do the length of arms and legs compare to the total body height? Where do elbows divide the arms and knees divide the legs?

3. Have your subject assume several different poses. How are body parts arranged when standing, reaching, bending, or sitting?

4. Decide on a position you wish to sketch. Look often at your subject. Begin by lightly sketching the form and body parts. Compare your drawing with your subject. Have you drawn the figure proportionally? Make any changes or adjustments in your drawing that are needed. Then add details and shading to make the figure look three-dimensional.

Art Materials

Pencil and eraser   Drawing paper

Ruler

Strand F: Faces and Figures

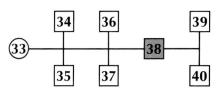

To evaluate your artwork, turn to the Learning Outcomes *section at the back of this book.*

39 Different Ways of Drawing

Observing and Thinking Creatively

Everyone draws differently. Some people like to draw every detail very carefully. Others do their best work when they scribble their ideas quickly. Some artists use thick, heavy lines, while others prefer thin, wispy lines. There is no one way of drawing that is right for everyone. It may take some time for people to discover the ways of drawing that are best for them.

Many artists learn to draw several different ways so they can choose the **style** of drawing that best fits their subject or art **theme**. Observe the artwork in this lesson. Note how each artist has used a particular style to draw the forms and faces of people. Observe how the different styles and feelings of the artists are reflected in the expressions of the people.

Artists also experiment with different kinds of drawing materials to learn which ones they prefer. Some artists like to use pencil to make sketches. Others use charcoal, pen and ink, pastels, or paint. Many artists use a variety of art materials to express different styles of drawing.

A good way to explore different ways of drawing is to experiment with a variety of **media**. This practice will enable you to discover the **medium** you like best and a drawing style that is uniquely your own.

One of the first published cartoonists was Francisco Goya, a Spanish painter and printmaker. His quick line drawings, with expressive figures and humorous comments, quickly became popular about 200 years ago. Why do you think the artist chose the title *You Make a Mistake If You Marry Again?*

Francisco Goya, You Make a Mistake If You Marry Again, Brush and India ink on white paper (black ink and grey wash), 267 × 181 mm (10½ × 7⅛"). Courtesy of the Fogg Art Museum, Harvard University.

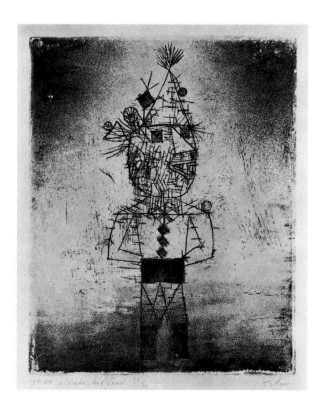

Childlike drawing is characteristic of Paul Klee's style. Note the variety of simple lines and shapes used here to depict the clown.

Paul Klee. Prickle, the Clown. 1931. Aquatint, printed in black, plate: 11⁹/₁₆ × 9⁷/₁₆". Collection, The Museum of Modern Art, New York. Gift of Victor S. Riesenfeld.

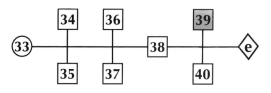

Käthe Kollwitz used black crayon and charcoal in this drawing to create a feeling of desperation. Note how she used only a few light lines in the faces to express the beggars' weariness.

Käthe Kollwitz, Bettelnde (Begging), Lithograph, The Metropolitan Museum of Art, Harris Brisbane Dick Fund, 1928. (28.68.7)

Instructions for Creating Art

1. Look at the drawings in this lesson. How are they alike? In what ways are they different? Note the variety of art styles and **media** used by the artists. Then look through the book for other styles of drawing.

2. Decide on a subject matter to draw that includes a person or people. You might draw someone you know or people from a photograph or magazine picture. Or you can create a figure from your imagination, as Paul Klee did in his picture, *Prickle, the Clown.*

3. Then choose a medium for drawing from the Art Materials box that best suits your subject matter. Make a preliminary sketch with pencil, and complete your drawing using the art materials of your choice.

4. Now draw the same subject once again, using a different medium from the materials list. Compare your two drawings and notice the different effects achieved by using two different drawing media.

Art Materials

Your choice: pen and ink, charcoal, crayons, pastels, etc.	Pencil and eraser Drawing paper

---

Strand F: Faces and Figures

```
        [34]   [36]              [39]
  (33)───┼──────┼─────[38]────────┼──────◇e
        [35]   [37]              [40]
```

To evaluate your artwork, turn to the Learning Outcomes section at the back of this book.

40 *The Genius of Leonardo da Vinci*

Observing and Thinking Creatively

Leonardo da Vinci lived over four hundred years ago during the **Renaissance** period in Italy. He is considered by many to be one of the greatest geniuses who ever lived. He was an artist, scientist, inventor, and engineer. He filled stacks of notebooks with drawings and writings about many of his ideas. His sketches reveal that he was a man far ahead of his time. He designed a number of things like airplanes, bicycles, machine guns, and armored tanks—things that were not actually invented until modern times.

Leonardo was a keen observer of nature, animals, and the human body. He would often sketch the same subject from different angles and in various positions. He also studied and drew the bones and muscles of people and animals to gain a new understanding of how they were made.

Not only did Leonardo observe, experiment, and invent, he also designed buildings, painted pictures, and made sculpture. His paintings, including the *Mona Lisa,* reproduced on page 89, and the famous *Last Supper* are among the greatest artworks of all time.

This pen drawing illustrates Leonardo's fascination with studying human nature. Here he has pulled together a most distinctive assortment of physical features into an unusual looking group of men. Who do you suppose these men may have been?

Leonardo da Vinci, Five Grotesque Heads. 1490. Pen. Royal Library, Windsor Castle. Reproduced by gracious permission of Her Majesty Queen Elizabeth II.

In the *Mona Lisa*, Leonardo has utilized his extensive studies of the human form to create one of the world's most famous portraits. How does the use of subtle colors, subdued background details, and the appearance of light radiating from the face help to show the character of this woman? Note how her steady gaze and luminescent appearance give the feeling of self-assurance and inner peace. What other techniques has the artist used in creating this portrait?

Leonardo da Vinci, Mona Lisa, *Louvre, Paris, Scala/Art Resource.*

Leonardo's appreciation for nature is seen in his drawing of *The Star of Bethlehem and Other Plants.* The artist made hundreds of sketches, which he used as records of visual reality in his continual search for the underlying nature, form, structure, movement, and dynamics of what he drew. Study how this detailed drawing, made with red chalk and pen, reveals the delicate structure of the stems, buds, and leaves.

Leonardo da Vinci, Star of Bethlehem and Other Plants, *c. 1505-8, Red chalk and pen, 7⅝" × 6⅜", Royal Library, Windsor Castle, Reproduced by Gracious Permission of Her Majesty Queen Elizabeth II.*

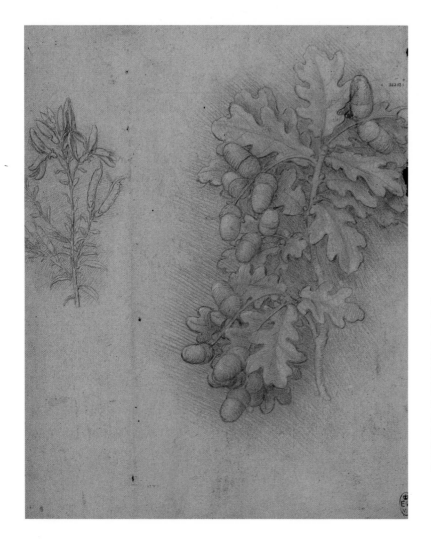

Oak Leafs with Acorns and a Spray of Greenwood is a drawing from one of Leonardo's sketch books. Great artists often draw simple, everyday objects from their immediate surroundings. Note how Leonardo filled in the background with light strokes of his chalk to make the objects stand out.

Leonardo da Vinci, Oak Leafs with Acorns and a Spray of Greenwood. *Reproduced by gracious permission of Her Majesty Queen Elizabeth II. The Royal Library, Windsor Castle, England.*

Instructions for Creating Art

1. You can learn a lot about art by studying the work of great artists. Look at the pictures of Leonardo's art. Note how his sketches show how closely he observed the subjects he drew. Then choose a subject that interests you to study and sketch. The subject for your sketches might be a natural object, a person, or an animal.

2. First, observe and study whatever you choose to draw from all angles. Then make three pencil sketches of your subject, each showing a different angle or position. Start by sketching the main outlines. Then add the details. Shading should be done after the lines have all been drawn. Shade the lighter parts first, and then fill in the darker areas.

3. When you have completed the sketches, choose one as the basis for a finished piece of art. Select the **medium** of your choice to draw your final artwork.

Art Materials

Your choice: pen and ink, charcoal, pastels, etc.

Pencil and eraser

Drawing paper

Strand F: Faces and Figures

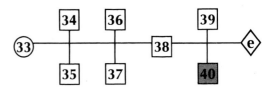

To evaluate your artwork, turn to the Learning Outcomes *section at the back of this book.*

90

Exploring Art

Keeping a Sketchbook

Great works of art usually start with simple sketches. In fact, most good artwork develops from a series of sketches. The sketching habit is essential to learning how to draw for both the amateur artist and the professional. Well-known artists, such as Leonardo da Vinci and Michelangelo, filled many sketchbooks with their practice sketches and drawings. Today, some of their sketches are famous works of art.

Start your drawing explorations by making or buying a sketchbook. You can make a sketchbook by folding and stapling drawing paper together, or you can purchase a sketchbook from an art supply store.

Use your sketchbook to experiment with different ideas and ways of drawing. Make sketches in your home, outdoors, and around your school or neighborhood. Sketch things that interest you—a tiny snail, an unusual tree, a child playing. Start with an object having simple lines. Make several sketches of it from different angles.

Then try sketching a more complex form, such as an animal or plant. Practice drawing the individual parts before drawing the whole. As your sketches progress, add details, shading, and **texture.**

Many different kinds of drawing tools can be used to make sketches, including pencils, crayons, felt pens, charcoal, pen and ink, pastel chalk, and brush and paint. Each drawing tool produces lines and **tones** with different qualities and characteristics. The way you use each tool will also affect the quality of drawing. Experiment by sketching with different materials and by making lines thin or thick, delicate or bold, dotted or scratchy, fine or blurred.

As you make your sketches, write brief notes about the colors, hues, sizes, and textures of the objects you've drawn. These notes will be helpful later when you want to create a finished artwork based on a sketch.

Showing an animal in motion requires much practice in observing and sketching the various positions. Leonardo's *Three Studies of Horses* show how he observed a prancing horse and drew it from different angles. Notice the corrections he made as he sketched.

Leonardo da Vinci, Three Studies of Horses *in black & white. Reproduced by gracious permission of Her Majesty Queen Elizabeth II. The Royal Library, Windsor Castle, England.*

91

Vincent van Gogh, The Starry Night. (1889) Oil on canvas, 29" × 36¼" (73.7 × 92.1 cm). Collection, The Museum of Modern Art, New York. Acquired through the Lillie P. Bliss Bequest.

Unit III

Composing with Colors

. . . when I paint, I never really know what I will paint. I look at the many colors before me. I look at my blank canvas. Then . . . I try to apply colors like words that shape poems, like notes that shape music.

Joan Miró

Artists use colors to communicate visual images, feelings, and imagination like writers use words to create stories and poems. Soft, subtle shades can express a peaceful mood. Explosions of vibrant colors in pictures might depict action, rhythm, and unrest. Brilliant colors can be joyful, while darker shades may seem more serious and somber.

Colors can be added to a composition using different **media**, such as colored paper, crayons, pastels, and paints. In this unit, you will learn how to use a variety of paints and explore different methods of painting. As you work, you will discover that paint can be applied with fine, delicate brushstrokes, or thick, bold ones. Paint can also be dabbed, dribbled, dotted, splashed, swirled, rolled and sprayed.

The lessons in this section will acquaint you with many well-known painters whose styles range from realistic to **abstract**. As you study their artwork, you will observe how various styles and methods of painting create different effects. For example, swirls of vibrant colors in van Gogh's paintings suggest motion and unrest, while Seurat used dabs of pure color to create a different effect. Through experimenting with a variety of media and techniques, you will develop your own painting style.

41 Colorful Creations

Observing and Thinking Creatively

Color is an important element in our world. It affects feelings, influences what we wear, and determines how we decorate our surroundings. Nature blends colors in a rainbow and splashes them across fields and sky.

In the world of art, color, or **hue**, is a major element of design. Artists use colors to express moods and ideas in their artwork. They experiment by mixing colors to produce new ones. You will find a knowledge of color helpful when planning your designs and pictures.

Colors are often arranged on a color wheel to show how they relate to one another. Every hue except white, can be produced by mixing different combinations of the three **primary colors**— red, yellow and blue—shown in the triangle in the center of the color wheel below. Two primary colors combine to make a **secondary color**. (See

the three colors adjacent to the triangle.) For example, orange is a secondary color made by combining the primary colors red and yellow. Can you find the other secondary colors on the color wheel below? What primaries were combined to produce them?

The colors between the primary and secondary colors on the color wheel are called **intermediate colors**. An intermediate hue is made when a primary color is added to a secondary color. Blue-green, for example, is an intermediate hue made by mixing the primary color blue and the secondary color green. Find the other intermediate colors on the color wheel. For more information about color, refer to page 3.

In this lesson, you will study the color wheel to learn about other color relationships. Then you will use paints to create a colorful design.

COLOR WHEEL

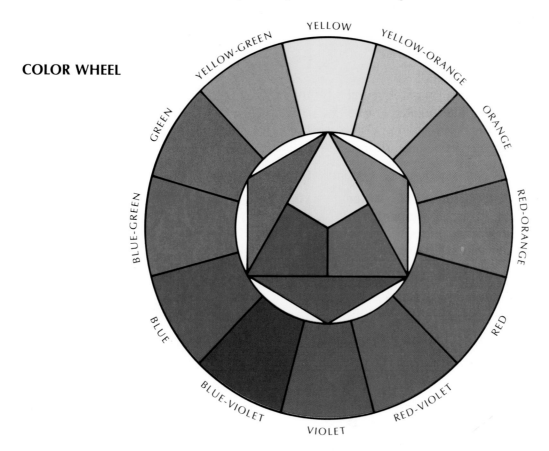

Lewis Junior High School. San Diego, California

Lewis Junior High School. San Diego, California

Instructions for Creating Art

1. Colors that are directly opposite on the color wheel are called **complementary colors**. Identify pairs of complementary colors by placing your pencil across the center of the color wheel. Colors that appear on opposite ends of your pencil are complementary colors. For example, green is the complement of red.

2. **Analogous** colors appear adjacent to one another on the outside ring of the color wheel. They are related colors that all share a hue in common. For example, yellow-green, green and blue-green all contain green. Can you find them next to each other on the color wheel? The analogous colors in the blue, green, and violet family are commonly referred to as **cool colors**. Which analogous colors on the color wheel are considered **warm colors?**

3. Experiment with groups of analogous colors to see how they combine and what effects they create. Begin by painting a large shape in the warm or cool color of your choice. Before the color dries, add splotches of other analogous colors from the group. Tilt the edge of the paper and watch the colors mix as they run together.

4. While your first paper is drying, develop another design with a totally different group of analogous colors. Look at the two designs. Do

the color combinations create a mood or give you an idea for a design?

5. Select one of your experiments to use as the background for a new design. Create a **unified** design using colors, shapes, and lines. For contrast, you may want to add complementary colors. You can emphasize certain areas with lines, details, and patterns.

Art Materials	
3 sheets of drawing paper	Colored markers
Pencil	Newspapers (to cover work area)
Watercolor paints and brushes	Water, paper towels

Strand G: Color and Composition

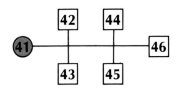

To evaluate your artwork, turn to the Learning Outcomes *section at the back of this book.*

95

42 Brushing with Rhythm

Observing and Thinking Creatively

If you recall your first attempts at painting as a small child, you might remember using large brushes and brightly colored paints. Most young children like to experiment with paints and brushes by making large brush strokes and simple shapes.

Many people use brushes to fill in spaces with color; yet brushes can also be used to draw lines. Using a brush to make lines is like drawing, except that a brush's lines can be more graceful and flowing than those of a pen or pencil. In learning to paint, it is important to use brushes in as many ways as possible. In this lesson, you will practice using a brush to draw a picture made of graceful, flowing lines that show **rhythm**.

For hundreds of years, artists in China and Japan have painted beautiful pictures by drawing with brushes. Some European and American artists have also used brush lines in their paintings and drawings to show rhythm. The paintings that are reproduced in this lesson are also good examples of this kind of art.

Japanese artist Hiroshige has used a variety of simple brushstrokes and empty spaces to create this striking composition of *The Cat*. Notice how your eyes first focus on the cat, then follow the long line of the string across the picture.
Photograph from Daniel J. Boorstin's 2 volume set of The Sketchbook of Hiroshige, *vol. 2, plate number 11.*

Charles Burchfield painted *Sun and Snowstorm* with strong, wavy brushstrokes. The rhythm of lines and contrasting yellows and blues create the effect of blinding, blowing snow.

Charles E. Burchfield, Sun and Snowstorm, 1917. Watercolor. Private Collection, photograph courtesy of Kennedy Galleries, Inc., N.Y.

Benton Central Jr. High School. Oxford, Indiana

Instructions for Creating Art

1. Look at the pictures on these pages. They may give you some ideas about different ways of showing rhythm with a brush, but show your own kind of rhythm in your artwork.

2. Fill a sheet of paper with practice work, using a soft brush and watery paint. Make all kinds of curving, rhythmic lines; don't try to make a picture of anything. Loosen up your hand and arm, so the brush makes smooth, flowing lines that twist and turn all over the paper. When you have filled a sheet with practice lines, look carefully for any rhythmic lines you think are good.

3. Think of a place you have seen or imagined that makes you feel happy, peaceful, or contented. Now make a drawing of this place on a clean sheet of paper, using only a brush and water paint (no pencil). It doesn't have to look real. All the lines you use should be flowing and rhythmic, like the best ones from your practice sheet. Some can be big and bold, and others can show detail, but all should show rhythm. Select colors that reflect the mood or feeling you want to express. Add an extra splash of color or finer, detailed brushwork to create a center of interest.

Art Materials

Paints and brushes

Drawing paper

Mixing tray

Newspaper (to cover work area)

Water, paper towels

Strand G: Color and Composition

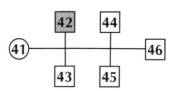

To evaluate your artwork, turn to the Learning Outcomes *section at the back of this book.*

43 *Painting over Wax*

Observing and Thinking Creatively

Have you ever tried to wash greasy dishes without soap or detergent? If so, you probably discovered that water alone will not get rid of grease. This is because water will not mix with anything that is oily or greasy. Artists sometimes use wax and watercolors together in an artwork, even though these two materials will not mix. You may have tried a similar kind of art if you have ever made a crayon drawing and then brushed over it with thin, watery paint. The background paper absorbed the paint, but the crayon wax did not. This kind of art is called wax **resist**.

Watercolor paints are **transparent**, and the color is usually mixed with large amounts of water. Because of this, any pencil drawing on the paper underneath often shows through the paint. For this reason, watercolor artists usually do not make detailed pencil drawings before they begin painting. Instead, they draw in important details at the end, using dark paint and a small brush, or pen and ink.

Like all artists, watercolor painters frequently experiment to discover ways of making their pictures more interesting. For this lesson, you will explore the effects that you can create with wax and watercolor paints.

If you have ever tried drawing with the end of a wax candle, you will realize why the shapes Henry Moore drew are composed of straight lines and simple curves. The watery paint also helps us see the wax lines, because it will not stick to the wax. Do these gentle curving shapes make you think of stillness and sleep?
Henry Moore, Pink and Green Sleepers. *The Tate Gallery, London.*

Finnish student

Meridian Middle School. Indianapolis, Indiana

Instructions for Creating Art

1. Look at the pictures in this lesson and note how the artists achieved interesting effects with wax and watercolors.

2. Practice drawing some designs on a small piece of paper with an ordinary white candle or crayon. Press down heavily on the paper as you draw.

3. When the wax drawing is done, paint over the paper with thin, watery paint. Notice that the paint runs off any areas where there is wax.

4. Now think of a new picture or design and draw it with candle wax or crayon on another sheet of paper. Work with the wax in as many different ways as you can. Paint over the waxy drawing, as before. You can paint with one color or several.

5. When your picture is dry, add details or designs using any combination of paint, pencil, crayon, or pen and ink. If you used colored crayons underneath, you may want to scratch away some of the paint to let the color show

through. Your finished art may be a realistic picture or an abstract design.

Art Materials	
White drawing paper	Crayons
Candle (white)	Mixing tray
Watercolor paints	Pen and ink
Brushes	Water, paper towels

Strand G: Color and Composition

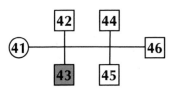

To evaluate your artwork, turn to the Learning Outcomes *section at the back of this book.*

99

44 A Watercolor Painting

Observing and Thinking Creatively

You may have noticed how colors seem to blend in the sky to create special effects. Perhaps you have seen a sunset glowing with reds and violets, or clouds drizzling with shades of gray and dull blues. Artists sometimes try to capture scenes such as these by using watercolor paints, which are an effective medium for this kind of artwork.

Watercolor paints are **transparent**, which means that you can see through them as if you were looking through a colored glass window. Other paints that you mix with water, such as **tempera** paint, are **opaque**; you cannot see through them. Watercolor works best when you mix it with plenty of water and then paint on white paper. The paper quality is very important, be-cause the whites and highlights in a watercolor painting depend on the whiteness of the paper.

As you look at the pictures in this lesson, you will see the beautiful effects that can be created with watercolors. The artists began by making only a few light pencil lines to show where the main objects should be. The palest, most watery background colors were painted in first. When they were dry, darker colors were added on top to show things that are in the **foreground**, or front of the picture. The closest parts and details were done last, using a small brush and thicker paint.

In this lesson, you will use transparent water-colors to paint a picture.

American artist Winslow Homer is famous for his watercolor paintings. In *Bermuda Sloop,* he achieves the effect of light on the boat, sails, and waves by letting the white paper show through. Note the wash techniques he has used.

Homer, Winslow (1836–1910), Bermuda Sloop. *Watercolor on paper. H. 15 in. W. 21½ in. The Metropolitan Museum of Art, Amelia B. Lazarus Fund, 1910.*

Montgomery Junior High School. San Diego, California

Montgomery Junior High School. San Diego, California

Instructions for Creating Art

1. Learning how to apply a transparent *wash** is often the first step in painting with watercolors. A watercolor wash sometimes forms the background of a picture.

   Before beginning a wash, first tape or tack the paper to a flat surface. Then lightly dampen the drawing paper with a clean, watery brush. Do not use so much water that the paper becomes soaked. If puddles of water begin to form, blot them up with dry paper towels, but do not rub the paper.

2. Experiment by making several watercolor washes. Make your first wash using only one color. Then make another using two or three colors. Vary the shades by using lesser and lesser amounts of color as you work down the paper. After dampening your paper, apply the color using quick brushstrokes back and forth, alternating the strokes from side to side in an even, rhythmic fashion. Add more color and water to the brush only at the end of a brushstroke, not in the middle of the page. Be careful not to make your wash too wet. Washes usually look best if they are painted fairly quickly.

3. After you have practiced making several watercolor washes, lightly sketch an idea for an outdoor scene on another sheet of paper. Think about the kind of background you want to show in your picture—a misty day, a vivid sunset, a sunlit sky, etc. With your pencil, lightly sketch in the objects in the distance, such as hills, houses, buildings, or trees. Show only a few simple shapes and do not add the details. Then sketch in the objects in the **foreground**, or closest part of your picture. Pencil marks will show through watercolors, so make your sketch very faint.

4. Next, paint in your background with a light watercolor wash using pale, watery paint. First, dampen the paper slightly. Then lay in the colors for your sky in light, flowing brushstrokes from top to bottom. Leave some white paper showing through if you want to create the effect of highlights or white clouds. If the color is too strong, or too much water collects, blot it with paper towels.

5. When the background wash is dry, add objects and shapes in the distance using thicker paint. Make your background shapes simple. To paint in closer shapes and details, use a smaller brush with more paint and less water.

6. When the paint has dried, add the finer details using thicker paint and a very small brush.

*For an explanation, turn to the How to Do It section at the back of this book.

Art Materials

Several sheets of drawing paper	Mixing tray
Masking tape	Newspaper (to cover work area)
Watercolor paints and brushes	Water, paper towels

Strand G: Color and Composition

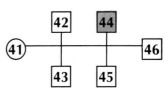

To evaluate your artwork, turn to the Learning Outcomes *section at the back of this book.*

101

45 Shapes Without Outlines

Observing and Thinking Creatively

Look closely at the objects around you. Observe the outside edges in particular, and note how they are defined. As you observe, you will discover that there aren't definite outlines; rather, the shapes and their shading appear to form outlines. If you look at a car, house, or school desk, you will see it does not have a line around its outside edge. Yet, people often drawn lines around the shapes in their pictures because the edges of things define their shapes.

Because artists understand that shapes do not have lines around them, they often draw and paint pictures that show the edges of objects without actually showing outlines. In this lesson, you will learn about the way things look realistically. You will paint a picture without outlines.

Frederic Clay Bartlett has defined these shapes by using the contrast of light against dark colors, rather than starkly outlining each object. Notice the far side of the table against the wall and the woman's arm against the back of the chair.

Frederic Clay Bartlett, Blue Rafters, 1919, Oil on Canvas, 28" × 30½", Friends of American Art Collection. 19.107 © Courtesy of The Art Institute of Chicago. All Rights Reserved.

Tecumseh Jr. High School. Lafayette, Indiana

Tecumseh Jr. High School. Lafayette, Indiana

Instructions for Creating Art

1. For this lesson, gather several interesting objects that you can closely observe. Select objects that vary in size and shape. If you cannot find anything at school for your picture, bring something from home. Ask your teacher for ideas and suggestions. You might use a vase of flowers or dried weeds, fruit, rocks, shells, pinecones, plants, candles, ceramic pots, figurines, etc.

2. Create an arrangement in which the sizes, shapes, colors, and textures are balanced and show **unity** of design. Place them against an uncluttered background, overlapping some objects in front of others. A group of nonliving objects arranged in this way for a painting or drawing is called a **still life**.

3. Lightly draw in the main shapes of your still life with pencil. Make the arrangement fill most of your paper. Then paint the picture without using any outlines; let the shapes of the objects form their own outlines. Be sure to fill in the background spaces around the still life so that your paper is completely filled. You may want to paint the background before

painting the objects. You can achieve **unity** by making the objects and the background appear as though they belong together.

The pictures in this lesson show how different artists have done this, but you can also invent your own ways of painting without outlines by closely observing shapes.

Art Materials

Objects for a still life	Paints and brushes
Drawing paper	Mixing tray
Pencil and eraser	Water, paper towels

Strand G: Color and Composition

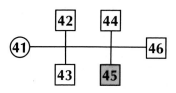

To evaluate your artwork, turn to the Learning Outcomes *section at the back of this book.*

46 Viewfinder Pictures

Observing and Thinking Creatively

Do you know that you have an artist's vision each time you look at the world? Every day you choose to see only what interests you. You do this artistically when you take a photograph. When you look through the little window in the camera called a **viewfinder**, it shows what will be in the picture. Other artists besides photographers use their own kinds of viewfinders. These viewfinders help them see which view of a scene would make the best picture. Viewfinders also block out all the parts of a scene that the artist does not want in a drawing or painting.

When artists create pictures from their imaginations, they arrange objects and **compose** their pictures any way they wish. Artists who create pictures based on actual scenes have to solve a very different problem. They have only two ways of altering a scene. First, they can move themselves to a place where the shapes look good together and form a naturally artistic composition. Second, they can select a few things from everything in front of them to put in their picture. In this lesson, you will use a viewfinder in both these ways to compose a picture.

The Cleaning of the Fish, painted by Pieter de Hooch, shows a backyard in which every object and person has been carefully arranged to pull us into the scene. Notice the man in the distance walking towards us, while the women busily work. What directs our eyes to the fish?

Pieter de Hooch, The Cleaning of the Fish. *Reproduced by courtesy of the Trustees, The National Gallery, London.*

Lewis Jr. High School. San Diego, California

Instructions for Creating Art

1. Cut a window shape in a piece of paper or thin cardboard. The easiest way to do this is to fold the paper in half and cut out an opening along the fold. Practice once or twice until your window opening is about the same **proportions** as your drawing paper.

2. Study the pictures in this lesson and decide whether or not they are composed well. Now, hold up the viewfinder and look through it to find an interesting group of objects or people in your classroom, around your school, or outside. Adjust the viewfinder until the objects or figures look balanced and form a **unified** picture that you want to draw.

3. First, draw the large shapes you see through the viewfinder on your paper using whatever drawing instrument you prefer. Outline the shapes so that they fill the paper. Strive to reproduce the same scene you see.

4. Next, draw in all the details that seem important to the scene. Choose one part of the picture as a **center of interest** and emphasize this area by adding finer details.

5. You may want to use a **monochromatic color scheme** to paint your picture. A monochromatic color scheme consists of a pure hue and its variations, produced by adding varying amounts of white (**tints**) and black (**shades**).

Art Materials

Piece of paper or thin cardboard	Drawing paper
Scissors	Paints and brushes
Pencil and eraser	Mixing tray
Ruler	Water, paper towels

Strand G: Color and Composition

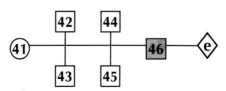

To evaluate your artwork, turn to the Learning Outcomes *section at the back of this book.*

105

47 From Dark to Light

Observing and Thinking Creatively

Have you ever stood on top of a hill and looked off into the distance? Do you remember how mountains, water, or buildings look from far away? In the distance, things like hills and trees seem to turn a whitish-purple or blue-gray color because the dust, mist, and smoke in the air have a fading effect on colors.

As a painter, consciously think about what happens to colors in the distance and try to reproduce that effect. To do this, you need an understanding of distance and depth. Because pictures are flat and the scenes that appear in them have depth and distance, artists must use lines and colors to make things look near or far away. Using lines to show depth and distance in a picture is called **linear perspective**. Distance can also be shown with color, a technique known as **atmospheric perspective**. You will practice atmospheric perspective in this lesson by using color to show distance.

In the *Bathers*, Impressionist Georges Seurat used both lines and colors to show distance. Notice how the objects in the foreground are brighter in color and larger than those in the distance. Seurat used tiny dots of color that appear to blend together as you get farther away from the painting.

Georges Seurat, Bathers. *Reproduced by courtesy of the Trustees, The National Gallery, London.*

The distant gray-blue mountains compose almost half of *House in Provence* by Paul Cézanne. The trees and house are balanced by the horizontal lines and brighter colors in the foreground. Note the kinds of perspective Cézanne used in this painting.

Paul Cézanne, French, 1839–1906, House in Provence, ca. 1885. Oil on canvas 45.194. Indianapolis Museum of Art, Gift of Mrs. James W. Fesler in memory of Daniel W. and Elizabeth C. Marmon.

Instructions for Creating Art

1. Think about a **landscape** picture you want to paint that will show distance, such as a seacoast or mountain scene. Make a preliminary sketch showing some objects in the **foreground** and others in the distance.

2. Paint your landscape with thick **tempera** paint on medium-colored paper. Tempera paint is **opaque**: you cannot see the paper through it. Begin by painting the parts that are farthest away. Add white paint to the colors you use for things in the distance. To make the sky seem distant, add more white paint as you get closer to the horizon in your picture. Mix purple and blue with the colors of objects like mountains to achieve a hazy, far-off look.

3. As you come nearer to the foreground, use brighter colors to make things appear closer. Vary your colors by mixing others with them. If you are painting green fields, for example, try adding other colors such as blue-green, yellow-green, yellow, or brown. Keep your paint thick and creamy as you work.

4. When the paint is dry, add details to the objects in the foreground to make them appear even closer.

Art Materials

Medium-colored paper	Newspaper (to cover work area)
Tempera paints and brushes	Water, paper towels
Mixing tray	

Strand H: Styles of Painting

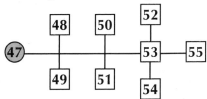

To evaluate your artwork, turn to the Learning Outcomes *section at the back of this book.*

48 Bright Blobs and Splashes

Observing and Thinking Creatively

When you paint, do you feel that your picture is good only if it looks like the real things it portrays? Years ago, most painters felt that way. They painted **realistic** pictures that represented the world as they saw it.

The trend away from realistic painting began with the invention of the camera. A group of painters began to change the ways they painted in order to do things cameras could not do. They began to paint outdoors instead of in a **studio**. As they moved outdoors, they noticed that sunshine seemed full of different colors. They also noticed how the movement of the sun during different times of day changed the appearance of things and created different moods.

These painters painted **landscapes** showing how sunlight brought out the brilliant colors in nature. They invented new ways of using color by painting with blobs of pure color placed next to each other on a painting surface. In this way, they were able to create rich, vibrant colors unlike paints mixed on a palette.

Because these artists wanted to capture the mood or impression of a scene, they became known as **Impressionists**. They began the first great modern art movement of our time, breaking away from the realistic approach to art.

The first Impressionists, who began working in this way about a hundred years ago, were led by a Frenchman, Claude Monet. Observe his painting in this lesson and notice how he used color and the effects of light. There are many artists today who also use this style of painting. In this lesson, you will use an impressionistic style to paint a landscape picture.

Claude Monet is one of the most famous French Impressionist painters. His style of painting with short strokes of color to capture the sparkle of sunlight is shown in this painting of waterlilies.

Claude Monet, Waterlilies, *Oil on Canvas. 34.75" × 36.25". Collection: Mr. and Mrs. Martin A. Ryerson. Courtesy of The Art Institute of Chicago.*

Meridian Middle School. Indianapolis, Indiana

Lenape Jr. High School. Doylestown, Pennsylvania

Instructions for Creating Art

1. Look at the Impressionist art shown here and throughout this book, especially paintings by Pierre Auguste Renoir, and Claude Monet. Studying the work of these great artists is a good way of learning a new style of painting and improving your own artwork. Note how these artists applied color. Before the Impressionists, artists blended their colors so that brushstrokes were rarely visible. Most Impressionists did not blend their colors. Instead, they used streaks and dots of pure color. By using this technique, they were able to achieve the effect of shimmering sunlight and vibrant colors in their artwork. Their experiments had a lasting effect on art.

2. If possible, before completing this lesson, observe an outdoor scene that you would like to paint. Notice the effects of light on different objects. Make a quick sketch of the scene and take brief notes about the colors and lighting effects you observe.

3. If you are unable to observe an outdoor scene, quickly sketch a picture of a landscape you remember and like. It can be the same kind of subject as an Impressionist painting, or it may be something quite different.

4. Paint the picture you have sketched. Apply your paint in the Impressionist style, using quick strokes and bright colors. Make your landscape appear as though sunlight is shining on it.

Art Materials

Drawing paper	Mixing tray
Pencil and eraser	Water, paper towels
Paints and brushes	

Strand H: Styles of Painting

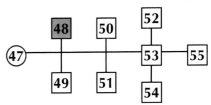

To evaluate your artwork, turn to the Learning Outcomes *section at the back of this book.*

49 Paint with Matisse

Observing and Thinking Creatively

One successful way of learning about art is to study the work of an important artist and then use that artist's **style** to make your own art. In this lesson, you will learn about the work of a great French artist, Henri Matisse.

Matisse lived from 1869 to 1954. The use of bright colors, freely flowing lines, and fanciful decorations marks his style. Matisse knew how to paint and draw things to look real, but he did not believe that artists should merely copy what they saw. He liked to look at people and places and then give his creative imagination all the freedom it needed as he painted his pictures.

Throughout his lifetime, Matisse worked in a variety of art **media**, including painting, print-making, and collage. He also designed the entire chapel of the Dominicans at Vence in France. In his later years, confined to his bed or wheelchair, he created fascinating designs with cutouts made from colored paper. (See Lesson 2 for an example of Matisse's cutouts.)

As you look at Matisse's art, notice his emphasis on light, color, and rhythm. In this lesson you will learn more about Matisse's style as you practice using it in your own painting.

Interior with Etruscan Vase, by Henri Matisse, shows the freely painted curving lines, bright colors, and stripes that are characteristic of his style. Look closely to see how Matisse uses repeating patterns to draw your eyes around the picture.

Henri Matisse, Interior with Etruscan Vase, *1940. Oil on canvas. The Cleveland Museum of Art, Gift of the Hanna Fund.*

Intense colors and unusual color combinations mark Matisse's style. *The Purple Robe* is so full of swirls and stripes that the woman's face stands out in contrast. Note how these designs create a sense of rhythm and movement.

Henri Matisse, The Purple Robe, 1937. The Baltimore Museum of Art: The Cone Collection formed by Dr. Claribel Cone and Miss Etta Cone of Baltimore, Maryland. BMA 1950.261

Oak Hill Jr. High School. Converse, Indiana

Instructions for Creating Art

1. Look at the pictures by Matisse in this lesson. Notice how he painted and what he painted —usually ordinary things, like people sitting down and the insides of rooms.

2. Sketch a picture of a subject similar to one that Matisse painted, using light, color, and rhythm the way he did. First draw the outlines of the shapes and figures. Include the background space as part of your design.

3. Choose a color scheme that fits your subject matter. Note how Matisse used bright colors, striking contrasts, and interesting patterns. He often painted solid areas of color, and then added details and patterns. Try using this same technique to paint your picture.

4. When your paint is dry, you may want to add details and patterns as Matisse did in some of his artwork.

Art Materials

White paper   Mixing tray

Pencil and eraser   Water, paper towels

Paints and brushes

Strand H: Styles of Painting

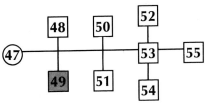

To evaluate your artwork, turn to the Learning Outcomes *section at the back of this book.*

111

50 *People at Work*

Observing and Thinking Creatively

Think about the kinds of activities you enjoy and those you dislike. Perhaps you love to study literature, but dislike history. Maybe you're really good at working with your hands, but have difficulty figuring out math problems. Eventually, you will match your skills and interests to a specific career.

In the same way, artists often become interested in one particular kind of subject or one particular mood or feeling. Sometimes artists will use the same style of art or work with one **medium** their entire lives. One artist may enjoy

modeling portraits in clay, while another prefers to paint landscapes. Other artists create art from dreams, paint scenes of the ocean, design art for churches, or do sculptures of animals. For this lesson, you will paint a picture of people doing work you find interesting.

Think about the kinds of workers you find interesting to watch: construction workers, mechanics, actors and actresses, window washers, beauticians, dancers, athletes, etc. If possible, closely observe this type of worker in action before you complete this lesson.

Mexican artist Diego Rivera often painted his people working at various difficult jobs. How does the composition of the design emphasize the work being done?

Diego Rivera, The Flower Carrier *(formerly* The Flower Vendor*). 1955. Oil and tempera on masonite. San Francisco Museum of Modern Art. Albert M. Bender Collection. Gift of Albert M. Bender in memory of Caroline Walter.*

Jacob Lawrence has tilted the head of the man to emphasize his concentration on sharpening the tool. *Builders #1* illustrates Lawrence's painting style which uses simplified shapes and flat colors. Why do you think the man's arms are so large?

Jacob Lawrence, Builders #1, 1972. St. Louis Art Museum.

Instructions for Creating Art

1. Observe the artwork in this lesson and note how each artist depicted people working. Also notice where the **center of interest** occurs in the pictures; it will be the place that shows the most action, or where your eyes look first.

2. Think of the kind of work you would like to show in a picture. It should be work that is interesting to watch, such as the construction workers pictured above. If possible, observe the workers, noting their movements, body positions, and facial expressions. Make a few quick sketches of them working.

3. Use your sketches to guide you in composing your final picture. If the work is done mainly with hands, like typing, make the hands the center of interest. The most important part of the artwork should be centered around the action. Paint your picture to complete it.

Art Materials

Drawing paper	Mixing tray
Pencil and eraser	Water, paper towels
Paints and brushes	

Strand H: Styles of Painting

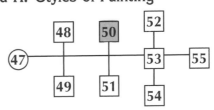

To evaluate your artwork, turn to the Learning Outcomes section at the back of this book.

51 Showing Action in Sports

Observing and Thinking Creatively

Think of some action sports you like to watch or play. Basketball, track, wrestling, soccer, tennis, swimming, and gymnastics are just a few that might come to mind. People who play these sports must move their bodies quickly and correctly. You may have observed how athletes' bodies bend, twist, turn, jump, and kick. Coaches and trainers often take photographs or make videotapes to study how their players move. In this way, both players and coaches can see what they need to do in order to improve.

The following poem, *Foul Shot*, captures the nervous tension and action of a basketball player. In this lesson, you will make an artwork that stops the action and shows what the athletes look like during the high point of a sport.

Foul Shot

With two 60's stuck on the scoreboard
And two seconds hanging on the clock,
The solemn boy in the center of eyes,
Squeezed by silence,
Seeks out the line with his feet,
Soothes his hands along his uniform,
Gently drums the ball against the floor,
Then measures the waiting net,
Raises the ball on his right hand,
Balances it with his left,
Calms it with fingertips,
Breathes,
Crouches,
Waits,
And then through a stretching of stillness,
Nudges it upward.

The ball
Slides up and out,
Lands,
Leans,
Wobbles,
Wavers,
Hesitates,
Exasperates,
Plays it coy
Until every face begs with unsounding screams—

And then

   And then

      And then,

Right before ROAR-UP,
Dives down and through.

     —Edwin A. Hoey

Calexico High School. Calexico, California

Rancho San Joaquin Middle School. Irvine, California

Instructions for Creating Art

1. Think about the kind of sport you know best because you have either played it or watched it. If possible, observe athletes playing the sport before completing this lesson. Notice how their bodies move. How does a basketball player dunk the ball into the net? How does a sprinter look crossing the finish line of a championship race? As you watch, make a few sketches of the players in motion. Observe changes in the position of body parts when the body is in action. Show the movement, the straining muscles, and the expressions on the faces of the players.

2. From your sketches, choose part of the action to draw in a picture. Create a **center of interest** by focusing on the movement of certain players or on a special feature of the sport. Show the action in the best way you can. (Refer to Lesson 38 for more information on drawing the human form.)

3. When you have completed your sketch, paint your picture. Select a color scheme that fits the subject matter and shows the action.

Art Materials

Pencil and eraser	Watercolor or tempera paint and brushes
Drawing paper	

Strand H: Styles of Painting

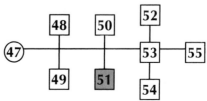

To evaluate your artwork, turn to the Learning Outcomes *section at the back of this book.*

115

52 *Geometry in Art*

Observing and Thinking Creatively

There is no single correct way of making art. Different people have different tastes, and many artistic problems have more than one solution. It is good to learn as many different ways of making art as you can.

Artists paint in a variety of ways. Sometimes they may choose to paint using wild, splashy colors. Other times, they may want to paint in a neat and careful manner. One way of being neat and careful is to use rulers, **compasses**, and other drawing instruments—instruments that are used in math and geometry. In this lesson, you will use drawing instruments to create an artwork with geometric shapes, such as squares, rectangles, and circles.

If you have not recently used the drawing instruments listed for this lesson, practice using them before beginning your design. You will be more successful in doing this lesson if you feel comfortable using each of the instruments.

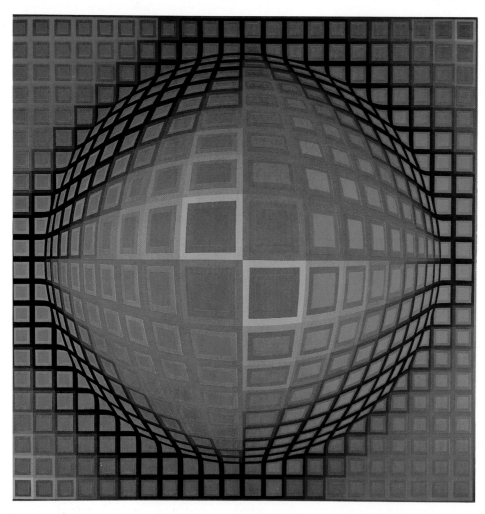

Victor Vasarely is famous for optical art. In *Vega-Nor,* he has created the illusion of a bulge on the flat surface. Notice how each square has been carefully drawn with precise instruments.

Victor Vasarely, Vega-Nor, *1969. Albright-Knox Art Gallery. Buffalo, New York. Gift of Seymour H. Knox, 1969.*

Beautiful and interesting designs can be created with simple tools like a compass and ruler. How many places can you identify where Frank Stella set the point of his compass to create this painting called *Lac Laronge IV*?

Frank Stella, Lac Laronge IV, 1969, Acrylic polymer on raw canvas, The Toledo Museum of Art; Gift of Edward Drummond Libbey.

Lewis Cass School. Walton, Indiana

Instructions for Creating Art

1. First, practice using a *ruler, set square, compass, protractor,** and a pencil to make various lines, shapes, and patterns. Also use a *T square** and drawing board if they are available. Experiment with using these instruments to make interesting designs.

2. Now draw a design. Use the most interesting ways you have discovered for drawing with instruments. Create a design or picture consisting of geometric lines and shapes. Be sure that every line in your design is made with a drawing instrument. All the lines will be either perfectly curved or exactly straight.

3. Paint your design with **tempera** paints using only two **primary colors**. The primary colors are red, yellow, and blue. All other colors except white can be made by mixing these three colors. Mix only the two primary colors you have chosen to make different colors. You may also add black and white to make light and dark **shades** and **tones**. Carefully fill in each part of your design with color. Be sure to paint exactly up to the pencil lines, making your edges even. Repeat certain colors and

patterns to achieve a **unified** design. When you finish, you will have created a piece of geometric art.

For an explanation, turn to the How to Do It section at the back of this book.

Art Materials

Drawing paper	Tempera paints and brushes
Pencil and eraser	Mixing tray
Drawing instruments: ruler, compass, protractor, and set square	T square and drawing board (optional)
	Water, paper towels

Strand H: Styles of Painting

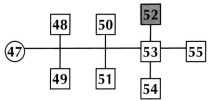

To evaluate your artwork, turn to the Learning Outcomes section at the back of this book.

117

53 *Losing Your Head*

Observing and Thinking Creatively

Have you ever watched a magician perform magic tricks? As you were entertained, were you also puzzled? Perhaps certain nagging questions kept entering your mind: Where did it go? How did she do that? Where did that come from? . . . It's that uncertainty that makes magic fun.

Art can be magical, too. Pictures often include shapes and forms that we can see only if we search for them. Artists also play tricks by showing objects that don't exist at all in the real world. Such magic helps make art interesting—even puzzling—at times.

It is not necessary for good art to look realistic; it can also be good because it does not look real. **Abstract** art uses shapes and designs that express moods and feelings rather than concrete reality. The pictures in this lesson show how artists in different parts of the world have combined magic with puzzles and dream-like ideas to create abstract art. These pictures may give you ideas that will help you think of a design for a picture with the title *Losing Your Head.*

Cubist Juan Gris painted this portrait to show Picasso as one of the most important Cubist painters. Notice the geometric shapes in the background contrasting with the shapes of Picasso that have more curving edges. Paintings by both Gris and Picasso often look like puzzles which do not fit together exactly. Do you get a sense of seeing the figure from several different angles at once?

Juan Gris, Portrait of Picasso, 1912. Oil on canvas, 29¼" × 36⅞". Gift of Leigh B. Block. 1958.525. Courtesy of The Art Institute of Chicago.

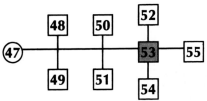

Jenkins Middle School. Haines City, Florida

San Diego City Schools. San Diego, California

Instructions for Creating Art

1. Make a simple drawing of a face. Draw the outline of the face to fill most of the paper.

2. Now divide the face and the rest of your paper into different shapes. Use the same kind of pencil line for dividing the face that you used to draw the outline. The parts of the face should almost disappear among the lines, just as they do in the pictures shown here.

3. Refer to the color wheel and the information on color in Lesson 41. Select a color scheme of three or four colors. Paint all the separate shapes of your design using these colors. Repeat certain colors to achieve a **unified** design. When the picture is finished, you should barely be able to recognize the original face. By changing your artwork in this way, you have created a piece of abstract art.

Art Materials

Drawing paper	Mixing tray
Pencil and eraser	Water, paper towels
Paints and brushes	

Strand H: Styles of Painting

47 — 48 — 50 — 52
      | | 53 — 55
      49 — 51   54

To evaluate your artwork, turn to the Learning Outcomes *section at the back of this book.*

54 Guess What It Was

Observing and Thinking Creatively

Have you ever looked at a piece of art and wondered what it represented? Perhaps you've seen a picture by a famous artist and asked, "What is it?" Some artists deliberately paint pictures that don't look like anything real. This kind of art is called **abstract**.

Some abstract artists do not try to portray anything real in their art. Others start with a real object and then change it into an abstract picture. This is one way of being creative.

Look at the pictures in this lesson and observe how the Dutch artist, Theo van Doesburg, began by drawing a realistic cow. In eight different sketches, he gradually changed the original drawing into rectangles, squares, and triangles. The first painting of *The Cow* on page 121 was based on one of the sketches shown below. Which sketch is the painting most like? The last picture, *Composition (The Cow)*, does not really look like any of the sketches, because the artist wanted to make it completely abstract.

In this lesson, you will begin with a realistic drawing and then make it into an abstract artwork with straight lines and geometric shapes.

In this series of sketches, Theo van Doesburg has shown us how he simplifies his image of *The Cow.* Notice the geometric forms that are drawn on top of the realistic image. At what point do you no longer recognize the cow?

Theo van Doesburg, The Cow. *Series of 8 pencil drawings, 4⅜" × 6¼" (nos. 1,2,4,5,6,7); 6¼" × 4⅜" (nos. 8,9). Collection, The Museum of Modern Art, New York.*

The Cow is now mostly geometric shapes. It is an abstract painting which looks only slightly like a black cow with a bright light shining down one side. Why do you suppose van Doesburg chose these particular shapes to represent a cow?

Theo van Doesburg, Composition (The Cow). 1916, Gouache, 15⅝" × 22¾". Collection, The Museum of Modern Art, New York. Abby Aldrich Rockefeller Fund.

Composition (The Cow) is a fully abstract cow. Do you know why it is called that? The titles of paintings often come from thoughts and ideas of the artists. Abstract art makes us spend more time looking at shapes, color, and lines, and we often find something new and exciting every time we look at it.

Theo van Doesburg, Composition (The Cow). (1916–17) Oil on canvas. 14¾" × 25". Collection, The Museum of Modern Art, New York. Purchase.

Instructions for Creating Art

1. Create a large outline drawing of an animal, bird or person. The lines and shapes of your drawing should make the subject appear as realistic as possible.

2. In your next sketch, begin to abstract your drawing by replacing realistic lines with straight lines. Replace some areas of the drawing with geometric shapes. Continue these changes by creating new sketches of your drawing, each one more abstract.

3. When the lines and shapes are as abstract as you wish them to be, use paints for additional abstractions. Refer to Lesson 41 and select a color scheme for your picture. You may want to use **complementary** colors to create contrast. You may wish to use **analogous** colors, or colors that are related.

4. Compare your original drawing with your finished painting. Decide how the painting is different. Write a few sentences telling about

these differences or be ready to discuss them with your classmates.

Art Materials

Pencil and eraser	Mixing tray
Two sheets of drawing paper	Water, paper towels
Paints and brushes	Writing paper (optional)

Strand H: Styles of Painting

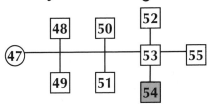

To evaluate your artwork, turn to the Learning Outcomes *section at the back of this book.*

121

55 *In Search of a Painting Style*

Observing and Thinking Creatively

Each person has an individual art **style** which only that person can discover. An artist's style is influenced by a combination of factors—personal experiences, feelings, preferences, background, as well as exposure to the styles of other artists. Each piece of art that you do is a way of searching for your own art style. Your particular style of painting will result from your choice of paints and the way you apply them. Style is also determined by the way shapes are shown and the artist's choice of subjects and colors. One way to discover your own style is to study the work of a particular artist and art style that you like.

In this unit, you have studied the work of many famous artists. You have also used various art **media**, including watercolor and tempera paints, and found that each one produces different effects. Think about the styles of painting you have seen. Then look over some of your own pictures. Which art style seems most appealing to you? This lesson will help you discover the style of painting that seems best for you.

With tiny strokes of bright paint, Impressionist Pierre Auguste Renoir catches the sparkle of sunlight on *A Girl with a Watering Can* and the delightful spirit of the little girl. What do you like about this painting style?

A Girl with a Watering Can; *Auguste Renoir; National Gallery of Art, Washington; Chester Dale Collection 1962. (Dated 1876)*

American artist Georgia O'Keeffe's style is uniquely her own. She is famous for her enlarged close-up studies of flowers. How does she make this *White Trumpet Flower* stand out against the background? What else can you say about her style?

Georgia O'Keeffe. The White Trumpet Flower, 1932. Oil on canvas, 30" × 40". San Diego Museum of Art. Gift of Mrs. Inez Grant Parker in memory of Earle W. Grant.

Dong Kingman's series of watercolor paintings depicting American cities is well known. Notice how he achieves unity here by linking the reds, yellows, and grays together with a brown mixture of all these colors.

Dong Kingman. The El and Snow. 1946. Watercolor. 21 × 29⅜ inches. Collection of Whitney Museum of American Art. Purchase. Acq#47.9.

Winslow Homer's life on the coast of Maine inspired him to paint the ocean and the hardworking fishermen there. Note how your eyes first focus on the men pulling in the fish. How would you describe Homer's painting style?

Winslow Homer, The Herring Net, *1885. Oil on canvas. 29¼" × 47¼". Mr. and Mrs. Martin A. Ryerson Collection 37.1039. Courtesy of The Art Institute of Chicago.*

Instructions for Creating Art

1. Observe the paintings by different artists in this lesson, throughout the unit, and in other art books. Also look at your own artwork, as well as art done by other students. Select one artist who uses an art style you like. Observe as many works as you can by this artist.

2. Then think of a subject for a picture you would like to paint. You can paint a **still life**, a **landscape**, a **portrait**, or any other subject you choose. When you have an idea for a subject, make a sketch for a picture. Sketch only the main shapes; you will add the details when you paint your picture. It may be necessary to make several quick sketches in order to create one that pleases you.

3. Select your best sketch and paint your picture in a style that is uniquely your own. Be sure to use a paint medium that is best suited for this style and subject. If you are not pleased with your first picture, try another. Professional artists often make several pictures of the same subject before they create one which satisfies them.

4. Display your finished painting so that it can be appreciated by others. (See the *How to Do It* section at the back of this book for instructions on matting and framing your picture.)

Art Materials

Several sheets of drawing paper

Pencil and eraser

Paints and brushes

Mixing tray

Water, paper towels

Strand H: Styles of Painting

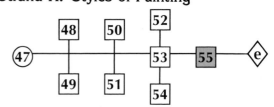

To evaluate your artwork, turn to the Learning Outcomes *section at the back of this book.*

124

Exploring Art

A Painter's Biography

In Lesson 55, you studied the artwork of a painter you liked, and employed a similar style in a painting of your own. For this activity, you may want to learn more about that same painter, or you may choose another artist to study. Before you decide, observe the paintings of various artists throughout this book and in other art books. If you have an art museum in your community, you may want to visit the museum and observe works of art firsthand. Then select one artist who uses an art style you like. Find out all you can by reading about this artist in various books and resources, and by observing his or her works of art.

Write a biography of the artist you choose to study. Tell about the artist's life and art background. During what major art period did this artist paint? Describe the artist's style—abstract, impressionistic, realistic, etc.—and explain what you like about it. Point out specific art elements and painting techniques, such as expressive use of color, rhythm of line, or simplicity of form, that you especially appreciate in the artist's work.

For your biography, you may choose one of the following master painters, whose works represent the major art periods. Or you may select a painter who is not listed below.

Vasily Kandinsky	Georgia O'Keeffe
Vincent van Gogh	Claude Monet
Pablo Picasso	Michelangelo
Rembrandt van Rijn	Pierre Auguste Renoir
Leonardo da Vinci	Thomas Gainesborough
William Turner	Winslow Homer
Frederic Remington	Henri Matisse
Mary Cassatt	Andy Warhol
Andrew Wyeth	Salvador Dali

The Russian artist Vasily Kandinsky experimented with many different styles before his paintings became abstract. This painting of *Blue Mountain* shows horses and riders against a colorful background. The figures and landscape are abstract. Where do you find a balance of shapes and colors in this painting?

Vasily Kandinsky, Blue Mountain, *1908–09. Collection, Solomon R. Guggenheim Museum, New York. Photo: David Heald.*

Antoine Pevsner. Twinned Column. 1947. Bronze, 40½" high. #54.1397. Justin K. Thannhauser Collection, Solomon R. Guggenheim Museum, New York.

Unit IV

Sculpting and Forming

There are three forms of visual art: Painting is art to look at, sculpture is art you can walk around, and architecture is art you can walk through.

Dan Rice

Drawings and paintings are art forms usually made on flat surfaces with two **dimensions** —height and width. Other art forms, such as sculpture, pottery, and architecture, have a third dimension—**depth**—the front-to-back measurement of an object. In this unit, you will have an opportunity to create a variety of three-dimensional art forms.

As you explore the world of three-dimensional art, you will discover the importance of touch and **texture**. Your hands will be your primary tools as you feel the rough edges and smooth contours of a piece of sculpture, or shape the wetness of a chunk of clay. The scope of your artistic vision will expand as you view your creations from all different angles. You will also discover that space is just as important as the solid forms themselves in three-dimensional art.

As you begin this unit, observe both the natural and man-made environment around you to see examples of three-dimensional art. Nature has two well-known sculptors —wind and water. The wind is a master at sculpting jagged mountain peaks or smoothing sand dunes into shifting patterns and ridges. Water sculpts minute grains of sand, smooths pebbles and rocks, and carves out cliffs and canyons. Look around you and observe the artistic forces of nature at work.

Inspired by their observations of nature, people from all cultures through the centuries have created three-dimensional art forms. In this unit, you will study the art of the Egyptian and African people and use their styles of art to create artworks of your own. Finally, you will learn how architects design the space in which we live.

127

56 *Sculpture from Found Objects*

Observing and Thinking Creatively

Every day we throw away all kinds of things that could be used in some way. For example, when we clean out the garage or attic, we throw away old toys, clothes, parts, and letters. Think about the kinds of things you have thrown away in the past week. Did you ever wonder if perhaps you could use some of these things?

Some sculptors collect things that people normally throw away and turn them into art. This kind of sculpture is called **assemblage**. Assemblage means art that is made by joining solid pieces together.

Sculptors often experiment with new and unusual ways of making sculpture. Instead of using clay, stone, or wood, they might weld pieces of metal together. Or they might construct sculpture out of objects that most people throw away.

In this lesson, you will construct a piece of sculpture from objects you have collected.

Some assemblages are fun to look at. *Le Roi de la Faim* by Robert Jacobsen is made of many recognizable metal objects, welded together to form a "King of Hunger" on a horse. Note how the artist gets us to look at familiar objects in a new way.

Robert Jacobsen. Le Roi de la Faim. *Museum of Art, Carnegie Institute, Pittsburgh; Rosenbloom Purchase Fund, 1958.*

128

Steven V. Correia Junior High. San Diego, California

Instructions for Creating Art

1. Look for interesting items you might use in an original piece of sculpture. These objects may be any shape or size and may be made of paper, plastic, wood, glass, or metal.

2. Choose some of the things you have collected and join them together to make your own sculpture. You may make your sculpture into a familiar shape, such as an animal, or you may arrange your things into an interesting **abstract** design. Be sure the pieces are joined together strongly; you may wish to use *plaster of paris,** glue, or wire to attach them. Also, be sure the sculpture is well balanced and looks good from every side.

3. You may paint your sculpture or leave it in its natural form.

*For an explanation, turn to the How to Do It *section at the back of this book.*

Art Materials

A collection of small objects: containers, boxes, cans, old toys, parts of clocks, plastic cups, etc.

Paints and brushes (or spray can if ventilation is good)

Plastic tape, masking tape, string, glue, wire, etc. (for joining pieces together)

Water, paper towels

Strand I: Sculpture, Molds, and Casts

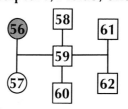

To evaluate your artwork, turn to the Learning Outcomes *section at the back of this book.*

57 *Redesigning Nature*

Observing and Thinking Creatively

One of the most important gifts you have is your imagination—and everyone has one. Your imagination helps you to see beyond the ordinary and dream of possibilities. Imagination is what stretches minds and creates new worlds.

The best way to improve your imagination is to use it as much as possible. You can do this every day by thinking of many different ways to accomplish something. In art, your imagination can help you think of different ideas for solving an art problem or creating an artwork. Then you can select the most creative and original idea.

Another way of improving your imagination is to think about how ordinary things might be changed into something else. For example, how many ways can you think of for using a paper clip? Could you change the original shape of a paper clip by bending it into the shape of a person or thing? Creative people stretch their imaginations in this way by looking for unusual ways of doing something.

In this lesson, you will use your imagination to make a sculpture out of natural objects by putting them together in new and interesting ways.

Children's Saturday Art Class. Indiana University, Indiana

Standley Junior High School. San Diego, California

Children's Creative and Performing Arts Academy. San Diego, California

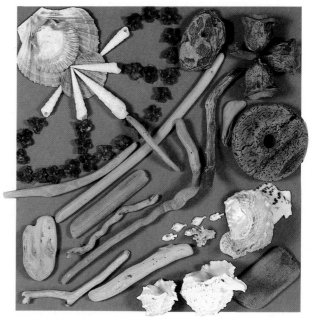

Standley Junior High School. San Diego, California

Instructions for Creating Art

1. Go for a walk in a wooded area or park and collect several kinds of natural objects such as leaves, grass, feathers, etc.

2. Study your collection. What kind of natural sculpture could you make with your objects? Dry grass can be used for hair, and parts of pinecones can represent bird feathers. Your sculpture could be a simple shape, or a more complex form.

3. Make a piece of sculpture using only natural objects. When you put your pieces together, try to make it difficult to tell where the pieces came from. The pictures that go with this lesson may give you some ideas, but use your imagination and creativity.

Art Materials

Natural objects: nuts, cones, corn-cobs, leaves, etc.	Newspaper
	Water, paper towels
Glue	

Strand I: Sculpture, Molds, and Casts

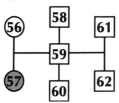

To evaluate your artwork, turn to the Learning Outcomes *section at the back of this book.*

58 *Building with Flat Shapes*

Observing and Thinking Creatively

Have you ever noticed how furniture or plastic toys are put together? Often they consist of flat pieces that fit into slots. Perhaps you have put together models using this idea. Artists sometimes use this process when they make a sculpture out of flat sheets of metal or wood.

In this lesson, you will construct a sculpture by slotting flat shapes together. These pieces can be attached by cutting slots in the materials and then pushing the pieces together. This sculpture is to be a small model for a large piece of modern sculpture. Imagine you are designing your sculpture for a special place such as your school library, a park, shopping mall, or community building where you live. It may look like a person or an animal, or it can be **abstract** and not look like a real object at all. Sculptors often make small models like this to help them with ideas; later they use these exact models for constructing large, finished sculptures.

Head No. 2 by Naum Gabo is made of sheets of metal cut into shapes that are slotted and welded into position. This sculpture is a study of flat planes arranged to define the shadowy empty spaces by the way they catch and reflect the light.

Gabo. Head No. 2 (1916). Enlarged version 1964. The Tate Gallery, London.

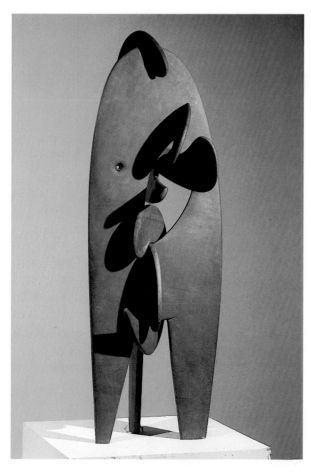

Isamu Noguchi's abstract sculpture *Humpty Dumpty* is made of interlocking pieces of polished slate. The shadows on the stone add more interesting shapes that are also part of the design. Can you imagine what the other sides look like?

Isamu Noguchi. Humpty Dumpty. 1946. Ribbon slate. 58¾ × 20¾ inches. Collection of Whitney Museum of American Art. Acq#47.7

Instructions for Creating Art

1. Decide on a subject for your sculpture. You can create either a realistic or an **abstract** form. Begin cutting a thin sheet of cardboard into seven or eight simple shapes. Some of the shapes can have straight sides, but try also using curved and irregular shapes.

2. Begin by *cutting** straight slots partway across one or two of the pieces of cardboard. Practice fitting two pieces of cardboard together in as many different ways as you can. When you decide which way of joining looks best, cut a slot in a third piece of cardboard and experiment with ways of joining it to the first two pieces. When the arrangement of these three pieces pleases you, cut a slot in another piece and add it to the others.

3. When all the pieces have been joined together, decide whether the sculpture looks pleasing from all angles. You may want to take a piece away, or change the position of a piece by cutting a slot in a different place.

4. When your sculpture looks just right to you, add glue to the joints where the cardboard pieces are slotted together. You may also

need to add cellophane tape to any joints that are loose.

*For an explanation, turn to the How to Do It section at the back of this book.

```
Art Materials

Thin cardboard or          Thick cardboard (to
thick paper (best if       protect desk when
each side is a differ-     cutting)
ent color)
                           Cellophane tape
Scissors
                           Glue
X-acto knife or single-
edge razor blade           Ruler
```

Strand I: Sculpture, Molds, and Casts

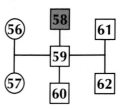

To evaluate your artwork, turn to the Learning Outcomes section at the back of this book.

133

59 *Bent Sculpture*

Observing and Thinking Creatively

Creative artists and designers are always experimenting with different materials to discover new ways of using them. For example, designers have discovered that thin sheets of iron and steel become much stronger if they are bent in different directions. This idea has been used in making cars, airplanes, refrigerators, filing cabinets, and many other factory-made objects. Some metal sculptors have used the very same idea in their work.

The same process works with paper. Once you crease a piece of paper, it will always bend, like a hinge, at that place. If you have ever made a paper airplane, you have used this principle. When a cardboard box is made, the corners are bent so that the box folds easily. The box becomes stronger because of the way it is folded together. An accordion uses a similar principle; it bends easily where there are many folds, and the folds give it strength and flexibility.

In this lesson, you will discover how to turn flat sheets of paper into a variety of curved and angled shapes by folding and creasing them to form a piece of sculpture.

Children's Saturday Art Class. Indiana University, Indiana

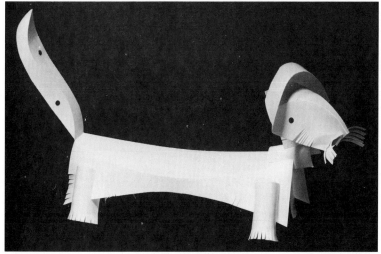

Shelbyville Junior High School. Shelbyville, Indiana

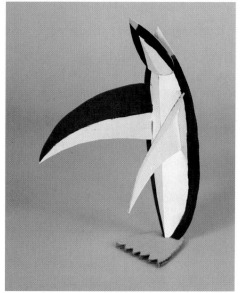

Children's Saturday Art Class.
Indiana University, Indiana

Instructions for Creating Art

1. Cut a strip of very thin cardboard or thick paper into three or more rectangles about five inches across.

2. Next, you will need a ruler and a pair of scissors. Using the pointed end of the scissors, press down firmly and draw a straight line across one of the pieces of cardboard from one side to the other. Be careful not to cut through the cardboard. The piece will now bend easily at the mark you made. This is called *scoring.**

3. Now score a curved line across another piece of cardboard. Curves can be made freehand, or they can be made around curved objects, such as plates. Notice how the curved scoring makes the cardboard bend differently than it does for the straight line. Experiment with scoring and folding wavy lines, **parallel** lines, zigzags, and lines that come to a point.

4. Now use what you have learned about scoring to make a piece of sculpture that looks like a familiar shape, such as an airplane, person, or sailboat. It doesn't have to be realistic. Try to capture the *feeling* or *main idea* of your

object. Tape or staple parts of it together to make the shapes you want. You can also cut holes in the paper for decoration. Your piece of sculpture should look interesting from all different angles.

*For an explanation, turn to the How to Do It section at the back of this book.

Art Materials

Sheets of thin cardboard or thick paper	Thick cardboard (to protect desk top)
Scissors with pointed ends	Tape, stapler
Ruler	Rubber cement or white glue

Strand I: Sculpture, Molds, and Casts

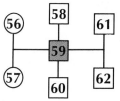

To evaluate your artwork, turn to the Learning Outcomes *section at the back of this book.*

60 Theme and Variations

Observing and Thinking Creatively

Think of your favorite musical group. Do they perform several songs that have a similar sound? Music composers often write a main tune and then develop different versions of the tune. In music, this is called a **theme and variations**.

Artists sometimes use this same idea in creating their art. For example an artist might create several abstract sculptures, each developed around a geometric shape, such as a square, a cone, or a cylinder. Even a single sheet of paper can be cut, scored, bent, and twisted into various arrangements. There are almost endless possibilities for variation.

In this lesson, you will develop variations using adaptable materials that are easy to obtain. Creating artwork in this way will challenge your imagination and inspire you to use materials in innovative and creative ways.

Correia Special Education Department. San Diego, California

Correia Special Education Department. San Diego, California

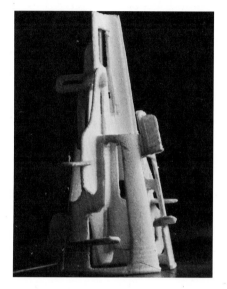

Children's Saturday Art Class. Indiana University, Indiana

Instructions for Creating Art

1. You will need at least three identical objects. Do not do anything to one of the objects. It will represent your theme.

2. Change the remaining two materials in interesting and creative ways. Each one should become very different from the other and should resemble the original only slightly. Develop your own unique changes. If you are working with paper or cardboard, you might use what you learned about bent sculpture in Lesson 59.

3. If you wish, add color to any of the variations, but make the shapes and **forms** more important than the decorations. Do not add other materials that are different.

4. Look at your finished variations. Compare each to the original theme. Observe your classmates' artwork. Discuss differences, similarities, and how variations were developed.

Art Materials

Five or six objects that are exactly alike: paper cups, egg cartons, milk cartons, small cereal boxes, etc.

Scissors

Paint and brushes, colored markers, pen and ink

Stapler or tape

Glue

Strand I: Sculpture, Molds, and Casts

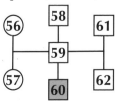

To evaluate your artwork, turn to the Learning Outcomes section at the back of this book.

61 *Handwarming Sculpture*

Observing and Thinking Creatively

Have you ever walked barefoot on muddy ground or damp sand? If you have, you made footprints. Footprints don't usually last very long because the mud or sand is too soft to hold their shape. When something happens to make the ground hard, however, footprints can be kept. Today we know about certain ancient animals because their tracks have been preserved in ground that froze or hardened.

If you squeeze a handful of mud, it will ooze through all the spaces between your fingers and hands. It is messy, but it can be fun to do. If you could make the mud keep its shape, it would make an interesting sculpture.

Plaster of paris is like white mud when it is freshly mixed, but it quickly dries and turns solid. If fresh plaster is poured over an object, it finds its way into every detail. If the plaster and the object it covers are kept perfectly still for a few minutes, the plaster will set and become solid.

In this lesson, you are going to make an artistic shape by squeezing fresh plaster in your hands until it sets. When you take your hands away, your plaster sculpture will show every detail of your fingers and hands, but they will appear in reverse. You will have made a plaster **mold** of the inside of your hands.

Westlane Junior High School. Indianapolis, Indiana

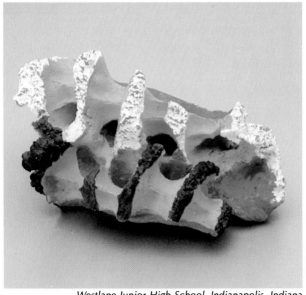

Westlane Junior High School. Indianapolis, Indiana

138

Instructions for Creating Art

1. In a bowl, mix a small quantity of *plaster of paris** with about one cup of water. When the plaster is ready to use, it will be thick and creamy. It will not drip.

2. Take a fairly large handful of plaster, spreading your fingers slightly apart. Gently squeeze the plaster between both hands until it begins to ooze between your fingers. Then hold your hands and fingers perfectly still until the plaster has set hard. Do not move your hands at all while the plaster is setting. As the plaster sets, it will become pleasantly warm.

3. Wait until the plaster is dry and hard, and then carefully open your hands. You will have molded an exact copy of the inside shape of your hands. Put your sculpture away until the next class period so it has time to become completely dry and hard.

   Make more hand sculptures that are different from each other if you have time.

4. Now, decorate your plaster sculpture with paints or marking pens. Select colors and add

lines, textures, or patterns that will make your hand sculpture an original design.

**For an explanation, turn to the* How to Do It *section at the back of this book.*

Art Materials

Plaster of paris	Measuring cup
Newspaper to cover work area	Water, paper towels
Large bowl	Paints, marking pens

Strand I: Sculpture, Molds, and Casts

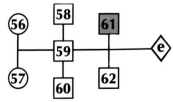

To evaluate your artwork turn to the Learning Outcomes *section at the back of this book.*

62 Sand Casting

Observing and Thinking Creatively

When you were a child, did you ever fill a cup or bucket full of damp sand, then tip it upside down on the ground and lift the bucket away? If you have done this, you have worked with a **mold**. Perhaps you have made jello in a mold. Jello that has been poured into a mold, allowed to set, and tipped onto a plate has been **cast** into the same shape as the mold, except that the jello is solid and the mold is hollow.

Molds are used by many different artists and designers. Some metal objects get their shapes from sand casting, which has been practiced for hundreds of years. An object of the desired shape is pressed into wet sand. The hollow shape in the sand serves as a mold. When molten metal is poured into the mold and allowed to cool, the metal cast can be pulled out of the sand.

For thousands of years, artists have reproduced exact copies of their sculptures by making molds around them and using these molds to make casts in plaster or metal. Perhaps you have seen a bronze or plaster statue of a famous person made in this way. Casting clay sculpture in plaster or metal makes it a stronger and more permanent piece of art.

In this lesson, you will make a simple plaster cast of a mold you design by pressing objects into wet sand.

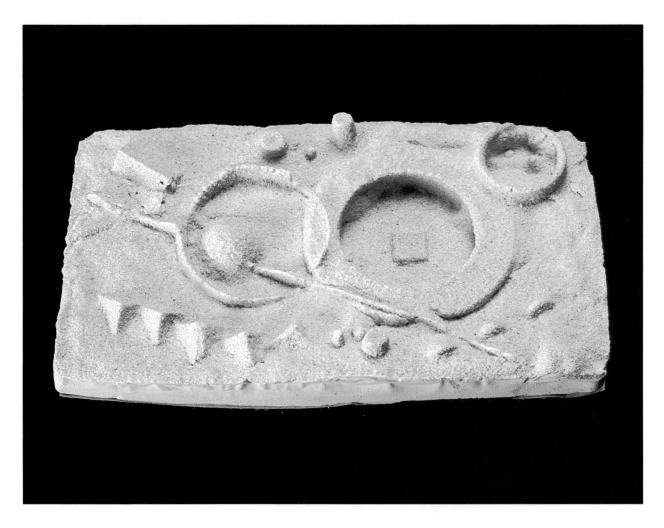

Instructions for Creating Art

1. Gather together several objects having simple but interesting shapes, such as scissors, keys, bottle caps, pieces of pipe, etc. See the Art Materials list for other suggestions.

2. Fill half of a wood or cardboard box with wet sand. Smooth out the surface of the sand.

3. Carefully press different shapes into the sand to make an interesting design. The shapes can overlap or be pressed to different depths. Make sure the sand is wet enough to hold the shape as you lift the objects out of it.

4. Mix *plaster of paris** with water in a bowl or bucket until it begins to thicken. Slowly pour it over the design you have made so that it fills all of the hollows but does not break the edges. Keep pouring the plaster until it is at least one inch thick at the thinnest places.

   If you put a loop of string or wire in the plaster while it is still wet, you will be able to hang your artwork.

   Lay a piece of cloth over the back of the plaster while it is still wet. The cloth will hold the artwork together in case it ever cracks.

5. When the plaster is completely dry, lift the casting away from the sand. Gently brush off

the extra sand, and your sand casting is ready to hang.

**For an explanation, turn to the* How to Do It *section at the back of this book.*

Art Materials

Sand

A collection of objects to press into the sand: cup, banana, chalk, bottles, pieces of rope, etc.

Plaster of paris

Shoe box or similar box container

Large bowl or bucket for mixing plaster

Thin cloth (to use for backing)

String or wire (for hanging loops)

Water, paper towels

Strand I: Sculpture, Molds, and Casts

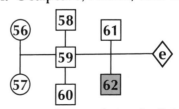

To evaluate your artwork, turn to the Learning Outcomes *section at the back of this book.*

63 Alligators, Lions, and Other Wild Beasts

Observing and Thinking Creatively

Imagine a painting of an animal. Now imagine a statue of that same animal. The painting would be flat, and the statue would be solid. Halfway between the painting and the statue, there is another form of art called a **relief**. A relief is a kind of picture in which some parts rise up from a flat background, and other parts are hollowed out. Relief sculpture can be made from a variety of materials, like metal, wood, and clay.

In this lesson, you will use soft clay to make a relief of a wild animal. Instead of making the whole body, as you would in a sculpture, you will make only one side of the animal. Look closely at the examples before you begin.

The Parthenon was an ancient Greek temple built entirely of white marble. This relief is a section of the frieze, or band of sculptured figures, depicting the people of Athens in a procession honoring the city's patron goddess, Athena.

Parthenon Frieze, Horsemen, 447–432 B.C. British Museum, London.

Assyrian kings had stone carvings made to record their military victories and bravery in hunting. This very shallow relief carved in alabaster shows a lion hunt almost 3,000 years ago.

Ashur-nasir-pal Killing Lions. Mesopotamia, from Nimrud, circa 850 B.C.
Reproduced by Courtesy of the Trustees of The British Museum.

Instructions for Creating Art

1. Flatten a piece of clay into a *slab** that is a square or rectangle. Your slab should be about six inches across and one inch thick.

2. Decide on an animal that you would like to model. Then scratch a picture of it into the clay slab. Fill most of the space on the clay with your animal shape.

3. Dig out the background area, leaving your design as a raised shape in the clay. Form and model your animal from this slightly raised clay so that the thickest parts protrude from the background, making a relief. Smooth the main shape of the animal and form the body and muscle structure.

4. Use a pencil or *carving tool** to press in details and interesting surface textures, such as skin, hair, fur, eyes, and nose.

5. Leave your relief in a warm place to dry for several days. If a **kiln** is available, *fire** your clay relief as your teacher directs. You may want to paint it with a red iron oxide stain, if available. Rub off some of the stain with a wet sponge so that raised, smooth areas are highlighted, and textured areas remain dark-

er. This stain can also be used on unbaked clay. Glue your finished relief on a burlap-covered background for hanging.

*For an explanation, turn to the How to Do It *section at the back of this book.*

Art Materials

Clay (water or oil-based)	Newspapers
Carving tool	Red iron oxide stain (optional)
Burlap-covered board (optional)	Water, paper towels

Strand J: Carving, Modeling, and Molding

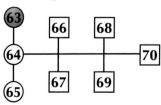

To evaluate your artwork, turn to the Learning Outcomes *section at the back of this book.*

143

64 Modeling and Molding

Observing and Thinking Creatively

Think of Halloween masks you have seen or worn. Did you ever wonder how they were made? Many of them are made by applying a thin sheet of plastic or rubber over a **mold**. The mold forms the shape of the mask. When the plastic or rubber is heated, it becomes soft and takes on the exact form of the mold. This process is also used for making some toys and plastic furniture. Automobile body parts are made using a similar process with molten metal. Can you think of other products that are made in this way?

Copies of molds can also be made using thin sheets of soft paper. For this lesson, you will use wet paper strips, or **papier-mâché**, for molding. The lesson will be done in two parts. First, you will carve your mold from a slab of clay to make a **relief** in which the shapes project or rise up from a flat background. Then you will reproduce your relief design by molding a thin layer of papier-mâché over it. When the papier-mâché dries, you can remove it from the relief. You will have made a **cast**, or an exact copy of your mold.

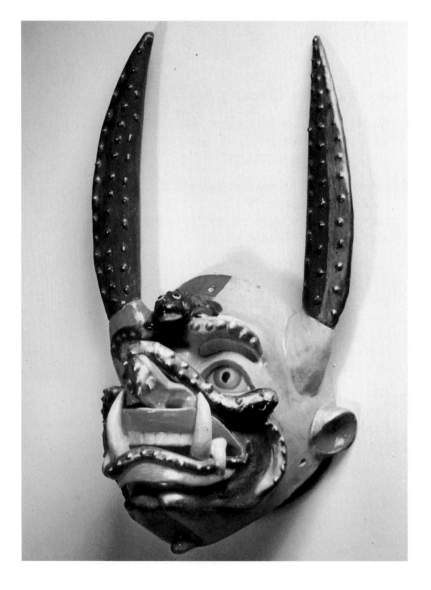

The Aymara Indians occupy the high Lake Titicaca plateau in western Bolivia. They believe in a multi-spirit world with devils and witches. Do you see the creatures creeping over this *Devil Dance Mask*? What other features make it look horrifying?

Aymara Indians, Bolivia, Devil Dance Mask repres. Supay the Evil One, 16" T. Museum of the American Indian, New York.

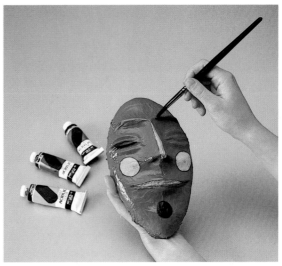

Instructions for Creating Art

1. Form a *slab** of clay about six inches square and one inch thick. *Oil-based clay** is best. If you use *water-based clay,** it may dry out and become too hard to work with.

2. Draw a simple picture on the clay slab. It could be a plant, a person, or an animal face. To make your relief, mold extra pieces of clay onto the slab so they stick out. Dig into the slab to make the hollow parts, but do not dig all the way through. Keep the shapes in your design fairly smooth and simple.

3. When the model is finished, cover it with a layer of petroleum jelly. Then make some strip *papier-mâché** by tearing strips of newspaper and mixing them with paste or glue, as your teacher directs. Build five layers of paper strips on top of the relief. Very carefully, press the paper onto the model, smoothing out unwanted bumps and air pockets.

4. When the papier-mâché is perfectly dry, carefully lift it off. Then paint and decorate it using tempera paints. Be as creative as you like, making your cast unique and exciting.

5. After the paint has dried, brush shellac over your cast. Shellac makes the colors look bright and shiny, protects the paint, and gives strength to the cast.

For an explanation, turn to the How to Do It section at the back of this book.

Art Materials

Clay (oil or water-based)	Newspaper (to protect work area)
Carving tools	Clear shellac and soft paintbrush
Strips of newspaper	
Wheat paste, bowl	Paint thinner (for shellac)
Petroleum jelly	Water, paper towels
Tempera paints and brushes	

Strand J: Carving, Modeling, and Molding

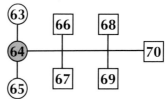

To evaluate your artwork, turn to the Learning Outcomes section at the back of this book.

65 Ancient Egyptian Art

Observing and Thinking Creatively

Where do you suppose some of the oldest buildings in the world are located? You may have seen pictures of the great pyramids of Egypt, which stood as high as tall skyscrapers. About five thousand years ago, Egyptians built these pyramids as tombs for their deceased kings, or pharaohs. They decorated them with wall paintings called **murals** which pictured special events and everyday activities in Egyptian life. Jewelry, pottery, clothing, statues, and other kinds of art were also placed inside the tombs of the dead pharaohs. Many of these tombs have been robbed of their precious treasures, but some of these things have been preserved and can be seen in museums today.

The ancient Egyptians were also great sculptors and carved many pictures, called **reliefs**, in the stone walls of their buildings. They also carved stone statues in many sizes; some fit easily into a person's hand, while others are hundreds of times larger than a human being.

In the Egyptian art shown here, you will notice a particular **style**, or way of drawing, painting, and sculpting, that reflects the Egyptian culture and way of life. Ancient Egyptian artists used simple, smooth outlines. Sometimes they added rich detail, using earthtone colors.

In this lesson, you will use Egyptian art ideas and styles to carve a drawing into clay or to make a clay statue.

Ancient Egyptian King Tutankhamun's tomb was filled with objects that had belonged to him. This gold mask covered the mummy face. "King Tut" reigned only briefly from age 8 or 9 to his death nine years later.
Tutankhamun Mask, *1339 B.C. Photo: Lee Boltin Picture Library.*

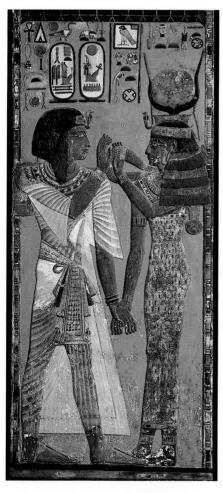

King Seti I and the Goddess Hathor are shown in profile in this painted limestone relief. The Egyptian king seems to be listening to the goddess. What do you notice about the clothing, jewelry, and hair?

King Seti I and the Goddess Hathor. *Painted limestone relief, The King's Tomb, Paris, The Louvre. SCALA/Art Resource, New York.*

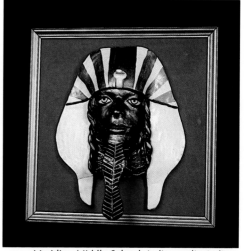

Meridian Middle School. Indianapolis, Indiana

Instructions for Creating Art

Choose one of the following activities. If you have time, you may do both. In your work, show ideas and styles used by Egyptian artists.

1. On paper, make a drawing of someone you know. Draw it the way the Egyptians showed people in their art, using smooth, simple outlines. Notice that in Egyptian painting and relief sculpture, heads are often turned to the side, with bodies facing front.

   After you have completed your drawing, roll out a flat *clay slab** until it is about an inch thick. Make a copy of your drawing by pressing a pencil gently into the clay. Then *carve** the clay out like the Egyptians carved relief sculpture, using a plastic knife or table knife. Work carefully.

2. Model a clay figure of someone you know. Shape it in the style the Egyptians used. Notice how Egyptian sculpture faces front and bodies appear very stiff, yet facial expressions are natural. You could also make a figure of your family pet, or some other animal, in the Egyptian style. The pictures in this

lesson may give you ideas for different subjects to model.

**For an explanation, turn to the* How to Do It *section at the back of this book.*

Art Materials

Pencil and eraser	Plastic or metal knife
White paper	Newspapers for working on
Clay	
Carving tools	Water, paper towels
Roller	

Strand J: Carving, Modeling, and Molding

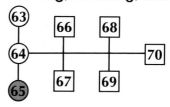

To evaluate your artwork, turn to the Learning Outcomes *section at the back of this book.*

66 *Hand Sculpture*

Observing and Thinking Creatively

Artists use two main ways of making **sculpture**. One is to join pieces together, and the other is to cut parts away. Pieces of clay can be joined by squeezing or pinching them together. Other materials, such as wood, wire, and plastic, have to be glued or twisted together. Pieces of metal can be joined by welding.

The main way to cut pieces away in sculpture is to **carve** unwanted parts from a solid lump.

Artists carve stone by using sharp steel **chisels** and hitting them with **mallets** to chip away pieces of stone. Wood is sometimes carved by using wood chisels, files, and sandpaper.

In this lesson, you will carve a simple shape that is interesting to touch and see. It does not have to look like something real. Your hand will tell you when the work is finished.

Sculptor Henry Moore portrayed the life spirit of the human form to look like rolling landscapes. To him, spaces around arches and holes were as expressive as the forms themselves. Note how the natural grain and character of the wood seem to give their own definition to the graceful curves of this *Reclining Figure.*

Henry Moore, Reclining Figure, *1935–36, Elmwood, 19 × 35 × 15". Albright-Knox Art Gallery, Buffalo, New York. Room of Contemporary Art Fund, 1939.*

Carving a piece of sculpture:
Carefully cut away from your hands
and body as you carve.

This abstract sculpture is almost four
feet tall and is carved from marble
and polished smooth. Even though
marble is a very hard stone, Hans Arp
has carved *Growth* to appear as if it
were soft. Imagine how it would look
from the other sides.

Hans Arp, Growth. *White marble. 1928–40.
43" high. Grant Jay Hick Purchase Fund.
65.357. Courtesy of The Art Institute of
Chicago.*

Instructions for Creating Art

1. As your teacher directs, choose a solid block
   of wax, soap, *plaster of paris** or anything else
   that can be carved easily. If you use wood, be
   sure that it is soft wood. Lumps of dry or
   nearly dry clay are also good to use. *Carve**
   your block to fit into the different shapes of
   your hand. Always carve away from your
   hands and body. Cut only the pieces of the
   block you do not want; you cannot put pieces
   back that have been accidentally cut off.

2. Make all the surfaces interesting to touch.
   Some parts can be rough, and others can be
   smooth. Some of the surfaces can have special patterns on them. Finish your sculpture
   so that all the surfaces feel good to touch.

3. The pictures that go with this lesson may help
   you, but be sure to use your own ideas in
   making your hand sculpture.

*For an explanation, turn to the How to Do It *section at the back of this book.*

Art Materials

Solid block for carv-
ing: paraffin wax,
Ivory soap (unwrap
and leave out for
one week to hard-
en), Styrofoam, soft
wood, clay (hard or
semi-hard), soft fire-
brick, plaster of
paris, or block salt

Cutting tools: knife,
rasp, sandpaper,
chisel and mallet

Surface polish (op-
tional)

Strand J: Carving, Modeling, and Molding

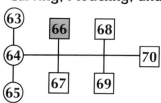

To evaluate your artwork, turn to the Learning Outcomes *section
at the back of this book.*

67 African Art

Observing and Thinking Creatively

Art in Africa reflects the customs, traditions, and art **styles** handed down from one generation to the next. Most African art is not only ornamental, but is also created to fulfill specific needs. The principal art forms are masks and figures, usually made for religious ceremonies. Art objects, such as decorated tools, pottery, and carved statues are also quite common. Many African tribal groups believe that all things, living or nonliving, have a spirit or life force. Where such beliefs prevail, the artist or sculptor of sacred objects must be purified before creating artwork to be used for religious or ceremonial purposes.

African art styles range from highly **abstract** to naturalistic. A few European artists were greatly influenced by the expressive nature and use of **imagery** in African art. The most famous of these artists was the Spanish painter, Pablo Picasso, whose work became quite different after he studied African art. He liked the look of the flat faces used by African artists, and he began using flat surfaces, or **planes**, in his art also. Other artists have used Picasso's ideas in their work. Thus, African art has had a great influence on Western art created during the past 75 years.

This distinctive brass sculpture comes from Benin, Nigeria. The beaded and decorated hair and neck coils illustrate an idea of beauty held by this culture in the 17th century. See if you can discover the meaning of wearing neck coils like these.

Benin Kingdom, Nigeria, West Africa. Memorial Head. Indiana University Art Museum. 75.98.

Many masks were used in African religious ceremonies. This one is made of wood and painted. It does not look much like an African face. What do you think it might represent?

Igbo Culture. Nigeria, West Africa. Maw Death Mask. Indiana University Art Museum. Gift of Frederick Stafford. 59.39.

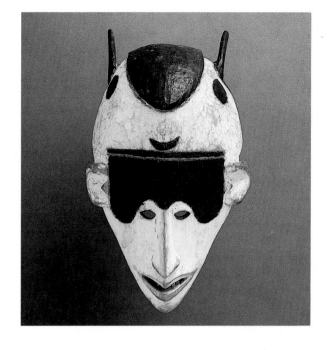

This wood carving of antelope from Africa is decorated with brass tacks, string, and cowrie shells. Notice the expressive quality of the simple lines and curves.

Africa, Female Antelope Figure; Bambara Tribe. Wood, brass, tacks, string, cowrie shells, iron, quills. 31⅜" h. Ada Turnbull Hertle Fund. 1965.7. Courtesy of The Art Institute of Chicago.

Instructions for Creating Art

1. Look at the pictures of African art in this lesson. Note how the artists represented their subjects by using simple shapes and flat surfaces, or planes.

2. Take a lump of fairly hard clay and press it into a shape or figure similar to those created by African artists. Then, use a *carving** tool to carve your figure. Use your own ideas, but make it in the African style.

3. If you use water-based clay, you may want to paint your figure after it has dried. African artists often used vivid colors to decorate their artwork, creating powerful figures.

**For an explanation, turn to the* How to Do It *section at the back of this book.*

Art Materials	
A large lump of clay	Newspaper (to cover work area)
Carving tool	
Pointed instrument or pencil (for small markings)	Water, paper towels
	Tempera paints

Strand J: Carving, Modeling, and Molding

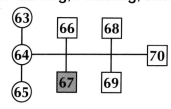

To evaluate your artwork, turn to the Learning Outcomes *section at the back of this book.*

68 Slab Buildings

Observing and Thinking Creatively

Once, the only way to build structures was by using bricks, stones, or logs. Buildings of these materials were constructed very slowly; each piece had to be carefully placed in the structure one by one, by hand.

Today there are new, faster ways of constructing buildings. Whole walls can be made in factories and delivered wherever they are needed. Perhaps you have used this idea to build a storage shed or pet shelter. The idea of building with large **slabs** of material is also used in art. Slabs of clay can be used to make vases, plates, and sculptures.

In this lesson, you will use clay slabs to construct a building. You may get some useful ideas from the model of a Chinese house, constructed from clay slabs hundreds of years ago. Be sure to use your own ideas in your design.

This model of a Chinese house is made from clay slabs which have been fired in a kiln and then glazed with decorations on every surface. Imagine how this building was constructed to support the weight of four stories and the overhanging roofs.

Chinese House Model. *The Nelson-Atkins Museum of Art, Kansas City, Missouri (Nelson Fund).*

Homecroft School. Indianapolis, Indiana

Homecroft School. Indianapolis, Indiana

Instructions for Creating Art

1. Think of the kind of building you would like to make, such as a house, church, or school.

2. Prepare some clay so that it is soft and ready to use. Roll your clay into a big flat *slab** about half an inch thick. Use a knife to cut out shapes for the walls and roof from the slab. When using sharp tools, always cut *away* from your hands and body. You may need several slabs of clay.

3. Build your model using your own ideas and imagination. Join the walls together at the corners. If you use water-based clay, *score** the pieces and seal them together using **slip**, a mixture of clay and vinegar or water. Supports such as blocks, sticks, or newspapers can be used to hold the slabs in place while the clay is drying. Before the clay begins to dry, you may want to *carve** designs or add **textures** and decorative details to the outside of your building.

4. If the buildings are to be *fired,** be sure the clay is completely dry and remove all supports. Follow the directions for firing that

come with the *kiln.** (Also see page 226 for more information on firing and glazing clay.)

*For an explanation, turn to the How to Do It section at the back of this book.

Art Materials

Clay (water or oil-based)	Blocks or sticks (as supports) clay tools
Dough roller or bottle	Vinegar or water
Two ½" thick wood strips (for rolling out clay slab)	Burlap or newspapers (to work on)

Strand J: Carving, Modeling, and Molding

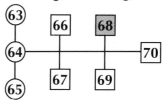

To evaluate your artwork, turn to the Learning Outcomes section at the back of this book.

69 Buildings Are Like Sculpture

Observing and Thinking Creatively

Think of the most interesting building in your town. Why do you find it pleasing to look at? Is there one side of the building that you like better than others? Do you find the inside as interesting as the outside? Some buildings are like sculpture; they are pleasing and interesting to look at from every angle.

Architects and sculptors create objects that are solid. An architect, however, must consider who will live and work in a building; the design of the building must be both **functional** and pleas-

ing. Sculptors have more freedom to create forms solely for people to look at and appreciate. Yet, both architects and sculptors must solve similar problems.

Like a sculptor, an architect must think carefully about the smooth and rough textures of materials. Both must pay attention to the design of their work, and plan their projects so that they will look good from every position.

In this lesson, you will construct a model building that is interesting from all angles.

Note the wide variety of ornamentation on the turrets and towers of the exquisitely designed and decorated *St. Basil's Cathedral* in Moscow, built in 1555–1560.

St. Basil's Cathedral on Red Square, Moscow, 1555–1560. TASS from SOVFOTO.

Salem Middle School. Salem, Indiana

Sleeping Beauty's Castle at Disneyland. © Walt Disney Productions.

Instructions for Creating Art

1. Collect boxes and other small cartons and containers from home or school. Gather a variety of containers of different sizes and shapes, such as oatmeal boxes, paper rolls, snack containers, and so on. Look at the pictures in this lesson for ideas.

2. Put some of the things you have collected together to make the shape of a building. It can be a house, church, airport terminal, hotel, sports arena, or castle. As you construct your building, *glue,** tie, or tape the parts together securely.

3. When the main sections of the building have been put together, add all the small parts that would make it look attractive. These might include swimming pools, chimneys, towers, steps, balconies, windows, and porches.

4. Finish your building by drawing and painting all the necessary details, such as windows and doors. Make sure your building looks good from all angles before you consider it finished.

5. Study the pictures that go with this lesson, and ask yourself why each building is unique.

What artistic qualities do you want to emphasize in your building?

*For an explanation, turn to the How to Do It *section at the back of this book.*

Art Materials

Cartons, boxes, containers of all kinds	Brushes
White glue	Mixing tray
String, thread, pins, and tape	Scissors
	Pencil and eraser
Paints	Water, paper towels

Strand J: Carving, Modeling, and Molding

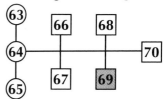

To evaluate your artwork, turn to the Learning Outcomes *section at the back of this book.*

70 *Being an Architect*

Observing and Thinking Creatively

An **architect** is an artist who designs buildings. Because buildings are very expensive to construct, the people who will be paying for them want to be quite sure the architect's design is exactly what they want before the building is started. To satisfy the customer, an architect will make a drawing or painting of what the building will look like when it is finished. Do you know of a housing area or office building that is under construction in your town? Perhaps there is a

drawing posted near it that shows what the finished structure will look like.

Quite often, architects will also make small models of the buildings they design, such as the models pictured here. Models are better than drawings, because they show what the building will look like from different angles.

In this lesson, you will design an imaginary home and make a model of it, just like an architect would do.

157

Instructions for Creating Art

1. Draw an idea for a building that you would like to live in. It can be any kind of building—an ultramodern home, a Victorian mansion, or a unique vacation hideaway. The main thing is to make the design an interesting one. For this lesson, it is more important to show the way the building will look from the outside: do not spend much time thinking about the inside. Study the illustrations in this lesson and note how the architect used materials, textures, and space as part of the total design. Then arrange the spaces and details of your building to create a good design.

2. As your teacher directs, make a cardboard model of the building you drew. Draw or color in details, such as windows, doors, steps, chimney, and balconies. You might add small bits of greenery to represent trees or shrubs.

Art Materials

Pencil and eraser	Scissors
Thin cardboard	Crayons, paints, or colored markers
X-acto knife	
Cardboard (to protect work area)	White glue or rubber cement
Drawing paper	Tape

Strand J: Carving, Modeling, and Molding

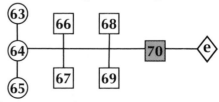

To evaluate your artwork, turn to the Learning Outcomes section at the back of this book.

Exploring Art

Designing a Bridge

For this project, you will draw a design for a bridge for a special area in your yard, neighborhood, or community. Think of a bridge as both decorative and functional. The Japanese are masters at creating bridges across ponds, lakes, or streams that beautify the environment and serve as passageways for people to observe and enjoy their surroundings. In some parts of the country, covered bridges are commonly used to keep roadways clear of snow in the winter. In other places, huge, steel expansion bridges link pieces of land separated by bodies of water or canyons. Some bridges, such as the Golden Gate Bridge across the San Francisco Bay in California, pictured below, are beautiful to behold and serve as a practical means of channeling transportation. Cities with several inland waterways, like Chicago, have drawbridges that open to let tall boats and ships pass through.

Look at pictures of many different kinds of bridges in books and magazines. Then decide on a bridge you would like to design. Imagine you are an architect hired to design a bridge for a particular area in your community. If possible, observe the area and make several sketches of its land formations, buildings, and special features. Write brief notes on your sketches about sizes of objects, amount of space, and specific details that will affect the construction of your bridge. Or you may also sketch an imaginary environment and design a fanciful but functional bridge to fit your drawing.

As you draw, carefully consider both the design and the environment, since the bridge must fit the land features and the surrounding space. Create a bridge design that will be functional and will enhance both the natural and man-made environment with its beauty.

Alice Parrott, Mesa Verde, 1976. Wool and linen, tapestry and soumac techniques. 48" × 62". Collection of Mr. and Mrs. Paul M. Cook, Menlo Park, California.

Unit V

Working with Ceramics, Crafts, and Textiles

Song of the Sky Loom

O our Mother the Earth, O our Father the Sky,
Your children are we, and with tired backs
We bring you the gifts you love.
Then weave for us a garment of brightness;
May the warp be the white light of morning,
May the weft be the red light of evening,
May the fringes be the falling rain,
May the border be the standing rainbow.
Thus weave for us a garment of brightness,
That we may walk fittingly where birds sing.
That we may walk fittingly where grass is green,
O our Mother the Earth, O our Father the Sky.

Tewa Indian Song

Whether you are awed by the vibrant reds of an evening sunset or the delicate surprise of a rainbow, nature offers many treasures for our visual memories. The visual memories and images stored in our minds are the stuff of which art is made. During the process of creating, these images emerge, often unconsciously, to be transformed into new creations—sketches, paintings, pottery, sculpture, and many other art forms.

In this section, you will tap your storehouse of visual memories as you create pottery, design various handicrafts, and use the art styles of different cultures. As you work, you will discover that making an original artwork, whether it is useful or purely decorative, is an exciting experience. Artistic expression ties ancient and modern peoples together, for people have always had a need to create—to make their mark on the world.

71 Clay Coil Pottery

Observing and Thinking Creatively

Can you remember working with clay when you were younger? Perhaps you rolled it between your hands until it became soft and warm. Then you may have formed it into the shape of an animal or a person. If you rolled it back and forth on a table, you may have made a clay rope or **coil**. Perhaps you experimented by using the coil in different ways. In this lesson, you will use the clay coil method to build a pot.

Clay pottery is made in every part of the world. Small pots can be made by pressing the shape from a lump of clay. Pots can also be pressed out by machines, **cast** in **molds**, or turned into shapes on pottery wheels.

The clay coil method of building pots has been used for thousands of years. Clay coils are easy to work with and require no other equipment except your own hands. A clay rope can be coiled around and around to build all kinds of interesting shapes. The coils can be left to dry as they are, or they can be pressed flat to make a smoother surface. Smaller coils can be added as designs and decorations. Experiment by using coils in some of these different ways.

Eastwood Middle School. Indianapolis, Indiana

Saturday Art Class. Indiana University, Indiana

162

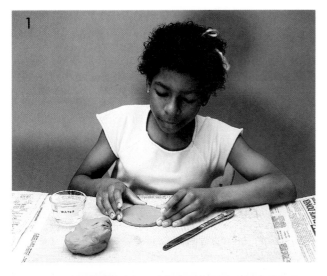

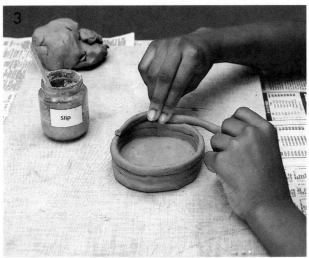

Instructions for Creating Art

1. First, make a flat, circular base out of clay, like the example in Illustration 1.

2. Roll your clay into a long rope, as in Illustration 2. Make the clay about one-fourth of an inch thick. Use the rope to build sides around the edge of your base piece, as in Illustration 3. Be sure to roughen or *score** all the places where the clay meets, using a pointed stick, pencil, or fork. Then cement the pieces together using *slip.** As you build, decide on the shape of your pot. Add decorations with designs made of the clay rope, as in Illustration 4. Remember to score the pieces and use slip to attach your decorations as well.

3. The clay pot will be dry when it no longer feels cold to the touch. You can leave the clay as it is or **fire** it in a special oven, or **kiln**, if there is one in your school.

**For an explanation, turn to the* How to Do It *section at the back of this book.*

Art Materials

Water-based clay (Oil-based clay may be used, but it cannot be fired.)

Dish (to hold slip)

Newspaper, burlap, or cardboard (to work on)

Popsicle stick or clay tool (for scoring clay and applying slip)

Vinegar (add several tablespoons to slip to prevent cracking)

Water, paper towels

Strand K: Pottery and Decorative Arts

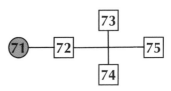

To evaluate your artwork, turn to the Learning Outcomes *section at the back of this book.*

72 Fancy Pots

Observing and Thinking Creatively

Think of some clay pots you have seen. Perhaps you have some pieces of pottery in your home that have unusual shapes. Some pots are used for cooking and serving food, and their shapes are usually simple. Other pieces of pottery are used mainly for decoration and can be formed into many interesting shapes. Useful pottery is called **functional**, because it has a practical use, or function. Pottery that is created mainly for decoration is called **nonfunctional**.

In this lesson, you will make a piece of pottery that is pleasing to look at. You may want it to be useful, but the most important thing is to create a pot that shows how imaginative you can be.

This beautiful Roman *Head Vase* was made in the early 4th century A.D. The face and neck were made by pressing clay into a mold. Do you think this would be an easy vase to use?

Early 4th century A.D. Roman Head Vase. *Clay, paint. Indiana University Art Museum. Gift of Dr. and Mrs. Henry R. Hope. 69.116*

This ceramic container is from the Pacific coast of ancient Mexico. The coatimundi's body forms the main part of the vessel, and there is no obvious handle. What do you think it was used for?

Colima Culture, Mexico, Coatimundi Vessel, *Ceramic, 9". Collection of Mr. and Mrs. James W. Alsdorf 1967.721. Courtesy of The Art Institute of Chicago. All Rights Reserved.*

Instructions for Creating Art

You will build your pot by shaping it with your hands using either the pinch method or the slab method, as illustrated in this lesson.

1. Look at the photographs and decide which method to use. Be sure your clay is nice and soft before you begin to shape it. If you use the *slab** method, the finished slab should be the same thickness all over.

2. Cut some pieces from the slab and fit them together, or pinch the clay out to make an interesting shape. Try building several shapes before you decide which one is the most imaginative. Your idea can look like an animal or a person, or it can just be a shape that looks pleasing to you.

3. When building objects out of separate pieces of clay, it is important to stick the parts together with a thick, creamy mixture of water or vinegar and clay called *slip*.* *Score** or scratch both surfaces with a fork or pointed instrument before applying slip. Apply slip to the scored surfaces, and smooth the pieces together. This helps to prevent cracking when the clay dries. Also smooth out any air bubbles that could be trapped inside the clay.

4. When you have decided on the shape you like best, finish it by smoothing the pieces together carefully. Then decide how to decorate it. You can add pieces of clay onto the surface, or you can cut into the clay to make interesting designs. Remember to score and use slip when adding clay pieces for decoration.

5. If you must set your work aside for longer than an hour, be sure to wrap it in an airtight plastic bag to keep it moist. Once it dries out, the clay cannot be worked further and any pieces

added will crack at the joints when it dries or is fired. Placing a damp paper towel around your work inside the bag is a good idea if you will be leaving it for more than two days.

6. Clay pots should be dried naturally in the open air. They may be left as is or baked in a hot oven called a **kiln**. This method is called **firing**. If there is a kiln in your school, fire your pot when it is perfectly dry.

**For an explanation, turn to the* How to Do It *section at the back of this book.*

Art Materials

Clay (water-based)	Modeling tools such as a spoon handle or a popsicle stick
Burlap (9″ × 12″), newspaper, or plastic sheet (to work on)	
	Pointed tool or fork for scoring
Water container	Rolling pin
Plastic bag (to keep pot damp between classes)	Vinegar
	Water, paper towels

Strand K: Pottery and Decorative Arts

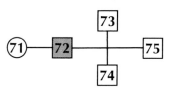

To evaluate your artwork, turn to the Learning Outcomes *section at the back of this book.*

73 Creative Mask-making

Observing and Thinking Creatively

No one knows when people first started wearing masks and using disguises, but they are found in every country in the world. When do you think people might want to wear masks, other than to attend a Halloween party?

Masks are used in some African religious ceremonies, in dances, and in the theater, as well as just for fun at fancy dress parties. Sometimes masks look very realistic, and sometimes they come from pure fantasy. Some look like famous people, and others represent character types, like pirates, Martians, or clowns. Masks can be made to look like animal heads, storybook characters, or creatures that exist only in the imagination. Mask-making is an activity in which artists can be very **creative**.

In this lesson, you will design your own original mask, and then make it out of papier-mâché.

Bella Bella Indians of the Pacific Northwest have long been expert wood carvers, making elaborate masks for ceremonial dances and dramas. Note the exaggerated features, deeply carved in the wood.

Bella Bella Indian (Canada) MASK, Wood, inlaid with haliotis shell, red, white and black painted decoration, 18". Photograph courtesy of the Museum of the American Indian. Heye Foundation.

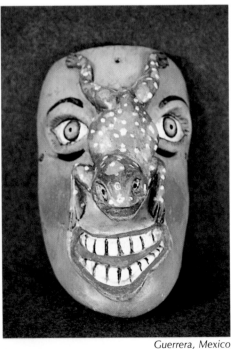

Guerrera, Mexico

166

Salem Middle School. Salem, Indiana

Salem Middle School. Salem, Indiana

Instructions for Creating Art

1. Look at the masks in this lesson and then make a few quick sketches of masks. Let your imagination help you design a creative mask.

2. When you have decided on an idea, think about how you want to make it. You can form a basic mask shape from cardboard, wire mesh, or an inflated balloon. After you have formed the shape that you like, cover it with strips of *papier-mâché.** If you are using an inflated balloon for your mask form, cover only the front half of the balloon. The mask should cover your face.

3. When the papier-mâché dries, add details and outlines by gluing on string and pieces of cardboard. You might want to create a special effect by attaching aluminum foil over your mask. If you brush paint over the foil and then rub it in, your mask will have a faint, tinted sheen to it.

4. When you finish adding details to your mask, let it dry completely. The final steps will be to apply paint and shellac to keep it bright and make it strong.

*For an explanation, turn to the How to Do It section at the back of this book.

Art Materials

Pencil and eraser	Painting materials
Sketch paper	Scissors
Wire mesh, cardboard, or balloons (for mask base)	Glue
	Wire clippers (optional)
Papier-mâché	Shellac and brush
X-acto knife and newspaper padding to protect surface	Paint thinner
	Elastic to hold mask on
String, aluminum foil, yarn, etc.	

Strand K: Pottery and Decorative Arts

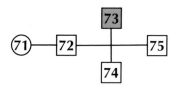

To evaluate your artwork, turn to the Learning Outcomes section at the back of this book.

74 Helmets, Hats, and Headdresses

Observing and Thinking Creatively

Think about the different kinds of hats and headdresses you have seen. What information do they give about the people wearing them?

Hats may be worn for many different reasons. Hats can be strictly practical; they keep heads warm or prevent the sun from shining in someone's face. Other hats are worn simply for decoration, because they please people. Certain headdresses, such as a king's crown or a soldier's cap, signify status or position, while others, like an astronaut's helmet, are related to someone's job. Hats may also give clues about where people come from—for example, an Arab sheik's turban or a tribal headdress. In some countries, headdress designs have been handed down over hundreds of years.

In this lesson, you will design and make a helmet, hat, or headdress out of cardboard and paper. It may be practical, decorative, or one that might be used in a ceremony.

For the first time in history, astronaut Bruce McCandless was able to move about in space independently of the mother ship because of his special helmet and nitrogen-propelled maneuvering unit. Note the reflection of Space Shuttle Challenger in the helmet visor.
NASA

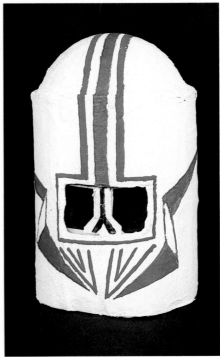

Martinsville East Middle School. Martinsville, Indiana

Asante Leather Caps

SWRL Inc. Los Alamitos, California

Instructions for Creating Art

1. Imagine a helmet, hat, or headdress that you would like to make. Will it be one that shows something important about you? Will it be attractive to look at? Will it show what kind of job you would like to do? Make some sketches showing how you would like it to look.

2. When you have chosen a design for your hat, begin putting it together. First, cut the basic form out of cardboard, making sure that it fits your head. Then glue or staple on other shapes of paper, cardboard, etc., until you have the shape you want.

3. When your basic hat form suits you, paint it. You may want to attach colored construction paper, cellophane, crepe paper, or aluminum foil to create special effects.

4. When you have finished, write a paragraph about why you chose that shape and design. Tape your explanation to the inside of your hat, or share your ideas and headdress design with your classmates and teacher.

Art Materials

Drawing paper	White glue
Pencil and eraser	Stapler
Large sheets of lightweight cardboard	Your choice: paints and brushes, crayons, or colored markers
Colored construction paper	Mixing tray (for paints)
Cellophane, aluminum foil, crepe paper, yarn, etc.	Water, paper towels

Strand K: Pottery and Decorative Arts

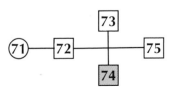

To evaluate your artwork, turn to the Learning Outcomes *section at the back of this book.*

75 *Inexpensive Jewelry*

Observing and Thinking Creatively

What catches your eye when you see a piece of jewelry? Perhaps you notice the color, shape, or material the piece is made of—the gold, silver, or precious stones. Jewelry is really a form of miniature sculpture, because it is solid and **three-dimensional**.

For many years, jewelry has been used as a symbol of wealth, status, and prestige. But many people enjoy wearing jewelry just because it is beautiful.

In this lesson, you will create an inexpensive, decorative piece of jewelry from papier-mâché. Use your imagination in designing and painting it to make it attractive, colorful, and original.

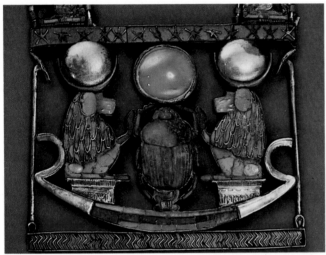
Egyptian Baboon Pendant

Ashante Pendant. Ghana, Africa

Pseudo Penannular Broach. Ross County, Tipperary, Ireland

Christenberry Middle School. Knoxville, Indiana

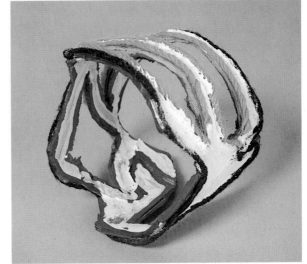

Bedford Junior High School. Bedford, Indiana

Instructions for Creating Art

1. Think about what kind of jewelry you would like to make. You might make a **pendant**, bracelet, lapel pin, necklace, ring, chain earrings, or cuff links.

2. Make the shape you want out of *papier-mâché strips.** You may want to wrap the strips around a form, such as a can or bottle. Use *papier-mâché pulp** to make details or smooth out your shape. If you make a pendant or necklace, leave a small hole to thread a leather thong, string, or chain through.

3. Wait several days to allow your piece to dry thoroughly, and then paint it. Use your imagination to create an attractive, original piece. You might want to glue on sequins, colored paper, string, or even part of a photograph.

4. When the paint and glue have dried, brush shellac over your piece to protect the colors and make it strong. If you made a pin or earrings, glue on pin backs, clips, wires, or posts after the shellac is dry.

*For an explanation, turn to the How to Do It section at the back of this book.

Art Materials

Newspaper for strip papier-mâché	Sequins, photograph, colored paper, string, etc.
Facial tissue for papier-mâché pulp	Clear shellac
Wheat paste and bowl	Paint thinner
Round objects to use as forms for making circular shapes	White glue
	Water, paper towels
	Your choice: jewelry clips, pin backs, wires, posts, etc.
Scissors	Leather thong, yarn, string, or chain for hanging pieces
Tempera paint	
Small brushes	

Strand K: Pottery and Decorative Arts

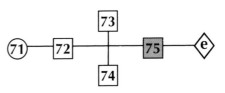

To evaluate your artwork, turn to the Learning Outcomes section at the back of this book.

76 A Picture to See and Touch

Observing and Thinking Creatively

Observe the different kinds of fabric people wear. These fabrics, or **textiles**, have a variety of **textures** and feel different next to your skin. Fabrics evoke certain images or moods: velvet is soft and elegant; burlap is rough and earthy; lace is thin and delicate; denim is tough and practical. Fabric also comes in different colors and designs. The designs are either printed on or woven into the cloth.

Because of their interesting designs and textures, textiles can be used to make effective **collages**. Just about any kind of fabric can be used in a collage, from bits of rags to pieces of lace and ribbons. When fabric is arranged in a collage, it becomes a picture you can see and touch. In this lesson, you will create different effects in a textile collage, working with a variety of colors, textures, and designs.

Student Art Workshop. San Diego, California

172

Azalea Middle School. St Petersburg, Florida

Madison High School. San Diego, California

Instructions for Creating Art

1. Collect different pieces of cloth. Select textiles that are interesting and unusual. Look for a variety of colors, textures, and designs.

2. Think about something from the outdoors that you would like to use as the subject of your collage. Cut out some shapes you like, and arrange them on a piece of cardboard or thick paper. Emphasize one area of your collage to create a **center of interest**. It can be highlighted by adding the most interesting colors, shapes, patterns, or textures to this part of your design. The other parts of your design should provide background for your center of interest.

3. When you have decided on a pleasing design, glue the pieces to your background paper. Write the title of your work, and sign your name. Display your textile collage.

Art Materials

A variety of pieces of cloth: cotton, burlap, velvet, denim, lace, wool, felt, etc.

Scissors

White glue

Cardboard or thick paper (12″ × 18″ or larger)

Newspaper (to cover work area)

Strand L: Textiles, Designs, and Symbols

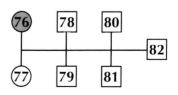

To evaluate your artwork, turn to the Learning Outcomes *section at the back of this book.*

77 Folk Art Yarn Pictures

Observing and Thinking Creatively

We often think that pictures must be painted or drawn, but some pictures are printed, and others are stitched with needle and thread. Some are made by arranging different materials in a collage. One kind of picture-making is done by gluing colored wool, string, or yarn to fill all the spaces in a picture. This kind of art is called yarn painting, or **nearika**.

Yarn paintings are a kind of **folk art** first made by Indian people living deep in the mountains of central Mexico. Early yarn paintings showed pictures of the gods and spirits the Indians worshipped. Today, many of these yarn paintings show other things, because the Indians design them for tourists who like to buy their work.

In this lesson, you will make a yarn painting. Use your own ideas, but make the picture similar to those done by Mexican Indian artists.

American artist Lucas Samaras decorated this wooden box sculpture like a Mexican nearika, using yarn. Notice how the swirling designs sweep your eyes in toward the center and then around the box. Where do you see asymmetrical balance?

Lucas Samaras, Box 45, 1966, Wood, wool, paint, 12 × 22 × 12 inches. Gift of Mr. and Mrs. George H. Schlapp, Courtesy of City Art Museum of St. Louis.

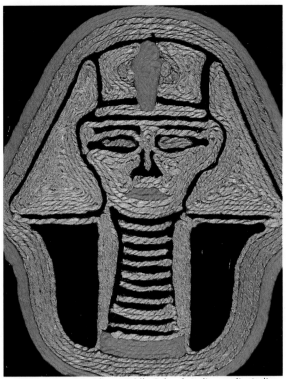

Meridian Middle School. Indianapolis, Indiana

Meridian Middle School. Indianapolis, Indiana

Instructions for Creating Art

1. Draw the outline shape of an animal, house, or simple outdoor scene to fill a piece of cardboard no bigger than nine inches by twelve inches. Simple shapes usually make the best designs.

2. Fill all the spaces in the drawing with yarn or wool. First spread some glue over a space in the picture. Then gently press the yarn into the shape, winding it in spirals to fill the space. It is usually best to begin in the middle of a shape and work outwards. You can link two or three shapes together by outlining them with one color of yarn.

3. The pictures in this lesson may give you some ideas, but use your own imagination to make an original yarn painting.

Art Materials

A 9″ × 12″ piece of cardboard

Pencil and eraser

Scissors

Different colored yarn, wool, string

White glue

Newspaper (to cover work area)

Water, paper towels

Strand L: Textiles, Designs, and Symbols

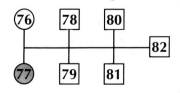

To evaluate your artwork, turn to the Learning Outcomes section at the back of this book.

78 Pennants, Flags, and Banners

Observing and Thinking Creatively

Think about the last parade you watched. You probably saw several people carrying and waving the American flag. And right in front of the marching bands, there were people who carried long, decorated **banners** that stretched across the street. Perhaps the parade passed by a car lot or supermarket that was decorated with strings of small, triangle-shaped flags, called **pennants**. All of these things were designed by artists.

Pennants, flags, and banners often have special designs or **symbols** on them. Think about sports pennants: what designs or symbols do they carry? The American flag is known for its stars and stripes. Do you remember what they stand for? Perhaps you know what your own state flag looks like. The symbols on a flag tell who or what the flag represents.

In this lesson, you will design a pennant, flag, or banner, using symbols that tell about a group you belong to.

San Diego High School. San Diego, California

176

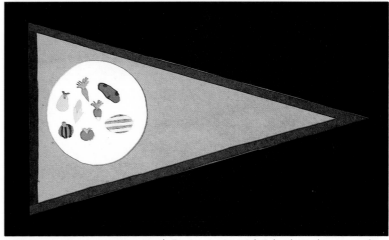

North Daviess Junior High School. Washington, Indiana

North Daviess Junior High School. Washington, Indiana

Instructions for Creating Art

1. Think about a flag you might like to make for a group you belong to. You may want to make a flag for your family, your ball team, club, or church youth group. What shapes or symbols might represent your ideas? Sketch some ideas, keeping your design simple.

2. When you decide on a design, draw it on a sheet of paper. You may want to choose colored paper for the background of your design; select a color that you like.

3. Most flags are made from pieces of material that have been cut out and sewn on the flag background. For your flag, you will cut out parts of your design from construction paper and glue them in place. Choose bold colors that will stand out clearly, and think about the symbolic meaning of the colors you select.

4. Display your flag in the place where your group meets. Tell the other members about the meaning of your flag and how its colors and design represent the group.

Art Materials

Sketch paper	Scissors
Colored construction paper	Glue
Pencil and eraser	

Strand L: Textiles, Designs, and Symbols

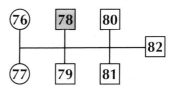

To evaluate your artwork, turn to the Learning Outcomes section at the back of this book.

79 Badges and Patches

Observing and Thinking Creatively

For thousands of years, people have used designs and pictures to communicate ideas. Today many people wear badges or patches with designs or symbols that tell something about their jobs or positions.

Think about badges or patches you have seen. What kinds of jobs were represented? What information was given on the badges? Some badges include both words and a design, and others consist of only a design. What kinds of badges and patches do soldiers, police, and scouts wear?

Badges and patches can be any shape, but some favorites include hearts, stars, suns, moons, and arrows. These shapes are called **symbols** because they stand for certain ideas and have special meaning.

In this lesson, you will design a badge or patch using symbols that communicate information.

Alexandria Middle School. Alexandria, Indiana

San Diego High School. San Diego, California

Instructions for Creating Art

1. Think about the patch or badge you want to make. Your badge might be a button for a school election campaign, or an emblem for a club or favorite hobby. When you have an idea, make some small sketches of possible designs for your badge. Most of your design should be symbols.

2. Decide on one design, and draw it carefully on a large piece of paper. Keep your design simple, and color it so it can be seen clearly from a distance. You may want to cut out your design and glue it to a different colored background.

3. On a separate sheet of paper, explain the meaning of the symbols you used.

Art Materials

White paper	Scissors
Pencil and eraser	White glue
Colored construction paper	Crayons or colored markers

Strand L: Textiles, Designs, and Symbols

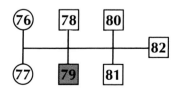

To evaluate your artwork, turn to the Learning Outcomes *section at the back of this book.*

80 Creating with Stitches

Observing and Thinking Creatively

Have you ever seen a picture, wall hanging, or banner made with colored yarn, wool, string, or thread? **Textile** designs such as these are sometimes done with **stitchery**—the art of designing on cloth. Artists who create designs with materials such as threads, yarn, cloth, and needles are said to be working in the field of **fiber arts**.

Many **tapestries**, long wall hangings, are also made with stitchery. They are meant to be attractive and interesting to look at. Some tapestries have simple designs, while others show whole, intricate scenes.

Stitchery can be very interesting when various stitches, yarns, and materials are used. Some artists create special effects by stitching buttons, feathers, twigs, or beads into their designs.

In this lesson, you will create your own piece of stitchery using a variety of stitches and threads.

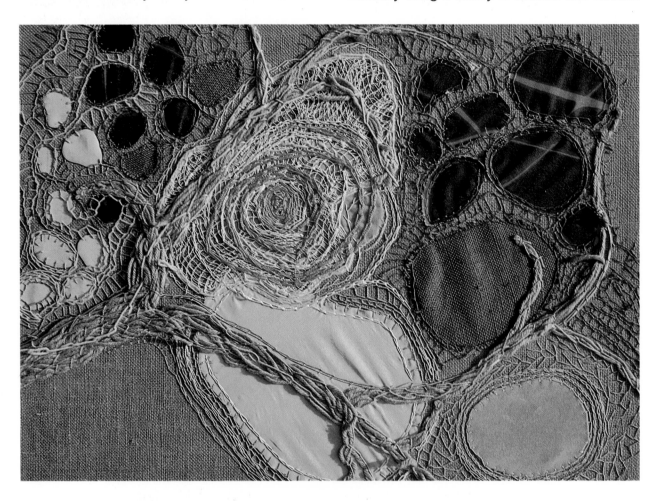

Stitchery can be used to create abstract shapes as well as realistic images. Phyllis Danielson created *Golden Opportunity* with colorful pieces of fabric appliquéd onto a background with large stitches branching over and around them. The twining chains of stitches link the varying oval shapes and textures into a unified whole. How is this work expressive of its title?
Phyllis Danielson, Golden Opportunity.

During the 17th and 18th centuries in America, young girls learned many embroidery stitches so they could later decorate household linens for their marriages. This piece by Polly Bedford is a sampler showing her skill with many stitches. Note how the medium of cloth and thread can be used to "paint" a picture.

Worked by Polly Bedford, *Sampler*, framed, *18th c. Bequest of Elizabeth R. Vaughan. Courtesy of The Art Institute of Chicago.*

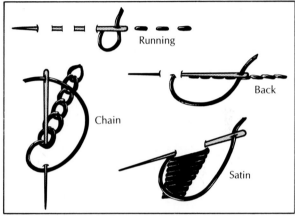

Instructions for Creating Art

1. Sketch some ideas you might use for your stitchery. When you decide what you want to do, make a simple line drawing of your design on a piece of cloth with pencil or chalk.

2. Thread a needle and use another piece of cloth to practice different kinds of stitches. The illustrations in this lesson show how to make these stitches. *Running* or *back stitches* are often used to outline big shapes. *Satin stitches* and *chain stitches* work well for filling in solid spaces.

3. Next, plan the types of thread or yarn and stitches you will use, and select colors to fit your design. You can add solid shapes to your design by sewing other pieces of cloth onto your background. This is called appliqué.

4. Now, stitch your design. Be sure to knot your yarn on the back when you start and as you finish each strand, so it can't pull loose. You can create special effects by using different kinds of threads and materials, as well as using a variety of stitches.

5. When your work is complete, decide how you might like to display it. You can use it for a wall hanging, frame it as a picture, or make it into a cover for a pillow.

Art Materials

Large darning or tapestry needles

Drawing paper

Chalk or pencil

Background cloth: burlap, linen or poplin

Stitching materials: twine, raffia, embroidery silk, or yarn

Scissors

Cloth remnants for appliqué

Strand L: Textiles, Designs, and Symbols

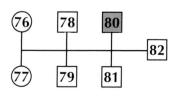

To evaluate your artwork, turn to the Learning Outcomes *section at the back of this book.*

81 *Flat Loom Weaving*

Observing and Thinking Creatively

How do you suppose weaving began? It may have originated when people first wove grass into crude mats to sit or sleep on. Today, most fabrics made for clothing, drapery, and carpets are made by weaving threads of wool, cotton, silk, and other materials. Woven materials and fabrics are called **textiles**.

Although most weaving today is done by machine, it can also be done by hand using a **loom**, a frame used for interlacing yarns. Yarn that is attached to the loom is called the **warp**. When the warp is prepared, other strands of yarn or string, called the **weft**, are woven over and under the warp. The yarns are pressed together to produce a tightly woven cloth.

In this lesson, you will weave a piece of cloth using a cardboard loom.

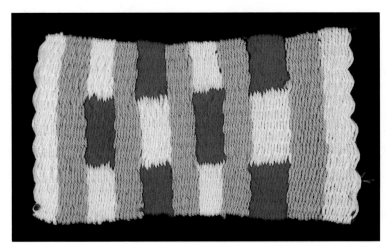

Keystone Middle School. Indianapolis, Indiana

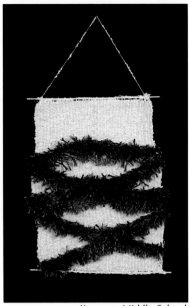

Keystone Middle School.
Indianapolis, Indiana

Keystone Middle School. Indianapolis, Indiana

Preparing the warp

Weaving the weft

Instructions for Creating Art

1. Look at the examples of weaving on these pages and decide what you would like to make. It may be something useful and functional, such as a table mat, or something to hang on a wall for decoration.

2. Make your loom by cutting a piece of thick cardboard into a square or rectangle. Then carefully cut out the center of the cardboard using a ruler and an *X-acto knife.** Leave approximately an inch of cardboard on all four sides. Cut matching notches one-fourth of an inch apart on opposite sides of the cardboard, as shown in the illustration.

3. Knot some yarn or string at one end, and tape it to the back of your loom. Then pull the strand through the end notch, across the loom, and through the notch on the opposite side. Wrap the yarn around the back and pull it through the next notch. Do this until all the notches are filled. Then tape the end of the yarn to the back of the cardboard. This process is called preparing the warp.

4. Next, thread another piece of yarn into a big needle. Using a single strand of yarn and starting at one side, go over and under the warp you just made. When you reach the other side of the loom, loop around the last strand and come back in the opposite direction. Continue doing this until the loom is filled. Keep the weft yarns fairly tight by pushing each new row up against the one before it. When you need to tie on another piece of

yarn, make the knot on the back so it won't show. You might want to use a variety of yarn colors and thicknesses to make your design.

5. To remove your piece of weaving, tie any loose ends, and cut the weft threads at the ends where they curve around the cardboard. These ends must be tied, or your piece will unravel. Starting at the ends, tie each pair of strands in a hard knot, close against the weaving. You can make a fringe by cutting the loops at the top and bottom.

For an explanation, turn to the How to Do It section at the back of this book.

Art Materials

Heavy cardboard	Yarn, string, or weaving material of medium thickness
Pencil and ruler	
X-acto knife	
Scissors	Blunt-ended tapestry needle
Masking tape	

Strand L: Textiles, Designs, and Symbols

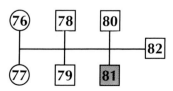

To evaluate your artwork, turn to the Learning Outcomes *section at the back of this book.*

183

82 American Indian Art

Observing and Thinking Creatively

When you think of American Indians, what kind of art comes to mind? North American Indians were creating art long before this continent was discovered, but the type of art they did depended on where they lived.

Indians who lived in the Northwest became known for carving totem poles, making masks, and weaving baskets. Indians in the East were recognized for their beadwork, wood carving, and leatherwork. From the Southwest came pottery, weaving, sand painting, and jewelry. Indians who lived in the Midwest carved stone sculpture and made pictures on the sides of cliffs.

Some of the most interesting art comes from the Indians of the Great Plains. They made feather headdresses, painted and carved their tools and weapons, did leatherwork, made blankets, and painted stories on animal hides. They used simple pictures and **symbols**, or designs that stand for something real, to tell stories and record important events.

In this lesson, you will create designs and symbols in the art style of the American Indians and use them in your own artwork.

Buffalo Hunt was created by this Indian artist in a contemporary stylistic manner. The rhythmic repeating curves express the large bulk and forward rushing movement of the animals. Note the repeated groups of three in the design.

Velino Shije Herrera, Buffalo Hunt, Tempera. *University of Arizona Museum of Art, Gift of R. Vernon Hunter.*

Pershing Junior High. San Diego, California

Pershing Junior High. San Diego, California

185

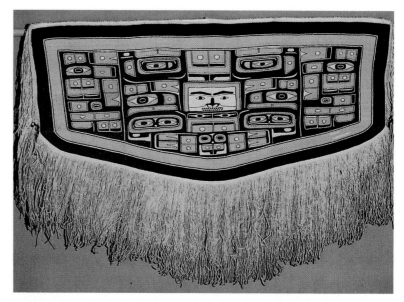

The Tlingit Indians were the original inhabitants of Alaska. This chief's blanket is woven of mountain goat wool colored with cedar bark dyes. Note the abstract face image. Is there symmetry in the design?

Tlingit Indian culture, Chief's Chilkat Blanket, c. 1870-80, Mountain goat wool, cedar bark, native dyes. Indiana University Art Museum. 79.79.2

This *Acoma Indian Jar* was made with thick coils that were smoothed out, and then decorated with geometric designs and lines that echo the curves of the jar shape. Ceremonial water jars like this take four to five days of concentrated work to make. During this time the artist eats and sleeps very little, and his soul is thought to be possessed by the pot.

Acoma Pueblo Jar, Arizona, late 19th century, Baked clay, slip, pigment. Indianapolis Museum of Art, Julius F. Pratt Fund.

Instructions for Creating Art

1. Look at the examples of Indian art in this lesson. These artists used geometric designs and painted figures and symbols with earth colors: red-browns, rusts, and browns.

2. Decide on the kind of artwork you would like to make using Indian designs and symbols. You may want to make an Indian mask, headdress, weaving, piece of pottery, jewelry, or carved figure.

3. After you decide on a subject, make a sketch of your Indian design on a sheet of paper. Using this sketch as a guide, create a finished piece of art. Color your artwork with the **medium** of your choice.

Art Materials

Sketch paper

Pencil and eraser

Your choice of art materials

Strand L: Textiles, Designs, and Symbols

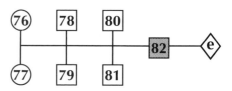

To evaluate your artwork, turn to the Learning Outcomes *section at the back of this book.*

Exploring Art

The Winter Count

Black Elk, an old Dakota Indian artist, knelt beside the picture-filled buffalo hide. He pointed to a picture of a man with red marks all over his body and explained, "This was Smallpox-Used-Up winter. The red spots killed many of my people."

Moving his finger to a figure with an arrow in his leg, Black Elk said, "This was White-Eagle-Died winter. White Eagle was a brave warrior."

Next he pointed to a figure surrounded by stars and said, "We call this Storm-of-Stars winter. Many stars fell from the sky." This drawing represented the great meteor shower of 1833 and appeared on the *winter count* of almost every Dakota tribe.

The Dakotas and other Plains Indians did not have a word for "years." They kept track of time by winters. Each year, a council of tribal leaders chose the most important event of that year.

Then the keeper of the winter count made simple pictures, called pictographs, to represent that event. Year after year, pictographs were added to a single buffalo, deer, or antelope skin until all the space was filled. These calendar records, called *winter counts,* were kept from about 1700 until the early 1900s. They provided tribes with a pictorial record of their ancestral history.

For this Exploring Art activity, recall important events that have occurred in your life during the past year or so. Select three major events or experiences and illustrate them using Indian designs and **symbols**. You may also make up your own designs, but draw them in the Indian style. As your teacher directs, you may want to transfer your designs to a class winter count which can be made on a large sheet of brown paper with edges torn to look like an animal hide.

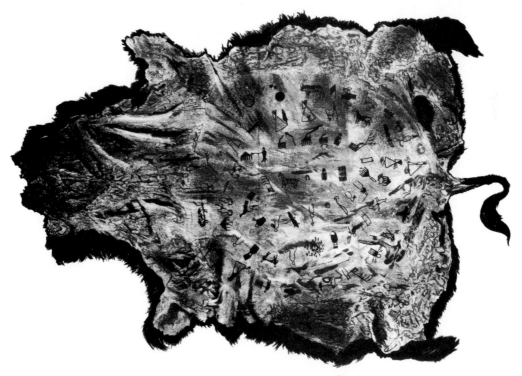

This *Winter Count* gives a history of the Yanktonai Dakota Sioux from 1800-71. It begins in the center, with the symbol of parallel lines representing 30 Dakotas killed that year by the Crow Indians, and progresses in an outward clockwise spiral. Can you find the "year when the stars fell," 1833-34, when there was a great meteor shower observed all over the U.S.?

Yanktonai Dakota Sioux, Winter Count of Lone Dog, *1800-1871. Smithsonian Institution National Anthropological Archives, Neg. #3524-B.*

Quincy Tahoma, In the Days of Plentiful. Philbrook Art Center, Tulsa, Oklahoma.

Unit VI

Expressing Feelings and Imagination

When you can do the common things in life in an uncommon way, you will command the attention of the world.

George Washington Carver

Throughout this book you have seen great works of art created by many different artists. They painted ordinary things—fields of flowers, faces of people, and shapes and forms of familiar objects. How, then, do artists transform these common subjects into artistic creations?

Art is based on how each artist perceives the world and the things in it. For example, one person may see clouds covering the top of a hill. Another person may see strange shapes and faces in those same clouds. A third person might see a mythical beast lurking over the hill. Artists see with their imaginations. Seeing, feeling, and imagining give artists their own individual styles.

Lessons in this final unit of the book invite you to use your skills and ability to explore the world of your imagination and to express your thoughts and feelings through art. You will have an opportunity to portray wishes, dreams, feelings, and fantasies. You will use your imagination to create mythical beasts and fanciful castles, and become the illustrator of a story or comic strip. You will also explore art from other cultures and ancient times. You may use the medium of your choice, and be as original as you dare.

As you work through these lessons, let your artwork express your individual way of seeing "the common things of life in an uncommon way."

83 Wishes and Daydreams

Observing and Thinking Creatively

Have you ever had a dream that you vividly remembered when you woke up? In your dream, you saw colors, things, and people. Perhaps your dream was like something that could happen in real life, or perhaps it was pure fantasy. The creative ideas artists express in their work sometimes come from their dreams, hopes, and wishes. Through pictures they express what they dreamed or imagined.

As you look at the pictures in this lesson, you can see that these artists were not concerned with making their pictures look like photographs.

Their main objective was to capture the feeling and force of their dream experiences or their hopes and wishes.

In this lesson, you will express some of your wishes and daydreams in a picture. You will picture in your art what you imagine and feel. You may draw something that looks real, or you may draw in an unrealistic or **abstract** style. Whatever style you choose, try to portray an impression or feeling of your wish or daydream in your artwork.

Can you imagine from this painting how Charles Burchfield felt about this brilliant garden? Sunlight touches the tops of clouds and flowers. The abstract forms and repeating parallel curves remind us of the rhythm of wind and sun on plants. What features give this painting a dreamlike effect?

Charles Burchfield, Childhood's Garden, *1917, Watercolor, 27 x 18 ¹⁵⁄₁₆". Munson-Williams-Proctor Institute, Utica, New York. Edward W. Root Bequest.*

Notice the striking use of color and abstract shapes in Joan Miró's *Person Throwing a Stone at a Bird.* This hard-edge painting seizes our attention and immediately sets us to wondering about its symbolism. What do you see expressed in the forms of the person and the bird?

Joan Miró, Person Throwing a Stone at a Bird, *1926, Oil on canvas, 29 x 36¼" (73.7 x 92.1 cm). Collection, The Museum of Modern Art, New York.*

Maple Dale School. Maple Dale, Wisconsin

Instructions for Creating Art

1. Relax for five or ten minutes; sit comfortably in your chair and clear your mind of any thoughts. Don't talk to anyone, and try to block out all sights and sounds from your awareness. Close your eyes and let your mind flow, daydreaming or wishing whatever you want. Imagine colors and scenes, and be aware of your feelings.

2. As soon as you have visualized an idea, wish, or daydream, make a picture of it. You might draw just a part of what you imagined or a combination of different dreams and wishes. Use an art style that is comfortable and pleasing to you. Be ready to explain what your picture is about.

Art Materials

Your choice: paints and brushes, crayons, pen and ink, oil pastels, colored markers, etc.

Paper: any color

Water, paper towels

Strand M: Imagineering

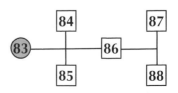

To evaluate your artwork, turn to the Learning Outcomes *section at the back of this book.*

84 Demons and Dragons

Observing and Thinking Creatively

Have you ever imagined or drawn a strange, frightening animal? Perhaps you have had nightmares about monsters chasing you, or imagined one hiding in your room when you were a small child. Did you know that people in many countries of the world tell stories about strange animals? From Scotland, for example, comes the legend of the Loch Ness Monster. In China, many stories and pictures about dragons have been passed down from one generation to another. Perhaps you have read about or seen pictures of imaginary Chinese dragons.

Imaginary animals that come to us from ancient legends or myths are called **mythical** beasts. Many descriptions have been written about them, and artists have portrayed them in artwork. Because these creatures do not actually exist, artists have used their imaginations to picture them.

Look at the pictures in this lesson to see examples of how creative artists can be in showing mythical beasts. In this lesson, you will create your own mythical beast, using these ideas and your own creative imagination.

Sharp, jagged lines of the whiskers, teeth, claws, spikes, and ball of flames accent the fierceness of this Chinese dragon embroidered on a silk robe.

China: early Ching Dynasty, 17th century. Panel from Dragon Robe, *Silk gauze embroidered with silk.*

Eastwood Middle School. Indianapolis, Indiana

Warsaw Middle School. Warsaw, Indiana

Warsaw Middle School. Warsaw, Indiana

Instructions for Creating Art

1. Look through some books to find out about different kinds of mythical animals, and take brief notes describing what they were supposed to look like. You can find information in dictionaries, encyclopedias, art books, and your library. You might choose to research one of the following fantasy creatures: dragon, unicorn, Minotaur, centaur, griffin, satyr, basilisk, sphinx, phoenix, or Cerberus. You and your teacher may have other ideas of mythical beasts to add to the list.

2. Select one of the mythical beasts to illustrate. Use your own imagination and art style to make a drawing, painting, or piece of sculpture. Your mythical animal may look frightening and fearsome, but it should also look beautiful. Add details to show exact features.

3. Look at the pictures in this lesson. Each one shows an imaginary animal, yet each one is different. Your animal should be as different from all of these as possible, coming from your own unique imagination.

Art Materials	
Drawing paper	Your choice of art materials
Pencil and eraser	

Strand M: Imagineering

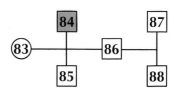

To evaluate your artwork, turn to the Learning Outcomes *section at the back of this book.*

85 *Fantasy Tower*

Observing and Thinking Creatively

Think about some of the fairy tales that you heard or read as a young child. Do you remember fearsome giants, trolls, or evil wizards and witches? Did they live in faraway castles and towers, such as the ones pictured below? Even though they are not real, stories such as these delight our imaginations with their fantastic crea-

tions. You may still enjoy reading or watching fantasies in which strange beings live in magical lands and enchanted castles.

In this lesson, you will invent a structure from your imagination. You might imagine the tower to be the dwelling of an animal or person from the story or fantasy you like best.

Sabatino Rodia, an Italian tile-setter, built what are commonly called the "Watts Towers." He titled them NUESTRO PUEBLO. For 33 years, he methodically constructed these Gothic-like spires out of such things as steel rods, mesh, and mortar. Then he creatively covered their surfaces with pieces of broken glass, tile, pottery, shells and other bits of found objects that he gathered from around his neighborhood.

American Fork Junior High School. American Fork, Utah

Instructions for Creating Art

1. Think of a fairy tale, story, television show, or movie that had a mysterious or strange dwelling or tower in it.

2. Select one idea as the basis for your art and use your favorite kind of art to invent a tower to fit your story. You can draw it, paint it, *carve** it, or build it out of sticks. When the fantasy tower is finished, it should look really strange and exciting.

3. The pictures in this lesson may help you decide what to do, but your tower should be an invention from your own imagination.

For an explanation, turn to the How to Do It section at the back of this book.

Art Materials

Your choice of art materials

Strand M: Imagineering

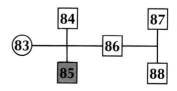

To evaluate your artwork, turn to the Learning Outcomes section at the back of this book.

Observing and Thinking Creatively

When you were a young child, what favorite picture book did you enjoy reading over and over? Perhaps you couldn't read the words then, but you could "read" the pictures. Later, when you could read, you probably still enjoyed the story's illustrations. Most people find stories more interesting if pictures are included.

In ancient times, many people couldn't read or write, and pictures were often used as a way of teaching stories. One of the pictures on these pages tells a story from the Bible. Pictures that tell a story are called **narrative** pictures. Narrative pictures appear in picture books, comic books, and storybooks, as well as in magazines and newspapers. Artists who draw and paint pictures to go with stories are called **illustrators**.

In this lesson, you will illustrate part of a story with a picture.

Edward Hicks draws us into this scene along the path the animals are walking, and up to the Ark with the dark storm clouds behind. What can you tell about the story of *Noah's Ark* from looking carefully at this painting?

Edward Hicks, Noah's Ark, 1846, Oil on canvas. '50-92-7 Philadelphia Museum of Art: Bequest of Lisa Norris Elkins (Mrs. William Elkins).

Nigerian student art

Instructions for Creating Art

1. Make a list of your favorite stories, including stories you liked as a young child. They may be about animals, beings from outer space, mythical creatures, or ordinary people. You may want to make up a story of your own or use one that you have written previously.

2. Choose one part of your favorite story to illustrate. Select a story part that describes a scene, character, or important event. Read this part carefully, taking notes about specific details, descriptions, feelings, or expressions. Then make a sketch based on your notes. Using your sketch as a model, make a final drawing or painting. Add color to your picture if you wish, and share or display it with the story it illustrates.

Art Materials

Your choice: crayons, paints and brushes, pen and ink, oil pastels, colored markers, etc.

White paper

Pencil and eraser

Strand M: Imagineering

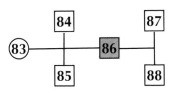

To evaluate your artwork, turn to the Learning Outcomes *section at the back of this book.*

Splat! Bonk! Varoom!

Observing and Thinking Creatively

Visualize a comic frame in which an egg is dropped. What word might be written in the frame to demonstrate the sound? (Splat!) What word could be included in a frame in which a heavy object lands on a man's head? (Bonk!) What word describes the sound of a car taking off really fast? (Varoom!) Now think of a television cartoon that uses sounds instead of written words. Do the sounds and the words reinforce the pictures in the same way?

Artists in the 1960s developed a style of art based on everyday popular things around us, like comic strips, popular foods and brand named packages. They call this type of art **Pop art** (for "popular art"). The Pop artists also got ideas from a kind of poetry called **concrete poetry**. The poem *Zigzag* is an example of this type of poetry. Notice how the meaning of the word "zigzag" is shown through repetition and the arrangement of letters and words.

In this lesson, you will illustrate sound words in your artwork in your own original way.

© 1984 United Feature Syndicate, Inc.

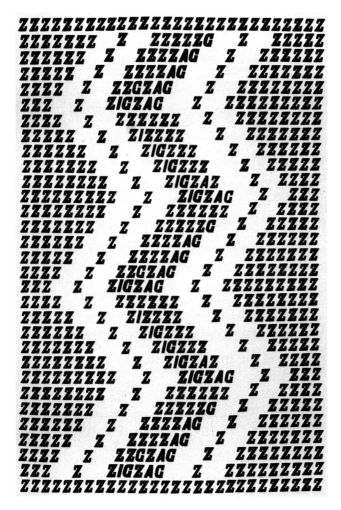

Mary Ellen Solt used letters to make a picture of the word *Zigzag*. How do you think this design was created? What might a concrete poem for the word *zoom* look like?

Mary Ellen Solt, Zigzag. *By permission of Mary Ellen Solt.*

Roy Lichtenstein, Whaam V. The Tate Gallery, London.

*Children's Creative and Performing Arts Academy.
San Diego, California*

Instructions for Creating Art

1. Think of two or three *sound words* and write them down. Here are some examples: zoom, pow, ping, hiss, splash, pop, and kerplunk. Invent some of your own.

2. Now, choose one word and draw a picture of what you imagine would be happening if you heard that sound. Your picture should be original. The sound word can be part of the picture, just as it is in comic strips. Perhaps you would like to create a concrete poem of a sound word similar to the poem *Zigzag*, using the letters of a sound word.

3. When you finish your picture, color it using any **medium** you like.

Art Materials

Your choice: paints and brushes, crayons, colored markers, etc.

Drawing paper

Pencil and eraser

Strand M: Imagineering

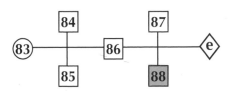

To evaluate your artwork, turn to the Learning Outcomes section at the back of this book.

89 Surprise and Fun in Art

Observing and Thinking Creatively

One of the things that makes art interesting is that it is full of surprises. Artists are always doing things in unexpected ways. This is part of what being **creative** means. Some works of art may be humorous, while others may be so unusual that people aren't sure about their meaning.

In this lesson, you do not have to be serious. You will create an artwork that will surprise people or make them laugh. The art you do for this project should not be a cartoon, comic strip, or **caricature** that is funny just because the shapes of people are **distorted**. Instead, think of something that is funny or surprising because your idea is creative. The pictures in this lesson and others in the book may give you some ideas for your art.

The main lines and shapes of this painting remind us of an envelope, and we are surprised to see them become the outlines for an abstract face and shoulders. What do you think Paul Klee meant by the title *Letter Ghost*? What other surprising ways might you decorate an envelope?

Paul Klee, Letter Ghost, 1937. Watercolor, gouache, and ink on newspaper, 13 x 19¼". Collection, The Museum of Modern Art, New York. Purchase.

Meret Oppenheim created an artistic surprise from familiar objects put together in an unexpected combination. How does it make you feel to think of drinking out of a fur-lined cup?

Meret Oppenheim, Object, 1936. Fur-covered cup, saucer, and spoon. Cup 4⅜" diameter; saucer 9⅜" diameter; spoon 8" long. Collection, The Museum of Modern Art, New York. Purchase.

*Children's Creative and Performing Arts Academy.
San Diego, California*

Westlane Middle School. Indianapolis, Indiana

Instructions for Creating Art

1. Look at the pictures on these pages. They show different kinds of surprises in art. Some are serious, and some are funny. How does each artist surprise the viewer?

2. When you have an idea that is really surprising, decide how you will express it. You might make a sculpture, print, or drawing. When you finish your artwork, give it a title. Your title might be clever and funny, making people laugh, or mysterious and surprising, causing people to wonder about its meaning.

Art Materials

Your choice of art materials

Strand N: Expressive Arts

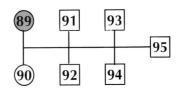

To evaluate your artwork, turn to the Learning Outcomes section at the back of this book.

90 *The Eyes Have It*

Observing and Thinking Creatively

You can learn a lot about people by looking into their eyes. Eyes can look open and friendly, or squinty and angry. They can give out and take in information. In fact, eyes are important in just about everything we do. Detectives use their eyes to search for clues. Scientists look through microscopes and telescopes to discover new things. Some people use their eyes to hypnotize others. Eyes are also very important in many kinds of art. Can you think of any paintings or drawings that emphasize eyes?

Eyes often have a magical meaning. Paintings and statues of gods are sometimes shown with fierce, all-seeing eyes. Eyes have been painted on boats and houses for thousands of years to guard against things that might harm their owners. In this lesson, you will make eyes the main focus of your artwork.

Fear and depression radiate from the eyes of these lifeless, solitary people in *The Subway,* each staring out in a different direction. What effect does George Tooker create with the many parallel lines and bars of the gates, walls, and railings? How does his use of color enhance this overall effect? What social statement do you think this contemporary painting makes?

George Tooker. The Subway. 1950. Egg tempera on composition board. 18 x 36 inches. Collection of Whitney Museum of American Art. Juliana Force Purchase. Acq#50.23.

Alexandria Junior High School. Alexandria, Louisiana

Evans School. Evansville, Indiana

Mexican Dance Mask

Instructions for Creating Art

1. The most important part of this artwork should be the eyes. Everything else should be done to make the eyes look important. Study the art pictured in this lesson to see how each artist made eyes the central feature.

2. The eyes you draw should communicate something or give a special feeling. Decide what feeling you want to communicate and how to express it in the eyes you draw. Use your idea to make a drawing, painting, **collage**, or sculpture, emphasizing eyes.

Art Materials

Your choice of art materials

Strand N: Expressive Arts

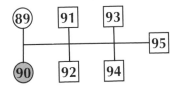

To evaluate your artwork, turn to the Learning Outcomes *section at the back of this book.*

91 A Feeling of Peace

Observing and Thinking Creatively

Peacefulness is a feeling everyone likes to experience. How do you feel when you are the most peaceful? Where do you like to be? What thoughts or images come to mind? You may think peacefulness is a feeling you experience when nothing goes wrong. Or perhaps you think it is a deeper feeling that remains even when things do go wrong. Someone else may feel peaceful sitting beside a mountain lake. Another person may think of peace as the absence of war. You may experience peace when you are sitting quietly at home watching TV, reading a good book, or listening to your favorite music. Peace can mean all these things. It may mean different things to different people, but most people agree that it is a pleasant, calm, gentle feeling.

Artists sometimes express their feelings about peace in their art. The painting *Peaceable Kingdom,* by American artist Edward Hicks, portrays his ideas of peace.

In this lesson, you will draw a picture with the title *Peace* to illustrate *your* meaning of the word.

Edward Hicks visualizes a perfect world with all people and all creatures living together in peace. The lion and the lamb lie down together while rosy-cheeked children play, the wild and tame animals feed side by side, and Pilgrims and Indians lay down their weapons and negotiate peace.

Edward Hicks, Peaceable Kingdom, *c.1848, Oil on canvas. '50-92-6 Philadelphia Museum of Art: Bequest of Lisa Norris Elkins.*

Lawren Harris was one of the "Group of 7" artists who painted landscapes depicting their love of Canada. Above, the timeless majesty of the mountains, the tranquillity of quiet reflections on still water, and subdued colors create a profound feeling of peace. Major lines of the painting form triangles that join at the meeting of land, sky, and water, suggesting the harmony of all nature.

Lawren S. Harris, Canadian, Maligne Lake, Jasper Park, 1924, Oil on canvas. National Gallery of Canada, Ottawa.

Instructions for Creating Art

1. Sit quietly for a few moments and let yourself experience a feeling of peacefulness. Close your eyes, relax, and picture a peaceful scene in your mind. Imagine colors and details in the scene. Or picture the word *peace* in another way, perhaps involving **abstract** designs or a piece of original **concrete poetry**.

2. When you have an image in your mind, draw or paint your idea of peace. The things in the picture do not have to look real, but people should be able to tell what the picture is about. Write the title at the bottom of the picture or on the back. Be sure to fill the whole sheet of paper with your artwork, showing what the idea of peace means to you.

Art Materials

Your choice: pen and ink, crayons, colored markers, or paints and brushes

White paper

Mixing tray (for paints)

Water, paper towels

Strand N: Expressive Arts

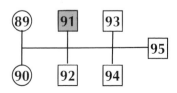

To evaluate your artwork, turn to the Learning Outcomes section at the back of this book.

92 Feelings That Are Opposite

Observing and Thinking Creatively

Think of ideas and feelings that are opposites, such as love and hate, strong and weak, war and peace, rough and smooth. Thinking about opposites is a good way to understand how artists depict moods. Some artists show happy, peaceful feelings in their work, while others portray anger, confusion, and distress.

Vincent van Gogh, a well-known artist of the late nineteenth century, is famous for communicating strong feelings in his pictures. He often combined opposite feelings in the same picture. Look at *The Starry Night* on page 92, and observe how van Gogh showed the turbulent action of the universe in a peaceful country village at night.

Observe how the artwork shown in this lesson expresses different moods. Compare the two sculptures on the opposite page. Notice how the sculpture by Roszak shows a feeling of violent action, while the one by Lipchitz conveys a sense of peacefulness and calm.

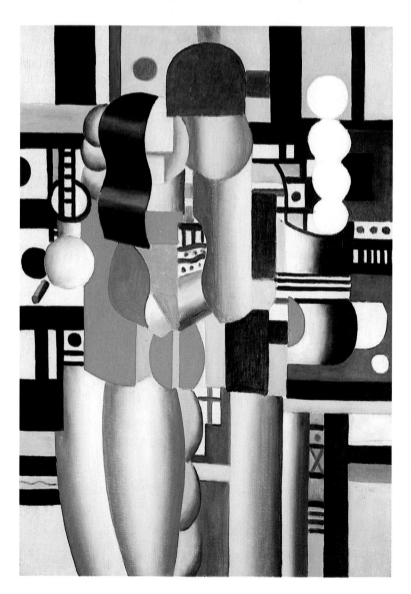

Opposites come together in this abstract painting by French artist Fernand Léger: horizontal and vertical lines, round and square shapes, and the man and woman represented by families of cool and warm colors. What is the overall feeling created by this union of opposites?

Fernand Léger, French, 1881-1955, Man and Woman, *1921. Oil on canvas, 52.28. Indianapolis Museum of Art, Martha Delzell Memorial Fund.*

208

Sharp points and acute angles reach out in menacing attack in *The Unknown Political Prisoner (Defiant and Triumphant)*. American sculptor Roszak is known for his expressionistic welded metal forms picturing strife and struggle.

Theodore Roszak, The Unknown Political Prisoner (Defiant and Triumphant), 1952, Metal. The Tate Gallery, Millbank, London.

Smooth, glossy surfaces and wide, relaxed angles create the calm, peaceful impression of a wet *Bather* drying with a towel in Jacques Lipchitz's abstract bronze sculpture. Do you see the influence of cubism in the composition of the overlapping, interacting planes?

Jacques Lipchitz, Bather, Bronze. San Diego Museum of Art.

Instructions for Creating Art

1. Think of two opposite feelings or ideas to express in your art. You may illustrate these feelings by drawing, painting, or sculpting. For example, if you create a picture of a fierce cougar, you might also draw a timid deer to contrast with it.

2. Express your first feeling or idea in a picture or sculpture. Color or paint it if you want. Don't make your picture or sculpture too large. Write the feeling expressed in your picture or, if you did a model, label it.

3. Now draw a picture or make a sculpture expressing the opposite feeling. Write the name of this feeling on your artwork.

Art Materials

Your choice: crayons, oil pastels, paints and brushes, or clay and sculpting tools

Pencil and eraser

Drawing paper

Strand N: Expressive Arts

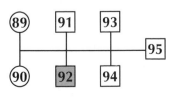

To evaluate your artwork, turn to the Learning Outcomes *section at the back of this book.*

93 The Original You

Observing and Thinking Creatively

Most artwork has to do with being **original**, or different from others. It involves a search for your artistic **style**—your own special way of doing art. Developing your art style takes time and practice. It involves experimenting with different methods, **media**, and ways of doing art. To be able to recognize and appreciate fine artwork, it is helpful to become familiar with the art styles of famous artists. With experience, you will come to appreciate some styles more than others, and you may begin to experiment by using them in

your own artwork. What, then, will make your artwork different from others'?

Using your own imagination and daring to be different are essential for developing your own style of art. Artists often work hard to be different. They want their art to say something unique—to express their thoughts, feelings, experiences, and views of the world.

In this lesson, you will discover your artistic style by selecting your own subject and art materials to create a finished piece of art.

Alfonso Ossorio created this assemblage from both man-made and natural objects like bones and shells. How many can you identify? Notice how he arranged these diverse materials, repeating shapes and colors to unify the composition.

Alfonso Ossorio. Empty Chair or The Last Colonial. *Assemblage: miscellaneous materials including glass, wood, plastic, bone, shell, stone, and metal on plastic sheets mounted on wood, 46⅜ x 39¼ x 15⅞". Collection, The Museum of Modern Art, New York. Gift of the artist.*

Abstract figures and a new way of applying paint distinguish Paul Klee's original style. Other painters used dots of paint 50 years earlier, but Klee used them to show a private world of his own. What about this painting reminds you of a *Traveling Circus?*

Paul Klee, Traveling Circus, *1937, Oil on canvas. The Baltimore Museum of Art: Bequest of Saidie A. May. BMA 1951.317*

Edmonton Art Gallery Classes. Edmonton, Alberta, Canada

Instructions for Creating Art

1. Observe the pictures in this lesson. They are all very different. Each artist used a variety of art materials and different subject matter. Some artwork is realistic, while other works express abstract ideas.

2. Choose the kind of art that you like best. You can make a piece of pottery, carve in plaster, draw with pen and ink, create a sculpture, or do any other kind of art you like.

3. Decide on a favorite subject for your art. If you like to draw faces, do a face. Perhaps you like to show action in art, such as dancing. Maybe you like to paint **abstract** pictures that don't show realistic forms. The choice is yours.

4. Gather your art materials and experiment by creating a piece of art expressing the subject you have chosen. Try to discover the art style that pleases you most. When you finish, dis-

cuss your art style with your classmates, as your teacher directs.

Art Materials

Your choice of art materials

Strand N: Expressive Arts

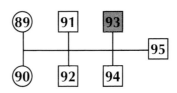

To evaluate your artwork, turn to the Learning Outcomes *section at the back of this book.*

94 The Sun as a Symbol

Observing and Thinking Creatively

As the source of all our light on earth, the sun has been important to man since the beginning of time. The ancient Egyptians worshipped it, and so did the Incas in Peru and the Aztecs in Mexico before the Spanish conquest. They painted pictures and made sculptures, carvings, and designs of the sun. Even today, the sun is portrayed in all kinds of art.

Think of an idea about the sun. You might picture the friendly, warm sun of a summer day.

Or you might portray an angry, merciless sun beating down on the desert. You might show the sun as a great, godlike spirit, as the ancient people thought of it. You could also show the sun as a small, insignificant star in our galaxy that seems large and bright only because we are close to it. The pictures in this lesson show some examples of how artists have portrayed the sun.

Egyptian Sun God *in the form of a falcon, from the tomb of Tutankhamun.*

Aztec Calendar Stone

International Collection of Children's Art, Illinois State University. Normal, Illinois

The bold contrast of gray clouds and dark hills silhouetted against the *Red Sun* evokes an ominous mood in this dynamic painting. Note how the artist has used various shades of gray. Find areas in the picture where there is a repetition of colors as well as undulating curves.

Arthur Dove, American, 1880-1946, Red Sun, 1935, Oil on canvas, 20 ¼ x 28 in. The Phillips Collection.

Instructions for Creating Art

1. After you have thought about what the sun is like, make a design, picture, or piece of sculpture that expresses your idea. Your art can be realistic or **symbolic**, showing a shape or design that reminds people of the sun.

2. Make your artwork as original as you can. Use your imagination both in expressing your idea of the sun and in the way you use your art materials. Can you think of unexpected ways to portray the sun? Keep in mind your own feelings about the sun as you work.

Art Materials

Your choice of art materials

Strand N: Expressive Arts

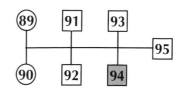

To evaluate your artwork, turn to the Learning Outcomes *section at the back of this book.*

95 Mexican Influences on Art

Observing and Thinking Creatively

The people of Mexico have an ancient history. For thousands of years, Mexican art was strongly influenced by the ancient cultures of the Mayans, Toltecs, Mixtecs, and Aztecs. Early artists from these cultures designed ceramic vessels and sculpture, wove beautiful fabrics, and made fine gold jewelry. They also constructed huge stone temples similar to the Egyptian pyramids. The ruins of these majestic temples, such as the one pictured at the top of page 215, can still be seen throughout parts of Mexico and Central America. These temples and buildings were decorated with carvings and wall paintings, or **murals**, reflecting religious beliefs and traditions.

In 1519, Spanish explorers led by Hernando Cortez conquered these ancient indian cultures and destroyed or plundered much of their art.

Under the influence of the Spanish, mission churches were built and designed with contrasting curves, carved figures, and elaborate ornamentation. At that time, Mexican art also began to reflect Spanish influences by emphasizing the use of contrasting colors, balance, and large-scale design.

Mexican-American artists in the United States today have brought with them this rich mixture of Indian and Spanish art. Some of these artists continue to create art as it has been done for centuries, while others develop new art styles.

In this lesson, you will create a piece of art in the style of Mexican artists from the past or present. Or you may decide to study the art from a different culture and create an artwork in a style similar to that culture's art.

A dark, shadowy foreground and bright sunlight in the valley emphasize the peaceful safety of the *Sanctuary*, a contemporary work painted by Joel Tito Ramírez.
Joel Tito Ramírez, Sanctuary.

Calexico High School. Calexico, California

215

Culturally advanced Mayan Indian civilizations designed expressive sacrificial burial figurines made of terra cotta, or "baked earth." This *Warrior* is probably a replica of an actual person, designed for a ceremonial burial.

Tatanac Warrior, *Terra cotta, Vera Cruz, Mexico, A.D. 400-800, St. Louis Art Museum.*

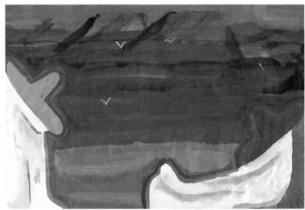

Calexico High School. Calexico, California

Instructions for Creating Art

1. Look at the variety of Mexican art represented in this lesson. Observe the art objects made by the ancient Indian artists, as well as those created by contemporary Mexican artists. Compare and contrast the different styles.

2. Think of a subject for an artwork you would like to create using Mexican art ideas and styles from the past or present. You might also combine certain ideas from different pieces of art to make your own original creation. Use any **media** you like to complete your work.

3. As another option, you can also learn about art from a different country or culture, perhaps one where members of your family came from. Then use these ideas to create a piece of art that reflects art styles from the country you studied.

4. When your work is finished, be ready to explain how you used art ideas and styles from Mexico or another culture.

Art Materials

Your choice of art materials

Strand N: Expressive Arts

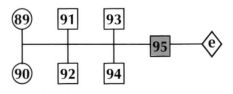

To evaluate your artwork, turn to the Learning Outcomes *section at the back of this book.*

216

Exploring Art

Creating a Wall Mural

In the early 1900s, following the Mexican Revolution, a new style of Mexican art emerged which often reflected the history of Mexico and the social welfare of the common people. Huge wall **murals** concerning social themes were painted on public buildings. Two of the best-known creators of Mexican mural painting were José Clemente Orozco and Diego Rivera. Rivera's simple, stylized paintings portray the struggles and everyday life of the working people in Mexico. He was greatly influenced by the French Impressionists and Post-Impressionists, and incorporated their uses of color, light, and balance in his artwork.

For this activity, design a picture for a wall mural that expresses something you feel strongly about or shows the life of people around you. Use the art style of Mexican muralists in your design after carefully studying their work.

Before you decide on a subject for your mural, think about where you want to display it. The place you have in mind will influence the subject you choose. For example, if you design a mural for your school, depict a subject that would be appropriate there. The picture you design can be a small **scale** sketch for a mural. Or you can design and complete a full-size mural with several classmates, and then display it on a wall.

This beautiful fresco, or mural, pictures the life of laborers in an orchard. Notice the illusion of space Diego Rivera has created between the children, the receding trees, and the man on the tractor. What sweeps your eyes around the picture?

Diego Rivera, Fresco, 1931. Photographed with permission of the Regents of Univ. of Calif., Berkeley, by Don Beatty © 1983.

217

How to Do It

DRAWING

Drawings may be done with light or heavy lines and shading, depending on the artist or the choice of subject. While many drawings are done in great detail, other drawings are made with a few simple lines. Yet another kind of drawing is the *sketch*, a quick, undetailed drawing that indicates only the main features of a person, object, or scene. A sketch is often used as a reference for a later drawing or other work.

Drawing instruments useful for drawing include pencils, pen and ink, crayons and oil pastels, felt or plastic-tipped colored markers, and charcoal, as well as brushes. Drawing instruments such as rulers, set squares, and compasses are useful for drawing exact shapes and dimensions.

Drawing Tools and Techniques

Pencils

Many different effects can be created with a pencil, depending on how it is held and how much pressure is exerted. Pencil lead varies from 6B, which makes the darkest, softest mark, to 9H, which makes the lightest, hardest mark. Note that very soft lead breaks and smears easily. Several pencils of different degrees of hardness can be used in one drawing if desired. Details are best made by medium-range, harder pencil leads, such as regular number 2 or 2½ pencils.

Shading is a technique of showing gradations of light to dark values in a picture by darkening areas in shadow and leaving other areas light. Various shading methods can also help to make objects and figures appear three-dimensional as well as show textures. The picture below illustrates different ways of using a pencil to achieve shading.

Colored pencils are most effectively used by first making light strokes, building up to darker tones.

Pen and Ink

Pen and ink are useful for creating line drawings, silhouettes, and calligraphy.

Ink is available in waterproof, or permanent, and non-waterproof varieties and colors. Permanent inks come in the deepest and longest-lasting colors. They produce better effects, but their stains are extremely difficult and sometimes impossible to remove from clothing and skin.

- **Safety Precautions:** Both permanent and non-waterproof inks stain badly. It is a good idea to wear old clothing or a bibbed apron when working with these inks.

When diluted with water, ink is useful for making washes. To get a lighter value, add more water to the ink. Inks can be put down with steel, reed, or bamboo pens, brushes, or pen nibs.

Pen nibs are small metal points that attach to a holder. They range in shape from very flat and broad to extremely narrow to make different kinds of lines.

- **Helpful Hints:** Pushing the pen *away* will cause it to dig into the paper and splatter ink. Press the tip against the lip of the ink bottle to remove excess ink. Ink flows more evenly if drawing is done on a sloped surface.

Pen Nibs

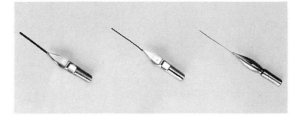

Shading and Texture Techniques

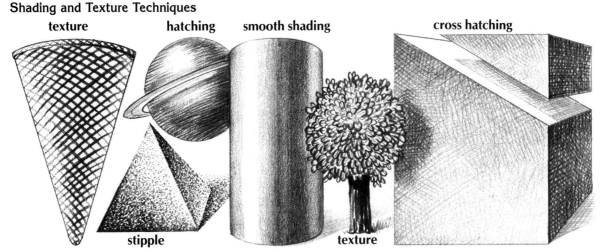

texture   hatching   smooth shading   cross hatching

stipple   texture

Crayons and Oil Pastels

Crayons. Made of hard wax, this medium is available in a great variety of colors. When applied with a heavy pressure, crayons produce rich, vivid colors. Strokes can be blended or softened by rubbing them with a cloth or paper towel. Preliminary sketches are better made with white chalk or a light-colored crayon because pencil lines will often show through the crayon color. Newspaper padding under the paper to be colored insures an even application of color.

Oil pastels are softer than wax crayons, similar to chalk, and produce bright, glowing color effects. They smudge more easily than crayons. As with crayons, drawing can be done with the points or with the unwrapped sides. Note: Oil pastels break easily once the wrapping is removed. Pressing hard creates rich, vibrant color; less pressure produces a softer color. Colors can be mixed by adding one over another, or by placing different colors side by side and smudging them. Rough paper makes the color lighter, and smooth paper makes the color appear brighter. (See illustrations below.)

Colored Markers

These felt or plastic-tipped instruments are easy to use and clean, and they are available in a wide range of colors and sizes. They are useful for sketching outdoors, making contour drawings, and for just about every art assignment imaginable. They dry out easily, so be sure to keep a cap on the tip when the markers are not in use.

Mechanical Drawing Instruments

Ruler. Hold the ruler firmly in place and measure a line of the desired length. Then put dots to mark the beginning and end of the line and connect them by drawing a line against the ruler's edge.

Set Square. This triangle has straight edges and may be set at any desired angle with the edge of a drawing board. It is used with a T square to draw lines at right angles.

Protractor. This instrument is a half-circle used to draw and measure angles.

T square. This instrument is a straight edge with a crosspiece or head at one end. The crosspiece is held against the edge of a drawing board to position the straight edge for drawing parallel or horizontal lines. It is also used as a support for a set square in drawing vertical lines at right angles.

Pencil Compass. This instrument is useful for making circles. First, be sure the legs are tight and will not move easily. When the pencil is securely attached to the holder on one leg, it should be the exact length of the pointed leg. Press the metal point into the paper, with the two legs apart. Hold the pencil at the top and turn the pencil leg around the pointed leg. This creates a perfect circle. Vary the size of the circle by spreading or closing in the legs of the compass. The measurement from the center of a circle to the outside edge is called the *radius*.

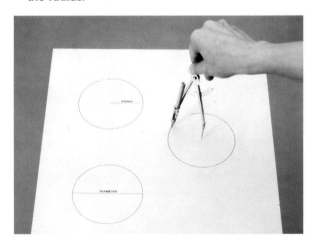

Using a Pencil Compass

Charcoal

This material is made from charred twigs or vine and is available in natural sticks, pencils, and compressed sticks. Its effects range from soft and dark to hard and light. Edges can be softened and light and dark tones blended by smudging with a finger or soft cloth. Changes can be made with a rubber kneaded eraser. Because it is dry and easily smeared, the final charcoal drawing should be sprayed with a fixative to preserve it.

PAINTING

Two of the most popular and readily available paints are tempera and watercolor.

Tempera

This paint works best when it has the consistency of thick cream. It is available in powder, liquid, and solid blocks of color. Tempera is opaque—the paper beneath cannot be seen through the paint.

Powder. Available in cans or boxes, tempera powder is mixed in small amounts. Water and powder are mixed to the desired consistency until there is sufficient paint. Only mix as much as is needed; dried tempera paint cannot be used again.

Liquid. Available in a jar, tube, or plastic container, tempera liquid is in a ready-to-use condition. Stir well if it has been stored for a long time. Make sure that any sticks, brushes, or spoons you use for stirring are clean so that the paint will remain clean and opaque. Keep the lid on when paint is not being used, and keep paint cleaned out of the cap to prevent sticking. Stuck bottle caps will usually loosen in warm water.

Blocks or cakes. Available in large, separate blocks or small blocks of different colors in paint boxes, it is made to dissolve easily when rubbed gently with a wet brush.

Watercolor

Watercolor paints come in tubes or small, solid pans or cakes. The solid paint dissolves very easily when it is rubbed gently with a wet brush. This kind

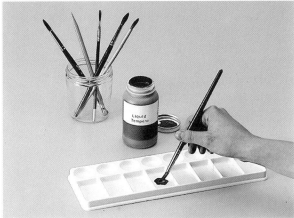

Tempera Paints

of paint is to be used with plenty of water and has a thin consistency. Because it is transparent, it is possible to see through it to the paper underneath.

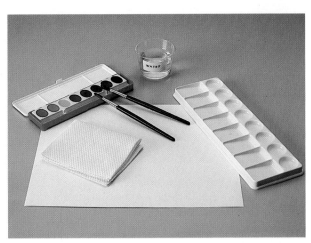

Watercolor Paints

Painting a Watercolor Wash

Color-mixing Tips

Be sure to keep the water in the rinsing container clean, and rinse the brush before dipping it into a new color.

1. With tempera paint, always begin mixing with light colors and add darker colors a little at a time. Never add a lot of black.
2. Never try to lighten tempera paint that has become too dark. The color will have to be used as it is or thrown away.
3. To make green, add blue to yellow.
4. To make orange, add red to yellow.
5. To make violet, add blue to red.

6. To make brown, try putting these colors together. Each combination will make a shade of brown.
   a. red and green
   b. red, yellow, and black
   c. red and black

7. To make gray, add black tempera to white. With watercolors, just thin down black paint with water. All grays look better with a dab of another color added.

8. To make watercolors lighter, add water.

9. To darken watercolors, use less water.

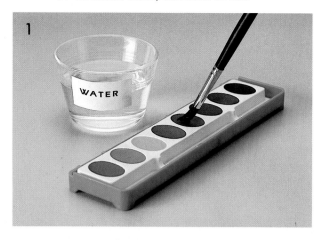

Painting with watercolors:
1) add clear water to moisten paint
2) clean the brush after applying paint
3) fill the brush with another color
4) mix paints to achieve desired color
5) apply mixed colors to picture

PRINTMAKING

Linoleum Techniques

1. Begin with a mounted or unmounted pliable block of linoleum.
2. Paint the block white and let it dry.
3. Draw a design on the linoleum.
4. Cut out unwanted areas with a U-shaped or V-shaped cutting gouge.

- **Safety Precaution:** Use linoleum cutting tools carefully. Always cut away from the body to prevent accidents.

5. Pour printing ink on an inking surface, such as a glass sheet, metal or plastic tray, or cookie sheet.

- **Safety Precaution:** Be sure to use printing inks in a well-ventilated room.

6. Roll the brayer over the ink to spread it so the brayer can pick up an even coat.
7. Roll the ink-coated brayer over the block of linoleum until the whole surface is evenly covered with ink. Roll first in one direction, then in another at right angles.
8. Turn the block over and lower it carefully onto the paper to be printed. Press it down firmly along all four edges. If there are textures or details in the design, turn the block over and press the paper onto it. Rub the paper against the textures with a covered finger or the back of a spoon to pick up all the details.
9. Peel the paper away from the block. The print is ready to dry.

Making a linoleum print:
1) cutting away parts from the design
2) applying paint with a brayer
3) printing the design

Other Printing Materials

Other materials recommended for making prints include man-made objects, natural objects, string designs glued to cardboard, roots, and wood.

Inks

Printing ink may be water or oil-based. Oil-based ink produces the best results but it dries slowly, has an unpleasant odor, and is difficult to clean up. Water-based ink dries quickly, needs thinning to keep it from becoming tacky, and cleans up easily.

Paper

Recommended paper for printing includes newsprint, construction paper, butcher paper, and tissue paper. Avoid using paper with a hard, slick finish because it absorbs ink and paint poorly.

Clean-up

If oil-based ink is used, use turpentine to thoroughly clean the roller, inking surface, and linoleum block when printing is completed. Ink that dries cannot be removed from these surfaces.

SCULPTURE

Sculpture refers to three-dimensional art. It is usually made by carving, modeling, casting, or construction. Sculptures can be created by adding to or taking away from a block of material. Materials appropriate for subtractive sculpture in school include firebrick, clay, chalk, soap, wax, soft salt blocks, plaster of paris, and soft wood. Materials recommended for adding on to a piece of sculpture include clay, papier-mâché, wood, and almost anything else that can be joined together. Specific *carving techniques* appear in the discussion of each medium.

Clay

Clay comes from the ground and usually has a gray or reddish color. It is mixed with other materials so that it is flexible and yet able to hold a shape.

Oil-based clay. This clay is mixed with an oil, usually linseed, and cannot be fired or glazed. It softens when it is molded with warm hands. As it becomes old and loses oil, it becomes difficult to mold and will eventually break apart. Oil-based clay is available in many colors.

Water-based or *wet clay.* This ceramic clay comes in a variety of textures and can be fired so that it is permanent. It should be kept in a plastic sack or covered with a damp cloth to keep it moist until it is used. If a piece begins to dry out, it may be kept damp with a fine spray of water.

Clay Methods

Clay can be molded and formed using the pinch, slab, and coil methods, or a combination of these.

With the *pinch* method, a chunk of clay is molded into a ball. Holding the ball in one hand, press the thumb in and carefully squeeze the clay between thumb and forefinger. Begin at the bottom and gradually work upward and out. Continually turn the ball of clay as it is pinched.

To make a *slab,* use a rolling pin to roll a chunk of clay into a flat slab about an inch thick. Shapes can be cut from the slab and joined together to form containers or sculpture.

To create a *coil,* use the palm of the hand to roll a chunk of clay against a hard surface until it forms a "rope" of clay of even thickness. Coils can then be scored, attached to each other with slip, and built into a shape or a base.

Textures can be created by pressing combs, coins, bolts, burlap, buckles, keys, chains, utensils, sticks, shells, straws, toothpicks, pencils, buttons, bottle caps, old jewelry, and other interesting objects into the clay.

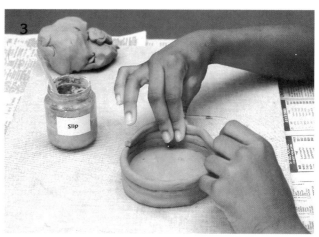

Making clay pottery: 1) a pinch pot; 2) a slab pot; 3) a coil pot

Carving Techniques

Use wire and wooden clay tools or an old table knife to cut away unwanted clay.

Preparing Clay

If clay is reused or made from a powder mix, it will be necessary to remove air pockets in the clay before it is molded. Clay that has air pockets in it can explode during firing in a kiln. Getting rid of air pockets may be done by wedging or kneading the clay thoroughly.

Wedging. Take a large chunk of clay and form it into a ball. Then use a wedging wire to cut the ball in half. Put one hunk on a hard surface and slam the other half down on top of it. Repeat this process until the cut clay has an even consistency. It should feel fairly soft and pliable.

Kneading. Take a large chunk of clay and press it down with the palms of both hands against a hard surface. Turn clay around, and press hard again. Keep turning and pressing in this manner until the clay has a smooth, even texture.

Wedging clay

Kneading clay

Joining Clay Together

Oil-based clay can be pressed together. Water-based clay pieces should be scored, painted with slip, and then pressed together.

Slip is a creamy mixture of clay and water. If clay has dried out, use vinegar instead of water to make the slip. Slip works like glue to adhere pieces of clay together.

• **Safety Precaution:** Check with your teacher on how to dispose of unused slip. It can block piping if it is poured down drains.

Scoring is done by roughening the surfaces that are to be joined with a fork, comb, or pointed instrument. Apply slip to the scored surfaces, press together, and smooth.

Joining clay: 1) scoring; 2) applying slip; 3) joining clay pieces

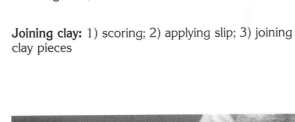

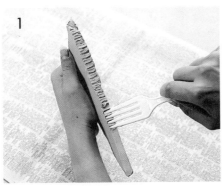

Drying, Glazing, and Firing Clay

Finished clay pieces should be allowed to dry naturally and completely for several days in a warm place until they no longer feel cold to the touch. The firing temperature required to mature various types of clays differs. You should select clay and glazes that mature at the same temperature—which may be determined by the capability of your kiln.

Firing is a two-stage process. Dried, unbaked clay (known as "greenware") may be stacked and loaded as closely as possible for the first firing. This firing will be to approximately cone 015, or 1500 degrees F., and will bring the clay to a "bisque" stage where it is halfway matured, but still porous enough to absorb liquid glaze.

Coat the base, or foot, of bisque ware with commercial *wax resist* or melted paraffin, or simply avoid getting glaze on areas that will touch the kiln shelf, to prevent pieces from fusing to the shelf. Bisque ware may be glazed either by dipping or pouring the glaze on, or by evenly painting on three coats with a soft brush. Glazed pieces must be loaded in the kiln so they do not touch anything for the very hot glaze firing.

Papier-mâché

This art material is made from mixing paper pulp or strips with paste or glue. It can be molded into various three-dimensional shapes when it is wet, and painted and shellacked when it is dry.

Preparing Pulp

Shred pieces of soft paper, such as newsprint, paper towels, newspaper, or facial tissue, into small bits or thin strips. Soak several hours in water. Then drain, squeeze out the extra water, and mix the pulp with prepared wheat paste to the consistency of soft clay. Let the mixture stand for an hour before working with it.

Preparing Strip

Tear newspaper or newsprint into long, thin strips about an inch wide. Dip the strips into prepared wheat paste, and then put down a layer of wet strips over the shape to be covered. Continue putting strips on the form until there are five or six layers. This thickness is strong enough to support most papier-mâché projects.

Sculpting Forms

Good forms that can be used as foundations for papier-mâché include the following: rolled newspapers secured with string or tape, blown-up balloons, plastic bottles, paper sacks stuffed with newspapers and tied with string, and wire or wooden armatures used as skeletal forms.

Pulp Papier-mâché

Strip Papier-mâché

Plaster of Paris

This very white powder comes in large paper sacks and must be kept dry before use. It quickly turns solid when it is mixed with water and feels warm to the touch as it dries. Let the plaster dry two or three hours before working with it. It is relatively soft and easy to carve and can be colored while drying or after it has hardened. The finished piece should be coated with an art spray or shellac to preserve and protect it.

How to Mix Plaster

1. Put as much water in a bowl or bucket as the teacher directs.
2. Quickly sprinkle plaster into the water until it begins to show through the surface of the water.
3. Mix the plaster and water together by hand or with a wooden spoon.
4. When the plaster begins to thicken, it is ready to pour.

Carving Techniques

1. Pour the plaster into a mold or directly onto a wooden board. Use hands to shape it as it hardens, forming it in the approximate shape desired.
2. Use a simple wood chisel and hammer to cut away large unwanted areas.
3. Use a small chisel, file, rasp, Sloyd utility knife, or an old table knife to further define shape.
4. Use a nail, nut pick, or dental tools to carve lines and descriptive details.

    Carving Hint: Proceed slowly and cautiously when removing plaster. Once a piece has been cut off, it cannot be re-attached to the form.

- **Safety Precautions:** Always put plaster that is to be thrown away in a special newspaper-lined wastebasket, *never* down a drain. If plaster powder ever gets in your eyes, immediately flush eyes with water and go to the school nurse.

Wood

Wood is a material whose grain, texture, and color may vary from piece to piece. It is available in a variety of thicknesses and forms for craft projects. Solid blocks about two to four inches thick are suitable for carving. Woods recommended for carving include pine, balsam, cypress, walnut, cherry, apple, mahogany, and rosewood.

Carving Techniques

1. Secure the wood to a surface so that both hands are free for woodworking.

Mixing and Pouring Plaster of Paris

2. Use a mallet and chisel to remove large areas of unwanted wood.
3. Use a saw to cut away areas close to the edges.
4. Use a pocketknife, gouge, or chisels to define shape.
5. Use sandpaper to smooth wood surface.

- **Safety Precaution:** Use sharp blades cautiously, always cutting *away* from your body.

227

BASIC MATERIALS AND PROCEDURES

Types of Paper

Butcher paper. Available in wide rolls and several colors, this paper is useful for murals and other large art projects.

Construction paper. Available in different colors, this fairly stiff paper is useful for tempera painting, collage, and paper sculpture.

Drawing paper. This fairly thick, slightly rough paper is useful for drawing and paper sculpture.

Newsprint. This thin, blank paper is used for printing newspapers. Inexpensive and easily torn, it is good for sketching, printing, and making papier-mâché.

Tissue paper. Very thin and strong and available in many bright colors, it is especially good for making collages and stained glass windows.

Watercolor paper. This thick, textured paper is especially suited to watercolors. Because it is expensive, it is seldom used in schools.

Techniques for Using Paper

Folding

Bend the paper so that one edge is exactly on top of the other, holding the two edges together. Smooth the paper until it creases at the center, then press the crease in between finger and thumb.

Tearing

Paper may be torn apart by hand, causing the edges to look ragged or fuzzy, or it may be folded, creased, and then torn along the creased fold, which gives a neater tear.

Cutting

Cutting may be done with scissors, a paper cutter, or an X-acto knife.

Scissors. If cutting a piece from a large sheet, cut what is needed from the edge, not the center.

Paper cutter. Several sheets may be cut at the same time with a paper cutter. Hold the paper down firmly and be sure fingers are out of the way when the blade is lowered. Pull the blade down slowly and firmly. Do not hack at the paper. If it does not cut smoothly, try cutting fewer sheets at a time. When finished cutting, always lock the blade in the closed position.

X-acto knife. Press this very sharp blade slowly and carefully when cutting.

- **Safety Precautions:**
  - ✔ Use caution when using sharp instruments.
  - ✔ Always keep sharp ends pointed away from your body.
  - ✔ Cardboard underneath materials to be cut will protect furniture.
  - ✔ Do not leave loose blades lying around.
  - ✔ Store blades in a safe place.
  - ✔ *Never* point a blade at anyone, even in play.

Scoring

With a pointed instrument, such as the tip of a pair of scissors, press into but not through a piece of paper or cardboard. The paper will then easily bend or fold on that line.

Scoring Paper

Glue, Paste, and Cement

Glue

White glue is a creamy liquid that comes in plastic squeeze bottles and in larger containers. It is useful for sticking cardboard, wood, cloth, styrofoam, and pottery. It will cause wrinkling when used with paper, especially if too much is used.

Water and white glue are recommended for making tissue paper collages. It should be mixed to a thin, water consistency.

Paste

School or library paste is thick, soft, and white and usually comes in jars. It is good for sticking paper and cardboard, but will often dry out so that the paper comes loose.

Wheat paste is a powder that comes in a package and must be mixed with water. Mix only as much paste as needed because it doesn't store well. This paste is good for sticking paper and cardboard, and for making papier-mâché.

Cement

Rubber cement is a clear, slightly thick liquid that comes in tubes, bottles, and cans. It dries quickly, so always keep the cap on tightly. It is a good idea to keep a can of solvent available to add to the cement so the proper consistency is maintained. It gives glued paper a smooth, unwrinkled look, and excess is easily removed by rubbing.

Applying Rubber Cement

How to Stick Things Together

Spread out some newspaper. Place the artwork to be glued face downward. Spread the glue, paste, or cement outward from the center. Use a spreader, brush, or finger. Be sure the edges and corners are all covered. Lift the paper up and carefully lay it in the desired place. Smooth the paper flat with clean hands. Place a sheet of paper over the top and smooth down on top of that, using the palm of the hand.

Always clean up thoroughly after using glue, paste, or cement with art projects.

- **Helpful Hints:**
  1. Always use the least amount of glue possible. Too much will spoil the appearance of the artwork.
  2. If a brush is used, be sure to wash white glue out of it before it dries. Rubber cement brushes will become stiff if allowed to dry with glue in them, so keep them in the cement bottle to keep them soft. They can be washed in special thinners if necessary.
  3. Both rubber cement and white glue dry very quickly. Don't put glue on until ready to attach the artwork to a surface.

- **Safety Precaution:** Be sure the room is well ventilated when you use rubber cement, and that you store it in a safe place away from open flames.

Attaching a Picture to the Background

Framing Artwork

Frames almost always improve the appearance of artwork and make attractive displays.

Mounting

The simplest kind of frame is a mount. It is made by putting a small dab of paste at each corner of an artwork. The artwork is then placed on the center of a sheet of construction paper or cardboard that is two to three inches bigger than the work on all sides. The border may be slightly narrower at the top and slightly wider at the bottom, for a well-balanced appearance.

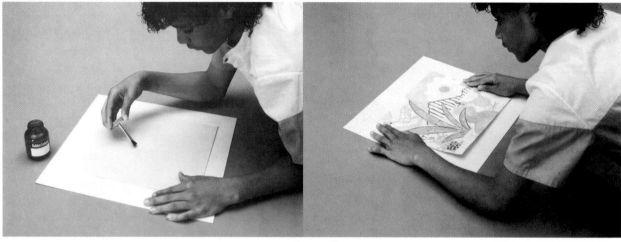

Mounting a Picture

Matting

A mat is a frame with a cut-out center. A picture is taped in place behind it, with the mat forming a border. To make a mat, take a piece of fairly thick cardboard, or matboard, that extends two or three inches beyond the picture on all sides. Measure the picture to be matted. Then, on the back of the matboard, mark the position where the art is to be placed. The mat will look balanced if the bottom margin is a little larger than the other sides. Then measure one-fourth inch in and mark it all around the frame. This will make the picture overlap the cut-out window on all sides.

Now take an X-acto knife and cut along your inside measurements. Cut very carefully when a corner is reached so the matboard is not cut beyond the mark. When all four sides have been cut, the center will come out. Fasten a picture to the back with tape, and the mat is complete.

- **Safety Precautions:** Work slowly and use caution when using an X-acto knife. Keep the blade pointed away from your body, and be sure to retract the blade or return the knife to its container when not in use. Place a pad of newspaper underneath the object to be cut so that you will not cut the table.

Matting a Picture

Learning Outcomes

Note: See page 2 for information on using the **Learning Outcomes.**

Unit 1 Exploring Creative Design

1 Collage from Unusual Materials

Understanding Art

1. Describe how to make a *collage.*

Creating Art

2. Did you cut or tear flat materials into a variety of shapes for your collage?
3. Do you have a center of interest in your collage? How did you emphasize the center of interest?

Appreciating Art

4. Describe the personal feelings or message you expressed in your collage.
5. Discuss everything you observe about the collage by Pablo Picasso in the lesson.

2 Artistic Messages from Music

Understanding Art

1. Explain the meanings of *collage, patterns,* and *textures.*

Creating Art

2. Did you cut and tear paper into a variety of shapes?
3. How do your paper shapes reflect the rhythm of the music?
4. How does your arrangement show unity of design?

Appreciating Art

5. Tell about the kind of music you think would go best with the collage by Henri Matisse.

3 The Glow of Tissue Paper

Understanding Art

1. Explain the meaning of *contrast.*

Creating Art

2. Did you use a variety of tissue paper shapes to make your collage?
3. Did you show color contrast in your artwork? Which colors contrast?
4. What colors did you repeat in your design?

Appreciating Art

5. Identify which pictures of student art you think show the most effective use of tissue collage, and explain why.

4 Stained Glass Windows

Understanding Art

1. Explain the meaning of *stained glass* and tell where stained glass windows have been used.

Creating Art

2. What colors did you use in your stained glass window? Did you repeat them in your design?

Appreciating Art

3. Tell which part of your stained glass window you think is most successful. Explain why you think so.

5 Shadow Pictures

Understanding Art

1. Explain the meaning of *silhouette.*

Creating Art

2. Did you glue your cut-out shapes on a contrasting color of paper? What colors did you use?
3. Which part of your picture was the most difficult to make? Why?

Appreciating Art

4. Explain what made you decide your silhouette shapes were arranged pleasingly on the paper.

6 Art from Nature

Understanding Art

1. Explain the meaning of *nature collage.*

Creating Art

2. List the natural objects you used in your collage, and tell where you found them.
3. Tell how the textures of your objects contrast with each other.
4. Tell which natural objects added any vibrant colors to your collage.

Appreciating Art

5. Explain how the natural objects you used fit the subject of your collage.

7 Printing with Natural Objects

Understanding Art

1. Describe how to make a print with natural objects.

Creating Art

2. Did you make good, clear prints with natural objects? What objects did you use?
3. Describe the patterns in your design.

Appreciating Art

4. Tell which natural objects make the best prints, and explain why.

8 Printing with Man-made Objects

Understanding Art

1. Explain how books were printed before the invention of the printing press.

Creating Art

2. Did you make good, clear prints with man-made objects? What objects did you choose?
3. How did you create *repetition* in your print design?

Appreciating Art

4. Show your favorite printing experiments and tell why you like them.

9 One-Time Printmaking

Understanding Art

1. Explain the meaning of *monoprint*.
2. Describe how to use a *brayer*.

Creating Art

3. Did you draw a design in the paint or ink using a pointed object?
4. What kinds of lines, shapes, and textures did you use in your design?

Appreciating Art

5. Choose your favorite monoprint and explain why it makes a pleasing design.

10 Relief Prints and Patterns

Understanding Art

1. Define *pattern* and give four examples of patterns found in nature.
2. Define *relief print* and explain how you made one for this lesson.

Creating Art

3. Did you design a block that made clear prints? Describe the difference between a clear print and one that is not so good.

4. Did you fill a large sheet of paper with a printed pattern? What did you do to create a feeling of unity?

Appreciating Art

5. Explain why you chose that particular arrangement of prints.

11 Block Prints with Vegetables

Understanding Art

1. Explain how to make a block print with a vegetable.

Creating Art

2. Did you practice making good prints? How can you tell a good print from one that is not so good?
3. Did you fill two sheets with carefully printed patterns? Explain how you used spaces and shapes in your pattern.

Appreciating Art

4. Tell which sheet of student prints in the lesson has the best repeating pattern. Explain why you think so.

12 Printed Lettering

Understanding Art

1. Explain how to transfer letter shapes so they will print the right way.

Creating Art

2. Did you cut your name in reverse on a linoleum block?
3. Did you print a complex design with your linoleum block? How did you make your design complex?

Appreciating Art

4. Tell how your letter design best reflects your personality.

13 Calligraphy and Fine Handwriting

Understanding Art

1. Explain the meaning of *calligraphy*.
2. Define pen *nibs*.

Creating Art

3. Did you hold the pen at a constant angle so the thin and thick lines occurred in the same places in each letter?
4. Did you practice lettering the alphabet? Describe how you made your lettering easy to read.

Appreciating Art

5. Tell which of your letters and words have the best shapes.

14 Letter Designs

Understanding Art

1. Explain the meaning of *proportion.*

Creating Art

2. Did you invent your own alphabet shapes? Describe the style of your alphabet.

Appreciating Art

3. Choose the student lettering in this lesson that you think is best and explain why.

15 Monograms and Trademarks

Understanding Art

1. Define *monogram* and *trademark.* Give an example of each.

Creating Art

2. Did you sketch different ideas for your own monogram?
3. Did you make a large, carefully drawn monogram? Describe your monogram.

Appreciating Art

4. Give the reasons why you chose the design for your finished monogram.

16 Word Pictures

Understanding Art

1. Explain the meaning of *unity.*

Creating Art

2. Did you design four words that look like what they mean? Tell the words you chose, and describe what you did to express their meaning.

Appreciating Art

3. Tell which of the four word pictures you designed is the best and explain why.

17 Art for Advertising

Understanding Art

1. Explain how artists use their art to influence the way people think and do things.

Creating Art

2. Describe how you achieved unity in your poster. Point out any colors, shapes, or patterns you repeated.
3. Describe how you designed your poster to catch people's attention. Tell how you wanted people to react to your poster.

Appreciating Art

4. Tell about some of the advertising art you have seen and why you think it is good.

Unit II Drawing Objects and Figures

18 Doodles That Come Alive

Understanding Art

1. Explain the value of doodling and how it can improve your artwork.
2. Explain how asking yourself questions can help you improve your art.

Creating Art

3. Did you turn your doodle into a design?
4. How did you choose which part of your doodle you wanted to emphasize?

Appreciating Art

5. Tell which of the pictures by Dubuffet and Tobey you think has the best ideas in it. Explain why you think so.

19 Contour Drawing

Understanding Art

1. Explain the meaning of *contour.*
2. Explain how observing objects helps artists in their artwork.

Creating Art

3. Did you make a contour drawing by drawing the edges of an object?
4. Did you make the first contour drawing without looking at your paper? What is this kind of contour drawing called?

Appreciating Art

5. Tell which of your two contour drawings you like best. Explain why you prefer it. Which method do you prefer?

20 Light on Flat Objects

Understanding Art

1. Explain the meaning of the term *plane* as it is used in art.
2. Define the meaning of *value* as it is used in art.

Creating Art

3. Did you draw outlines of objects made out of planes? What objects did you draw?
4. Did you shade in the different planes or objects with the proper grayness? Which parts did you make darker? Which parts did you make the lightest?

Appreciating Art

5. Tell how your shading of planes makes your picture look better.

21 Light on Rounded Objects

Understanding Art

1. Tell which changes more gradually, shadows on rounded objects or shadows on flat objects.
2. Explain the meaning of *gradation.*

Creating Art

3. Did you draw the outlines of a group of curved objects?
4. Did you use gradual shading on rounded objects with the proper grayness? Which parts did you shade the lightest?

Appreciating Art

5. Tell what you like about the way Rembrandt drew the elephant in this lesson.

22 Discovering and Drawing Textures

Understanding Art

1. Explain the meanings of *texture* and *contrast* in art.

Creating Art

2. Did you practice drawing textures?
3. Did you make a design in which the different textures stand out clearly? Which textures show the most contrast?

Appreciating Art

4. Identify the texture you drew that was most successful and the one that was least successful. Explain why you think one is better than the other.

23 Artists and Scientists as Observers

Understanding Art

1. Discuss some ways in which both artists and scientists learn about things.
2. Explain the meaning of *texture.*

Creating Art

3. Did you draw all the main parts and all the details of an object?
4. Is there a shape that is repeated on your object? If so, tell what it is.

Appreciating Art

5. Choose one of the pictures shown in this lesson and explain why you think it shows details well.

24 Drawing Shapes and Spaces

Understanding Art

1. Explain why spaces around objects are important in art.

Creating Art

2. Did you decorate the background shapes only? Describe how you used colors and lines to make a pattern.

Appreciating Art

3. Tell why you think your arrangement of objects makes a good design.
4. Tell which background of the pictures in the lesson you prefer, and explain why.

25 Drawing Without a Pencil

Understanding Art

1. List art materials other than pencils that are good for drawing.

Creating Art

2. Did you experiment with drawing with different art materials other than pencils?
3. Did you draw an object that has an interesting surface texture? What medium did you use to create the texture?

Appreciating Art

4. Tell which medium other than pencils you prefer to draw with, and explain why.

26 Drawing with Color

Understanding Art

1. Explain the meaning of *medium* in art.

Creating Art

2. Did you draw a picture using oil pastels?
3. What colors did you repeat to achieve unity?
4. Did you place light objects next to darker ones to achieve contrast? Which objects did you make the brightest colors?

Appreciating Art

5. Tell what effects you can create with oil pastels that can't be created with other art materials.

27 Joining Up Picture Ideas

Understanding Art

1. Explain the meaning of *visualize* in art.
2. Define *unity* in art.

Creating Art

3. Did you create a picture using photographs and drawings?
4. Did you join all the parts of your picture to create unity? Tell which parts you drew in.

Appreciating Art

5. Define the best way to fill in the empty spaces with drawing.

28 Above and Below the Horizon

Understanding Art
1. Define the term *horizon*.
2. Explain why the horizon line is important in showing depth and distance.

Creating Art
3. Did you draw a line on the chalkboard that is level with your eyes?
4. In your drawing, were all the objects in the correct places in relation to the eye level line? Which objects did you place above the eye level line?

Appreciating Art
5. Compare the two artists' pictures in the lesson. Tell which picture you prefer, and explain why.

29 Two Ways of Showing Distance

Understanding Art
1. Explain two ways of showing distance in a drawing or painting.

Creating Art
2. Did you make six separate, different-sized drawings of furniture?
3. Did you arrange shapes by size and overlapping to show distance? Which object looks closest? Which looks farthest away?

Appreciating Art
4. Tell which of the artists' pictures in the lesson you think shows depth and distance in the best way.

30 Near, Far, and in Between

Understanding Art
1. Define *foreground* and *landscape*.

Creating Art
2. Did you draw the outlines of objects in a picture?
3. Did you fill in details and shading on some of the objects?
4. Tell how you made some objects look closer and others far away.

Appreciating Art
5. Tell which of the pictures by Lozowick and Van Ruisdael you think uses dark areas and details best.

31 Using Your Visual Memory

Understanding Art
1. Explain why it is important in art to remember the things you see.

Creating Art
2. Did you make a list of everything you could remember about a place you know? What place did you choose?
3. Did you draw your place from memory? Which details did you have trouble remembering?
4. Did you check the accuracy of your drawing by going to look at the real place?

Appreciating Art
5. Tell what you did to improve your picture after you visited the place you tried to remember.

32 Inside an Artist's World

Understanding Art
1. Tell some important things to remember about indoor scenes.

Creating Art
2. Did you draw an interior scene that you know? What scene did you choose?
3. Did you put in all the details you could remember? List three to five details in your pictures.

Appreciating Art
4. Describe your feelings about either the Van Gogh or Folsom pictures.

33 Drawing Profiles

Understanding Art
1. Explain the meaning of *profile.*
2. Describe the correct placement of facial features in a drawing.

Creating Art
3. Did you draw a profile portrait of a person?
4. Did you put in all the details on the face to tell as much as possible about the person you drew? Describe three particular details you added.

Appreciating Art
5. Tell what you like about the profiles by Dürer and Baldovinetti in the lesson.

34 Create a Face

Understanding Art
1. Explain the importance of *proportion* in drawing facial features.

Creating Art
2. Did you draw a portrait of a person's entire face with all the features in proportion?

3. Explain what you learned about drawing by doing this assignment.

Appreciating Art

4. Tell which student drawing in the lesson you think is most successful, and explain why you think so.
5. Tell which part of your drawing was most difficult to draw.

35 Face Messages

Understanding Art

1. Explain the meaning of *portrait.*

Creating Art

2. Did you make a pencil portrait of your face showing a strong feeling?
3. Tell what feeling you expressed, and describe how you drew the mouth or eyes to show that feeling.

Appreciating Art

4. Look at the expressions on the faces of the people in the portraits in this lesson. Tell what you think each person is feeling from the look on his or her face.

36 Drawing Close-ups

Understanding Art

1. Describe two ways close-ups are used in art and communications.

Creating Art

2. Describe all the details you drew in your close-up picture.
3. Which feature did you emphasize? What did you do to emphasize it?

Appreciating Art

4. Tell what you think about the feelings shown in the pictures by Kollwitz and Doogan in the lesson.

37 Small into Large

Understanding Art

1. Explain how to use a grid to enlarge or reduce a drawing.

Creating Art

2. Did you use a grid to make a scale drawing of your original drawing?
3. Did you reproduce lines and spaces in your picture so that you produced the original shape?

Appreciating Art

4. Tell which scale drawing in the lesson is drawn best, and explain why you think so.

38 Human Measurements

Understanding Art

1. Explain the meaning of *proportion.*
2. Tell how the size of a person's head relates to the height of the whole body.

Creating Art

3. Did you draw your subject's body with all the parts in proportion? Did you compare the drawing to the subject?
4. Tell where you added details and shading to your picture, and explain how shading makes the person in your drawing look more three-dimensional.

Appreciating Art

5. Tell which part of your figure has the best proportion and looks most natural.

39 Different Ways of Drawing

Understanding Art

1. Explain how artists discover the best way of drawing for them.
2. Explain the meaning of *style* in art.

Creating Art

3. Did you make two drawings using a different medium for each one? Describe how the effects achieved are different.

Appreciating Art

4. Tell which of the two media you tried was most successful, and why you think so.
5. Tell which of the artists' drawing styles shown in the lesson appeals to you most, and what you like about it.

40 The Genius of Leonardo da Vinci

Understanding Art

1. Explain why you think Leonardo da Vinci was a genius. Name three things he is known for besides painting.
2. Decide whether you could best understand something by just looking at it or by drawing it. Explain your answer.

Creating Art

3. Did you make three sketches of a subject you studied carefully?
4. Explain how making the three sketches helped you improve your finished artwork.

Appreciating Art

5. Choose one of Leonardo da Vinci's artworks in this lesson or elsewhere, and explain what you like about it.

Unit III Composing with Colors

41 Colorful Creations

Understanding Art

1. Define *primary, secondary,* and *analogous* colors.
2. Name two families of analogous colors.

Creating Art

3. Did you make two designs using two different *analogous* color groups? Name the colors you mixed for each design.
4. Did you make a unified design using colors, shapes, and lines? Describe what you did to create unity.

Appreciating Art

5. Describe what things your best color mixtures remind you of.

42 Brushing with Rhythm

Understanding Art

1. Describe how *rhythm* may be shown in art.
2. Give an example of a country whose artists are known for using rhythmic lines in art.

Creating Art

3. Did you use watercolors to show a place that you imagined or remembered?
4. What did you do to create a center of interest in your picture?

Appreciating Art

5. Point out where you used different kinds of rhythmic lines in your art.

43 Painting over Wax

Understanding Art

1. Explain what happens when you paint over wax with watery paint.

Creating Art

2. Did you draw a picture with a candle or crayon and then paint over it with watery paint?
3. Describe how you used different kinds of lines to create a shape or pattern in your picture.

Appreciating Art

4. Tell what details or designs you added to your picture when it was dry, what medium you used, and why you chose it.

44 A Watercolor Painting

Understanding Art

1. Explain the difference between *transparent* and *opaque* paints.
2. Define *foreground* and *background.*

Creating Art

3. Did you paint a watercolor wash on your picture? Describe how you did your wash.
4. What did you paint in the foreground of your picture? How do the objects in the foreground contrast with the background of your picture?

Appreciating Art

5. Tell what effect you wanted to create with the colors you chose for your picture.

45 Shapes Without Outlines

Understanding Art

1. Explain the meanings of *still life* and *unity* in art.
2. Name some techniques for unifying a still life picture.

Creating Art

3. Did you paint a picture of a still life without any outlining?
4. Which objects in your picture have textures that provide contrasts?

Appreciating Art

5. What mood or feeling do you get from Frederic Clay Bartlett's *Blue Rafters* in the lesson?

46 Viewfinder Pictures

Understanding Art

1. Explain how to use a *viewfinder* in art.

Creating Art

2. Did you select a view of a scene to paint by using a viewfinder? How could you tell when you found a good view?
3. What is the center of interest in your picture?
4. Tell what you did to emphasize the center of interest in your picture.

Appreciating Art

5. Explain what you liked about using a viewfinder in choosing a scene to paint.

47 From Dark to Light

Understanding Art

1. Explain the difference between *linear* and *atmospheric perspectives.*

Creating Art

2. Did you paint a landscape with opaque paint?
3. Explain how you used color to show objects in the distance and objects closer to the foreground.

Appreciating Art

4. Look at Cézanne's *House in Provence* and Seurat's *Bathers* in the lesson. Tell which painting you think shows distance best, and explain why you think so.

48 Bright Blobs and Splashes

Understanding Art

1. Describe the art style of the *Impressionist* painters.
2. Tell who the leader of the Impressionists was and where Impressionists did their painting.

Creating Art

3. Did you paint a picture using the impressionistic style? Explain how you used paint to achieve this style.

Appreciating Art

4. Tell what you like or dislike about the impressionistic style of art.

49 Paint with Matisse

Understanding Art

1. Name two characteristics of Henri Matisse's style of art.
2. Describe two kinds of art Matisse made.

Creating Art

3. Did you paint a picture in the same style that Matisse used?
4. Describe what you did to make your picture in Matisse's style. What colors did you repeat to create unity? Describe any areas of striking contrasts and any interesting patterns you created.

Appreciating Art

5. Express your opinion of Matisse's painting style. Point out things you like or do not like about his artwork.

50 People at Work

Understanding Art

1. Explain the meaning of *center of interest* in art.

Creating Art

2. Did you make a painting of someone working? What work did you represent?
3. What is the center of interest in your picture?
4. How did you emphasize your picture's center of interest?

Appreciating Art

5. The pictures by Jacob Lawrence and Diego Rivera are very different from each other. Point out the parts you like best in each picture, and explain why.

51 Showing Action in Sports

Understanding Art

1. State two ways an artist might learn to draw an athlete in motion.

Creating Art

2. Did you draw a picture showing an athlete in action? What movement did you emphasize?
3. Did you make the parts of the body in the proper proportions?
4. Where in your picture did you create your *center of interest?*

Appreciating Art

5. Explain how the color scheme you selected relates to the subject matter of your picture. Tell what you like best about your artwork.

52 Geometry in Art

Understanding Art

1. Name three drawing instruments that can be used to make geometric art.

Creating Art

2. Did you draw a design using drawing instruments in creative ways? Describe the kinds of lines you made.
3. Did you paint a geometric design using only two primary colors and the additions of black and white?
4. Which parts of your design did you emphasize? What colors did you repeat?

Appreciating Art

5. List all the words and phrases you can think of that describe the center of the picture by Vasarely.

53 Losing Your Head

Understanding Art

1. Explain the meaning of *abstract.*
2. Explain why artists sometimes make ordinary shapes in unusual ways.

Creating Art

3. Did you draw a face and divide it into many small shapes?
4. Did you repeat certain colors to achieve a *unified* design? Tell what colors you used in your pattern.

Appreciating Art

5. Tell what you want people to notice most in your abstract picture, and why.

54 Guess What It Was

Understanding Art

1. Explain how Theo van Doesburg made an *abstract* picture of a cow.

Creating Art

2. Did you create an abstract design from a realistic drawing using straight lines and geometric shapes?
3. Did you use *complementary* colors or *analogous* colors in your design?

Appreciating Art

4. Point out which part of your finished abstract picture is most successful, and explain why you think so.
5. Tell what you learned through the process of making abstract art.

55 In Search of a Painting Style

Understanding Art

1. Explain the difference between *still life, landscape,* and *portrait.*

Creating Art

2. Did you first sketch only the main shapes for your picture, adding the details last?
3. Did you paint your picture in a style that is uniquely your own?
4. Describe what you did to make your picture in your own style.

Appreciating Art

5. Name the artist you selected. Explain what you like most about that artist's style, and why you like it.

Unit IV Sculpting and Forming

56 Sculpture from Found Objects

Understanding Art

1. Explain the meaning of *assemblage.*
2. Name four items that are normally thrown away that could be used to make an assemblage sculpture.

Creating Art

3. Did you make an assemblage that balances and looks good from every angle? Explain how you attached the assemblage pieces.
4. Describe any areas of contrasting texture or color in your assemblage.

Appreciating Art

5. Describe the parts of your sculpture that are most successful and explain why you think so.

57 Redesigning Nature

Understanding Art

1. Name two ways to improve imagination.

Creating Art

2. Did you make a sculpture from natural objects? What simple or complex shape did you choose?
3. Describe the different textures of your sculpture.
4. Describe the details of your sculpture.

Appreciating Art

5. Identify which natural objects in your collection were most useful in the making of your sculpture.

58 Building with Flat Shapes

Understanding Art

1. Explain how *slotting* is used to join sheets of flat material.
2. Explain the difference between a *realistic* form and an *abstract* form.

Creating Art

3. Did you build a piece of cardboard sculpture, joining the pieces together by slotting them?

Appreciating Art

4. What do you like or dislike about each of the sculptures in the lesson?

59 Bent Sculpture

Understanding Art

1. Explain how to *score* paper in art and tell how scoring affects paper strength.

Creating Art

2. Did you make a piece of cardboard sculpture, scoring the cardboard in several different ways?

3. Explain what you did to capture the feeling or main idea of the familiar shape you chose.

Appreciating Art

4. Identify the two best views of your paper sculpture and explain why you think they are best.

60 Theme and Variations

Understanding Art

1. Give an example of how an artist might use a *theme and variations* in art.

Creating Art

2. Did you change two of three identical objects in creative ways?
3. Describe the variations you made in the objects.
4. In what ways are the new *forms* still similar to the original object?

Appreciating Art

5. Identify the best sculpture variation you made. Explain why you think it is better than the other variations.

61 Handwarming Sculpture

Understanding Art

1. Name two characteristics of *plaster of paris.*

Creating Art

2. Did you create and decorate a plaster mold of your hand?
3. Describe what you added to your art form to create interest.

Appreciating Art

4. How did the decorations you added to your sculpture improve it? Does it look good from all angles?

62 Sand Casting

Understanding Art

1. Explain the meanings of *cast* and *mold* in art.
2. Explain why artists use molds.

Creating Art

3. Did you pour plaster into shapes you made in sand?
4. What did you learn about the mold you made?

Appreciating Art

5. Identify the objects that made the most interesting shapes when they were cast.

63 Alligators, Lions, and Other Wild Beasts

Understanding Art

1. Explain the meaning of *relief sculpture.*

Creating Art

2. Did you make a clay relief sculpture of an animal?
3. What part of your animal did you emphasize in your relief?

Appreciating Art

4. Tell which looks more exciting to you, the Greek or the Assyrian relief sculptures in the lesson. Explain why you think so.

64 Modeling and Molding

Understanding Art

1. Explain the meanings of *relief, mold,* and *cast* in art.

Creating Art

2. Did you press papier-mâché over a clay relief mold?
3. How did you decorate your cast?
4. What part of your cast did you emphasize?

Appreciating Art

5. Express your reaction to the mask from Bolivia, South America. What does it make you think about?

65 Ancient Egyptian Art

Understanding Art

1. Describe the characteristics of the Egyptian art style.

Creating Art

2. Did you carve a drawing into clay or make a clay statue using Egyptian art ideas?
3. Describe the Egyptian art features you used in your artwork.

Appreciating Art

4. Explain the kind of art you decided to do and tell why you chose it.

66 Hand Sculpture

Understanding Art

1. Name three ways sculpture pieces can be joined together.

Creating Art

2. Did you carve a piece of hand sculpture?
3. In forming your sculpture, how did you create various textures?

Appreciating Art

4. Explain how you knew when your hand sculpture was finished.
5. In a few words, describe the feeling you get from your own sculpture.

67 African Art

Understanding Art

1. Name the principal art forms of Africa.
2. Explain how Pablo Picasso's art was influenced by African art.

Creating Art

3. Did you carve a clay figure in the African style?
4. Describe the African ideas you used in your art.

Appreciating Art

5. Tell which piece of African art in the lesson you like best, and why.

68 Slab Buildings

Understanding Art

1. Define *clay slab* and name three things that can be made from clay slabs.
2. Define *slip* in art and explain how it is used.

Creating Art

3. Did you make a model building with clay slabs? Explain how you attached the walls.
4. Describe any decorations you added to create texture, make a pattern, or give unity to your house.

Appreciating Art

5. Explain how you used your imagination to design a clay slab building.

69 Buildings Are Like Sculpture

Understanding Art

1. Name two ways architects and sculptors are alike.

Creating Art

2. Did you make a model of a building that looks good from all angles?
3. Name details you added to your building to create a variety of textures, patterns, and shapes.

Appreciating Art

4. Identify the best view of your building and explain why it is better than other views.
5. Tell what features you like best about your building.

70 Being an Architect

Understanding Art

1. Explain why an architect's model is more informative than a drawing of a building.

Creating Art

2. Did you draw a design and make a model of a house?
3. Describe how you used space, textures, and details in your design.

Appreciating Art

4. Describe what you like about the model home you built. Would you build any parts differently if you had it to do over again? What parts would you change, and how would you change them?

Unit V Working with Ceramics, Crafts, and Textiles

71 Clay Coil Pottery

Understanding Art

1. Explain how to *score* clay and use *slip* to join clay coils together.

Creating Art

2. Did you build a pot with clay coils? Describe the shape of your pot.
3. Did you add decorations to your pot?
4. Describe details and patterns you used to decorate your pot.

Appreciating Art

5. What do you like best about your coil pot? Tell how you plan to use it or where you might display it.

72 Fancy Pots

Understanding Art

1. Explain the difference between *functional* and *nonfunctional* pottery.
2. Explain the meanings of *kiln* and *firing* in working with pottery.

Creating Art

3. Did you build an imaginative pot?
4. Describe the shape of your pot. What details did you add?

Appreciating Art

5. Tell how you plan to display or use your imaginative pot. Is it to be functional or nonfunctional?

73 Creative Mask-making

Understanding Art

1. Name three ways masks can be used.

Creating Art

2. Did you design and make an original papier-mâché mask? Explain the process you used to create your mask.
3. Describe special features or details of your mask.

Appreciating Art

4. Tell what kind of feeling you get from looking at the Bella Bella Indian mask.
5. Describe the expression or mood of the mask you created.

74 Helmets, Hats, and Headdresses

Understanding Art

1. Explain how the purpose of a hat might influence its design.

Creating Art

2. Did you design and make a helmet, hat, or headdress out of cardboard?
3. What shape did you give your hat? What is the hat's purpose?

Appreciating Art

4. Describe special effects or features of your hat, and explain what you wanted to achieve by adding them.

75 Inexpensive Jewelry

Understanding Art

1. Explain why jewelry is a form of miniature sculpture.

Creating Art

2. Did you make a piece of jewelry out of papier-mâché?
3. Describe the shape, color, and special features of your piece of jewelry.

Appreciating Art

4. Identify the piece of jewelry in the lesson that you think is most original.

76 A Picture to See and Touch

Understanding Art

1. Explain the meanings of *textile* and *collage.*

Creating Art

2. Did you create a textile collage with a variety of colors, textures, and designs?
3. Describe contrasting colors, textures, and designs you used in the collage.
4. How did you create a center of interest?

Appreciating Art

5. Explain why the arrangement of your fabric collage pleases you.

77 Folk Art Yarn Pictures

Understanding Art

1. Define *nearika.*

Creating Art

2. How did you create your yarn picture?
3. What colors or shapes did you repeat to unify your design?

Appreciating Art

4. Point out what is unusual and original about Lucas Samaras's box.

78 Pennants, Flags, and Banners

Understanding Art

1. Explain the meaning of *symbol.*

Creating Art

2. Did you design and make a flag? What materials did you use?
3. Name the colors and symbols you chose for your flag.

Appreciating Art

4. Explain the meaning of the colors and symbols you chose, and tell why you chose them for your flag.

79 Badges and Patches

Understanding Art

1. Explain why people wear badges and patches.
2. Explain the meaning of *symbol.*

Creating Art

3. Did you design, draw, and color a badge or patch?
4. Describe the badge or patch you designed.

Appreciating Art

5. Explain the meaning of the symbol you chose and why you used it. Tell what your badge or patch is to be used for.

80 Creating with Stitches

Understanding Art

1. Explain the meaning of *stitchery.*
2. Describe a *tapestry.*

Creating Art

3. Did you draw and stitch a design, using a variety of stitches and yarns? What stitches did you use?
4. Describe special effects, patterns, and details you created with yarn.

Appreciating Art

5. Identify which stitchery in the lesson you like best, and tell what you like about it.

81 Flat Loom Weaving

Understanding Art

1. Explain the meanings of *warp, weft,* and *loom* in weaving.

Creating Art

2. Did you make a cardboard loom and make a weaving on it?
3. Did you use a variety of yarn colors and thicknesses to make your design?
4. Describe the pattern you created with color and repetition.

Appreciating Art

5. Tell which weaving in the lesson you prefer, and why.

82 American Indian Art

Understanding Art

1. Name two facts about North American Indian art forms or styles.
2. Explain the meaning of *symbol.*

Creating Art

3. Did you create a piece of artwork using Indian designs and symbols?
4. Describe what you made and how you used color, shape, and symbols in an Indian design.

Appreciating Art

5. Identify which piece of artwork from the lesson you liked best, and explain why you prefer it.

Unit VI Expressing Feelings and Imagination

83 Wishes and Daydreams

Understanding Art

1. Explain the meaning of *abstract.*

Creating Art

2. Did you make a picture expressing an idea, wish, or daydream?
3. Describe how you expressed your idea.

Appreciating Art

4. Look at the pictures by Burchfield and Miró in the lesson. Choose the one that seems most like a wish or daydream to you, and explain why you think so.

84 Demons and Dragons

Understanding Art

1. Explain the meaning of *mythical beast.*
2. Tell where artists get their ideas for drawing mythical beasts.

Creating Art

3. Did you create a drawing, painting, or sculpture of a mythical beast from your own imagination?
4. Describe the special features you gave your mythical beast.

Appreciating Art

5. Identify which of the imaginary animals shown in the lesson you think is most unusual, and explain why.

85 Fantasy Tower

Understanding Art

1. Explain the meaning of *fantasy.*

Creating Art

2. Did you create a fantasy tower from your own imagination?
3. Describe your fantasy tower.

Appreciating Art

4. Describe what you think is really strange or interesting about your tower.
5. Tell what kind of creature or person might live in your tower.

86 Storytelling with Art

Understanding Art

1. Explain what *illustrators* do.

Creating Art

2. Did you illustrate part of a story you like? What story did you choose?
3. What characters and part of the story did you illustrate? How does your illustration portray the action in the story? Explain what is happening in the scene you illustrated.

Appreciating Art

4. Tell what part of your illustration you think is most successful.

5. Look at the picture by Edward Hicks in the lesson. Describe the scene you think might have happened right before that scene, or the scene that might happen next.

87 Comic Art

Understanding Art

1. Explain the meaning of *cartoon art.*

Creating Art

2. Did you make up a simple story and illustrate it in a comic strip?
3. Did you exaggerate or distort any features of your characters? If so, tell what you exaggerated and why.
4. Tell what action you emphasized in each frame.

Appreciating Art

5. Identify the television or newspaper cartoon feature you like best, and tell what you like about it.

88 Splat! Bonk! Varoom!

Understanding Art

1. Describe *Pop art.*

Creating Art

2. Did you choose a word and draw a picture of what you imagined might be happening if you heard that sound?

Appreciating Art

3. Explain how the sound word in your picture fits into the whole design.
4. Describe how the images in your artwork portray sound. Does your picture look like cartoon art, a concrete poem, Pop art, or a style of art uniquely your own?

89 Surprise and Fun in Art

Understanding Art

1. Explain the meaning of *caricature.*

Creating Art

2. Did you create a piece of artwork designed to surprise people?
3. Explain what colors, designs, or combinations you used to create your surprising artwork.

Appreciating Art

4. Look at the artwork in the lesson by Klee and Oppenheim. Tell which artwork you think is most surprising, and explain why.

90 The Eyes Have It

Understanding Art

1. Give two examples of ways eyes have been used in art.

Creating Art

2. Did you create an artwork in which the eyes are the most important part?
3. Describe how you emphasized the eyes in your artwork.

Appreciating Art

4. Describe the feeling you tried to communicate with the eyes in your artwork.

91 A Feeling of Peace

Understanding Art

1. Explain how different people might interpret the word *peace.* How do you define it?

Creating Art

2. Did you draw a picture that illustrates your meaning of the word *peace?*
3. Tell how you illustrated your feeling of peace, and explain why you chose to illustrate it that way.

Appreciating Art

4. Explain why you agree or disagree with the captions about the two artists' pictures of "peace" in the lesson.

92 Feelings That Are Opposite

Understanding Art

1. Explain what might be useful about studying opposite feelings and ideas.

Creating Art

2. Did you make two works of art that show feelings that are opposite?
3. Explain how your two artworks are different. Point out specific contrasts in shape, color, texture, size, details, expressions, and so on.

Appreciating Art

4. Tell which piece of art in the lesson you think best expresses a feeling or mood. Explain why you think so.

93 The Original You

Understanding Art

1. Explain the meaning of *style* in art.

Creating Art

2. Did you make an artwork that shows your own artistic style?

3. Tell which materials you used, and why you chose them.

Appreciating Art

4. Explain what you think is best about your artwork. Tell how it characterizes your particular style or personality.
5. Name the artwork in this lesson that seems most original to you, and explain why you think so.

94 The Sun as a Symbol

Understanding Art

1. Name three ways the sun has been portrayed in art.
2. Explain the meaning of *symbol.*

Creating Art

3. Did you make a piece of art that shows your idea of the sun? Was it realistic, or symbolic?

4. Describe how you used art materials to create your sun.

Appreciating Art

5. Explain the meaning of the sun in the art you created for this lesson.

95 Mexican Influences on Art

Understanding Art

1. Describe the contemporary Mexican style of art.

Creating Art

2. Did you create a piece of art in the style of Mexican artists or artists from another culture? Was the style you used from the past or present?

Appreciating Art

3. Explain how you used art ideas and styles from Mexico or another culture.

Glossary

abstract A style of art that uses shapes, designs, textures, and colors to depict an object in a way that may not look real but that emphasizes moods or feelings. Abstract art often uses geometrical shapes and bold, bright colors.

additive sculpture Making sculpture by adding, combining, or building up materials. Modeling with clay and welding steel parts together are forms of additive sculpture.

advertising Printed, painted, or spoken art that communicates positive aspects of a product or idea to an audience in order to persuade them to do or buy something.

analogous colors Colors that are closely related, such as blue, blue-violet, and violet—all of which have the color blue in common. Families of analogous colors include the warm colors (red, orange, and yellow) and the cool colors (blue, green, and violet).

architect A person who designs buildings and gives advice to builders about their construction.

armature A skeleton-like framework used to support constructions of clay or papier-mâché. It can be made of wire, piping, metal rods, rolled paper, or similar materials.

assemblage /ə-sem′-blij/ A piece of art made by combining a collection of three-dimensional objects into a whole. It can be either a free-standing sculpture or mounted on a panel, and is usually made from scraps, junk, or various man-made or natural objects.

atmospheric perspective A way of showing depth and distance in a painting by using fading colors and hazy details in distant objects. (*See also* linear perspective.)

background Parts of artwork that are in the distance and appear behind the objects in the foreground.

balance A principle of design that refers to the arrangement of elements in a work of art. There are three kinds of balance: symmetrical (formal balance); asymmetrical (informal balance); and radial (from the center).

banner A long flag that is hung on a pole or carried stretched out by two people. It may have a sign, name, or slogan written on it, as a banner that comes before a marching band in a parade.

Baroque /bə-rōk′/ A style of art that stresses fancy swirling curves, large works of art, elaborate detail and ornamentation, and dramatic contrasts of light and shade. The Baroque period followed the Renaissance in Europe during the 1600s.

blind contour drawing A kind of drawing made in one continuous line, keeping your pencil going and your eyes on the object without looking down at your paper. (*See also* modified contour drawing.)

block A piece of thick, flat material, such as cardboard, wood, or a potato, with a design on its surface, used to print repeated impressions of that design.

block printing A way of making a design, pattern, or other print on a material such as paper or fabric by using a block.

block relief A means of making prints by creating a raised design on a flat surface. The design is inked or covered with color and stamped on paper or another surface.

brayer /brā′-ər/ A small, hand-held rubber roller used to spread printing ink evenly on a surface before printing.

calligraphy /kə-lig′-rə-fē/ The art of writing letters and words in an ornamental style using brushes or pens.

caricature /kar′-a-kə-chər′/ A picture in which a person's distinctive features, such as nose, ears, or mouth, are distorted or exaggerated.

cartoon art The kind of art used in comics or cartoons. It usually has simple lines, uses basic colors, and tells a story in one picture or a series of pictures drawn in boxes called *frames.*

cartoonist An artist who draws pictures to make people laugh, tell a simple story, or point out problems in society.

carve To cut away unwanted parts from a block of wood, stone, or other material, using sharp tools such as a chisel, knife, or file. *Carving* is a way of making sculpture by cutting away unwanted parts.

cast To copy a solid object by pouring a liquid, such as melted metal, clay, wax, or plaster, into a mold and letting it harden. The mold is then removed and a copy, or *cast,* is left in the shape of the mold.

centaur /sen′-tor/ An imaginary animal that is half man and half horse.

center of interest The most important part in a work of art. All the other parts should center around, provide background for, or draw attention to the center of interest.

ceramics The art of making and decorating objects of clay that are fired in a kiln.

chisel A metal tool with a cutting edge at the end of a handle. Chisels are used by sculptors for carving stone, wood, and other materials. Some pens used in calligraphy have tips that are shaped like a sculptor's chisel.

clay   A powdery kind of earth that becomes pliable and can be molded when it is mixed with water or oil. Clay is used to make pottery and sculpture.

coil   A long rope-like shape that may be wound into a spiral. Clay coils can be used to make pottery.

collage /kə-läzh′/   A work of art created by gluing bits of paper, fabric, scraps, photographs, or other materials to a flat surface.

color   The hue, value, and intensity of an object. The *primary colors* are red, yellow, and blue; every color except white can be created by combining these three colors. Color is an important element of design.

compass   A mechanical tool that has two hinged, adjustable legs for drawing different sizes of circles and arcs. One of the legs has a sharp steel point that is placed on one spot on the paper. The other end holds a pencil that rotates around the pointed end, making a circle.

complementary colors   Colors that are opposites on the color wheel and contrast with each other. For example, orange is the complement of blue, violet is the complement of yellow, etc. When two complementary colors are mixed together, they make brown or gray. When they are used side by side in a work of art, they create interesting contrasts.

compose   To create or form by putting together and arranging.

composition   The arrangement or design of elements of an artwork to achieve balance, contrast, rhythm, emphasis, and unity and to make it an effective expression of the artist's idea. The term refers to any work of art.

concrete poetry   A kind of poetry in which meaning is reinforced by the visual shape of the poem on the page and the use of words to make a picture.

x **contour**   The outline or edge of a figure or object. In contour drawing, a single line is used to draw the outline of an object.

contrast   A large difference between two things; for example, hot and cold, yellow and purple, and light and shadow. Contrasting patterns or colors add excitement, drama, and interest to a picture.

cool colors   The family of related colors ranging from the greens through the blues and violets. (*See also* analogous colors.)

creative   Able to design or make something new and original, using the imagination rather than imitating something else.

critique   To analyze and evaluate an artwork, making judgements of its merit, value, meaning or relevance, technique, and design. The word also refers to such a written or spoken evaluation.

x **cross-hatching**   Shading done by drawing closely set parallel lines that crisscross. Cross-hatching is

used to show light and shadow in drawings, paintings, and engravings.

cylinder   A round shape with two flat ends. Cans and pipes are cylinders.

decorate   To add ornaments such as lines, colors, shapes, and textures to objects to make them look better.

depth   The third dimension of front to back or near to far, represented in an artwork by the actual or apparent distance from bottom to top or front to back. *Techniques of perspective* are used to create the illusion of depth in a two-dimensional painting.

design   An organized and creative arrangement of the elements of an artwork, such as lines, shapes, textures, spaces, and colors.

diameter   The distance across a circle, measured through its center.

dimension   A measurement of either length, width, or depth. Two-dimensional art, such as a painting, has length and width. Three-dimensional art, such as sculpture, includes depth.

distort   To change the way something looks to make it more interesting or meaningful, usually by twisting it out of its proper or natural form or by exaggerating some of its features. A work of art that is made in this way is *distorted.*

dominant   The part of a design that is most important, powerful, or has the most influence. A certain color can be dominant, and so can an object, line, shape, or texture.

drawing   A major art form in itself, drawing may be either an artwork that stands on its own, having shapes and forms sketched and/or shaded on paper, or it may be the basis for a painting or sculpture.

x **elements of design**   Basic parts which are put together to compose an artwork. These include line, shape, space, texture, color, and value.

embroidery   Decorative designs sewn on cloth with a needle and thread or yarn.

x **emphasis**   Accent, stress, or importance of a part of an artwork. Opposing sizes, shapes, and lines, contrasting colors, closer detail, and intense, bright color are all used to emphasize, or draw attention to certain areas or objects in a work of art. Emphasis is a principle of design.

enlarger   A machine used in photography to make pictures smaller or larger.

etching   A picture made by coating a paper, metal, or plastic plate with wax and cutting or scratching a design into the wax. A print of an etching can be made by covering the plate surface with ink and pressing it onto paper or another flat surface to transfer the design.

fantasy   Something unreal that is invented by the imagination.

fiber arts   The range of handicrafts created with

such materials as yarn, thread, and cloth. Stitchery, macramé, and weaving are among the common fiber arts.

fibers Threads or strands that make up a material and give it texture.

fire To bake shaped clay in a hot kiln to make it into hard pottery.

fixative A thin liquid that is sprayed over pastels and drawings to keep them from smudging or rubbing off the paper.

folk art Traditional art made by people who have not had formal art training but whose art styles and craftsmanship have been handed down over the generations.

foreground The part of a work of art that appears to be in front, nearest to the viewer.

form The organization of masses, shapes, or groups of elements in an artwork; the plan or design of a work of art; unit in an artwork that is defined or set apart by a definite contour; to give shape to an artwork.

frame One of a series of boxed pictures in a comic strip.

free-form Irregular; asymmetrical; not formed according to any preset rules or standard design.

freehand Drawing done without using tracing paper, ruler, compass, or any other drawing instruments.

functional Practical or useful.

genius A person with extraordinary intelligence and creativity.

geometric Based on simple shapes such as squares, triangles, or circles.

gesture Quick, scribbled drawing to capture the basic form and indicate the main movement of lines in a figure. Also, body positions and expressions shown in a work of art.

glaze A glasslike coating applied to the surface of pottery or ceramics by dipping or painting it on, and then fired in a kiln to produce a hard colored shiny or matte surface.

glue A sticky solution used to join surfaces together.

gradation /grā-dā′-shən/ A gradual, smooth change from light to dark, rough to smooth, or one color to another.

graphic design A category of art that includes designing packages, signs, and advertisements; illustrating ads, magazines, and books; cartooning; and making any kind of art for reproduction.

grid Horizontal and vertical lines drawn on a piece of paper, dividing it into equal squares. An artist uses a grid to copy pictures by drawing what is in each of the squares separately.

guild An organization of people in the Middle Ages who all did the same kind of work. Merchants, painters, sculptors, and other craftsmen each had their own guilds.

haiku An unrhymed Japanese verse form of three lines containing 5, 7, and 5 syllables respectively.

horizon A level line where water or land seems to end and the sky begins.

hue Another word for *color,* such as red, yellow, or green.

illustrator An artist who creates designs and pictures for books or magazines to explain the text or show what happens in a story.

imagery The imaginative expression of objects, feelings, ideas, and experiences in art. Imagery can depict both physical and nonphysical things.

Impressionist An artist who tries to show the effects of light on different things, especially color. Impressionists use unblended dots of pure color placed close together to create a mood or *impression* of a scene.

intensity The brightness or dullness of a hue or color. For example, the intensity of the pure color blue is very bright; if a lighter or a darker color is added to blue, the intensity is less bright.

invent To create something new that has never been made before by using imagination and creativity.

jewelry Ornaments that people wear, like rings, necklaces, bracelets, or earrings, often made of precious metals and gems.

kiln /kil or kiln/ A special oven or furnace that can reach very high temperatures and is used to bake, or *fire,* clay.

knead To prepare clay by working and pressing it by hand.

landscape A picture of natural outdoor scenery, such as mountains, rivers, flowers, fields, or forests.

line An element of design that refers to a path of a moving point through space which can vary in width, direction, movement, length, curvature, and color. Lines can be two-dimensional or implied, or they can define three-demensional contours.

linear perspective /lin′-ē-ər pər-spek′-tiv/ Showing depth and distance in a picture with converging lines. In linear perspective, lines that are parallel in nature get closer together and objects get smaller in the distance. (*See also* atmospheric perspective.)

logo A symbol that identifies a business, club, or other group. Logos are often made of a few artistically drawn letters or shapes. (*See also* trademark.)

loom Any type of framework used for weaving fibers at right angles to make cloth.

mallet A type of hammer with a large blunt, barrel-shaped head, often made of wood. Sculptors use a mallet to hit against a chisel when cutting wood, stone, or another solid material.

mat A cut-out cardboard border placed around a picture to display it.

media Materials, such as paint, charcoal, and clay, that an artist uses. Also the techniques, like painting, sculpture, or collage, used with these materials. Plural form of *medium.*

medieval /mēd-ē′-vəl/ From or characteristic of the Middle Ages in Europe, A.D. 500–1500.

medium The material an artist uses—oil, watercolor, pen and ink, chalk, and so on. (*See also* media.)

Middle Ages The period of time between A.D. 500 and A.D. 1500 in Europe. (*See also* medieval.)

modified contour drawing A line drawing made by looking at an object and drawing it with one continuous line, occasionally glancing down at the drawing to check the lines and proportions. (*See also* blind contour drawing.)

mold A hollow shape that is filled with a material such as plaster or metal and removed when the material hardens into the shape of the mold. A mold is used to make one or many copies of an object.

monochromatic color scheme Variations of one color in an artistic composition. A pure hue is combined with varying amounts of white or black, producing tints and shades respectively. (*See also* tint *and* shade.)

monogram A design made from the initials of a name. Monograms are often printed on caps, ties, shirts, towels, handkerchiefs, and linens.

monoprint A simple printing process that produces only one copy. Many techniques can be used to transfer the design to paper, but the same design cannot be printed more than once.

mount To attach a picture to a larger piece of paper or cardboard, leaving a wide border all around it.

movement A principle of design that refers to the arrangement of elements in an artwork organized in such a way to create a sense of motion.

mural A very large, permanent painting that covers a wall. It can be painted directly on the wall, or on wood or canvas to be attached to the wall.

mythical Made-up, invented, or imaginary. Mythical animals, people, and objects usually originated in ancient legends or myths.

narrative Telling a story or idea. Much art, such as drawings in picture books, comics, magazines, and newspapers, is narrative.

nearika /nā-är-ē′-kà/ A kind of art that originated in early Mexico in which colored yarn or string is glued on a background to form a solid design.

nib A point that fits on the end of a calligraphy pen and regulates the flow of ink. Nibs come in many sizes from very thin or fine to broad and flat.

nonfunctional Created mainly for decoration rather than practical use.

opaque /ō-pāk′/ Something that cannot be seen through; the opposite of transparent.

original Unusual, different, or creative, such as original art or ideas. Original can also mean the actual or initial work of art, rather than a copy.

overlapping One shape or part covering up some part or all of another. Overlapping objects appear closer, and this is a perspective technique used to show distance in pictures.

painting Artwork made using oil tempera, watercolor, acrylic, or other kinds of paint, applied with a brush or other tool. The term also refers to the act of creating such an artwork.

papier-mâché /pā′-pər-mə-shā′/ An art material made of paper torn into strips or made into pulp and mixed with paste or glue. It can be molded into various shapes when wet and produces a solid material that is quite strong when it dries. It is used to make molds of decorative and functional objects. The term is French for *chewed paper.*

parallel Two or more lines that are the same distance apart at every point, extend in the same direction, and never converge, or meet.

pattern The repetition of shapes, lines, or colors in a design. A pattern can also be a model or mold designed to be copied.

pendant A piece of jewelry that hangs around a person's neck, usually on a chain.

pennant A small triangular flag.

perspective The representation of three-dimensional objects on a flat, two-dimensional surface. Perspective is achieved by creating a sense of depth and distance. There are two types of perspective: linear and atmospheric.

photographing Taking pictures with a camera.

photography The process of creating art with a camera and film. Photography may be used to capture exact, realistic images or to create more abstract or impressionistic moods.

pigment Fine colored powder that, when combined with various liquid mixtures (water and a binding agent, for example), makes paint.

plane Any surface that is flat. Most sculpture surfaces are made up of many tiny planes, joining to form flat or curved sides.

Pop art A style of art based on the everyday, popular things around us, like comic strips, popular foods, and brand-name packages. The style developed in the 1950s and 1960s, mainly in New York and London.

portrait A painting, sculpture, drawing, photo, or other work of art showing a person, several people, or an animal. Portraits usually show just the face, but can include part or all of the body, as well.

primary colors The hues red, yellow, and blue, which in different combinations produce all other colors except white. The primary colors cannot be produced by mixing any other colors together.

principles of design Rules that aid in effectively arranging and composing designs. These include balance, contrast, variety, pattern, rhythm, emphasis, and unity.

print A shape or mark made from a printing block or other object that is covered with ink or paint and then pressed on a flat surface, such as paper or cloth. Most prints can be repeated over and over again by reinking the printing block. Prints can be made in many ways, including using an engraved block or stone, transfer paper, or a film negative. *Printing* is the art of making many copies of one image.

printing press A machine that can make printed copies by pressing an inked or colored metal plate containing lines of type or an image onto sheets of paper that are threaded through the machine. Printing presses are used to make books and newspapers, as well as copies of original art.

printmaking Designing and producing prints using a printing block, woodcut, etching, lithographic or photographic negative. (*See also* print.)

profile An outline of an object, usually a drawing or painting of the side view of a person's face.

proportion The relationship of the size of parts of the body to each other and to the whole. In painting and sculpture, for example, an artist tries to achieve the right size or *proportion* of a nose to a head, and a head to a body.

protractor /prō-trak´-tər/ A piece of wood or plastic shaped in a half or full circle and used to measure angles.

radius /rād´-ē-əs/ The distance between the center of a circle and the outer edge.

rasp A kind of file that has sharp, rough teeth that can cut into a surface. It is used in sculpture and ceramics to shape materials such as wood, clay, and plaster.

ratio /rā´-shē-ō/ The relationship in size or quantity between two or more things. For example, the ratio in height of an object two feet tall to an object one foot tall is 2 to 1.

realistic Looking like real people, objects, or places as we actually see them. Realistic art portrays lifelike colors, textures, shadows, proportions, and arrangements.

rectangle A shape with four straight sides and corners that meet at right angles.

relief An art mode that is halfway between solid sculpture and flat painting, in which figures rise up from a background that is flat or has hollowed-out parts.

Renaissance /ren´-ə-säns/ A period that began in Italy after the Middle Ages and lasted from about A.D. 1400 to 1600. The period was characterized by a renewed interest in ancient Greece and Rome and their philosophies, including an emphasis on human beings, their environment, science, and philosophy.

repetition Repeating lines, shapes, colors, or patterns in a work of art.

resist A type of art in which oil or wax, which will not mix with water, is used to block out certain areas of a surface that the artist does not want to be affected by paint, varnish, acid, or another substance.

rhythm Regular repetition of lines, shapes, colors, or patterns in a work of art.

ruler A flat piece of wood or plastic with a long, straight edge marked off in units of measurement, used for measuring and drawing straight lines.

scale Ratio of the size of parts in a drawing or artwork to their size in the original. If a picture is drawn *to scale*, all its parts are equally smaller or larger than the original.

scale drawing A reproduction of a drawing in which the dimensions and sizes are in the same ratio as in the original. Scale drawings are usually made by using a grid and can be smaller, larger, or the same size as the original.

score To cut into, but not all the way through, paper or thin cardboard in order to make a line where it will bend easily. *Scoring* is often done with an X-acto knife. Also, in clay work, to make small grooves or scratches in pieces of clay to be joined together. Scoring and applying slip to the roughened surfaces creates a firm bond that holds the pieces together.

sculpture A carving, model, or other three-dimensional piece of art.

secondary colors Colors created by combining two of the three primary colors, red, yellow, and blue. The secondary colors are orange, green, and purple: orange is a mixture of red and yellow, green a mixture of blue and yellow, and purple a mixture of red and blue.

set square A wood or plastic triangle used in technical drawing to make angles, shapes, and lines.

shade A color to which black or another dark hue has been added to make it darker. For example, black added to red produces a darker *shade* of red. (*See also* tint.)

shading Showing gradations of light and darkness in a picture by darkening areas that would be shadowed and leaving other areas light.

shape A spatial form depicted in two-dimensions and outlined by lines or a change in color, shading or materials. Shape is an element of design.

silhouette /sil-ə-wet´/ An outline of a solid shape without any details inside, like a shadow. Most silhouettes are of a person's profile, done in black or another dark solid color, and attached to a light background.

slab A thick, even plate or slice of clay, stone, wood, or similar material. Pottery may be made from a clay slab that is modeled and formed into shape.

slip A creamy mixture of clay and water or vinegar used to cement two pieces of clay, such as a handle and cup, together, or for dripping on pottery as decoration.

slogan /slō′-gən/ A short, attention-getting phrase used in advertising to promote a product.

slot A narrow opening or slit through which a tab of paper is threaded to join it to another piece of paper.

slotting A way of joining pieces of paper by cutting slits in one piece and threading tabs of paper from another into them.

space An element of design that refers to the visual or actual area within and around shapes and forms. Positive space defines the contents of a shape or form, bound by edges or surfaces. Negative space refers to the area around a shape or form.

sphere A round, three-dimensional shape. Balls, the sun, and the earth are spheres.

stained glass Pieces of brightly colored glass held together by strips of lead to form a picture or design. Stained glass was first used in churches during the Middle Ages.

statue A carved, modeled, or sculpted three-dimensional figure, especially of a person or animal, that stands up by itself.

still life A drawing or painting of an arrangement of nonmoving, nonliving objects, such as fruit, flowers, or bottles. Usually, a still life is set indoors and contains at least one man-made object, such as a vase or bowl.

stitchery A kind of artwork in which designs or pictures are made by stitching yarn, thread, string, or other materials to a fabric backing.

studio The place where an artist or designer works.

style An artistic technique or way of expressing, using materials, constructing, or designing that is characteristic of an individual, group, period, or culture. For example, the style of Egyptian art is different from the style of the Japanese.

subtractive sculpture Making sculpture by removing material from a large block or form. Marble, wood, and soap carving are some types of subtractive sculpture.

symbol Something that stands for something else, especially a letter, figure, or sign that represents a real object or idea.

symmetrical /sə-me′-tri-kəl/ Having a kind of balance in which things on each side of a center line are identical. For example, the two halves of a person's face are symmetrical.

tab A tongue of paper cut to fit in a slot in order to join sheets of paper or two ends of the same sheet. (*See also* slot.)

tactile Relating to the sense of touch; the way an artwork feels to the touch.

tapestry /tap′ə-strē/ A picture or design woven or stitched in cloth and hung on a wall.

tempera /tem′-pə-rə/ A thick, opaque paint made of powdered colors mixed with a medium to make it adhere and water.

template /tem′-plət/ A flat, stiff shape used as a pattern or guide for drawing shapes that are neat and uniform.

textile /tek′-stīl/ A piece of woven cloth; fabric. Cotton, velour, silk, polyester, and burlap are examples of textiles.

texture The way a surface looks and feels—rough, smooth, silky, and so on.

theme A subject or topic in an artistic work. A theme may be concrete—such as a realistic painting of a landscape—or abstract, such as a painting using symbols of change.

theme and variations A series of artworks composed on a single subject showing several interpretations or versions of it. The picture of the basic subject is the theme, and the later forms or versions are the variations.

three-dimensional Having length, width, and depth. A sculpture is three-dimensional, but a drawing is only two-dimensional since it is flat and has only length and width, not depth.

tint Lighter variation of a color produced by adding white to it. For example, white added to blue makes a lighter blue *tint*.

title The name given to a picture, sculpture, or other piece of artwork, reflecting the main idea of the work.

tone The tint, shade, brightness, or value of a color.

trademark A special design, name, or symbol that represents a company or business. Most trademarks are registered with the government and cannot be used by anyone else. (*See also* logo.)

transparent Allowing light to pass through so that objects can be clearly seen underneath; the opposite of opaque. Window glass, cellophane, and watercolors are transparent.

T square A long, flat ruler that is attached to a short crosspiece, making a T-shape. The crosspiece slides along the edge of a drawing board to position the ruler so that parallel lines can be drawn.

unified Having all parts look as if they belong together in a complete whole.

unity A principle of design whereby all parts of a work of art are interrelated, balanced, and organized to achieve a quality of oneness.

value The lightness or darkness of tones or colors. For example, white and yellow have a light value and black and purple have a dark value. Value is an element of design.

variety Different types or an assortment of lines, shapes, or textures in a work of art. Variety is a principle of good design.

viewfinder A small window in a camera or cut in a piece of paper that shows what will be in a photograph or picture.

visual Able to be seen and not just heard. For example, visual advertising includes TV commercials, billboards, magazine ads, and posters.

visualize To form a picture of something in the mind by using the imagination.

visual memory Being able to remember exactly what something looks like. A good visual memory is important to an artist, who may not always have the object to be drawn available as a guide while working.

visual texture See **Texture.**

warm colors The family of related colors ranging from the reds through the oranges and yellows. (*See also* analogous colors.)

warp The vertical threads that are attached to the top and bottom of a loom, through which the weft is woven. (*See also* weft.)

wash The background of a watercolor picture, prepared using thin, watery paint applied quickly with large, sweeping brushstrokes.

watercolor A transparent paint made by mixing powdered colors with a binding agent and water. The term also refers to a painting done with watercolors.

weaving The interlacing of yarn or thread to make cloth.

wedging Cutting, pounding, and kneading clay to mix it and knock air bubbles out until it has a smooth and even texture and is ready to use.

weft The threads or strands of yarn that are woven back and forth across the warp threads to make a solid textile. (*See also* warp.)

yarn A strand-like fiber made of cotton, wool, or a man-made material and used for stitchery, weaving, knitting, and appliqué.

Artists' Reference

All the artists and artwork presented in this book are listed here. Use this list to locate particular paintings and to find works by artists who especially interest you.

256

Index

Acknowledgments

We gratefully acknowledge the generous efforts of the art supervisors, consultants, teachers, and students all over the country and other parts of the world who have helped to make this book possible. Although it is impossible to list all of the contributors to this project, we express special thanks to the following individuals: Kay Wagner, Fine Arts Specialist, and Lou Moody, Fine Arts Resource Teacher, San Diego City Schools; Claire Murphy; Mary Lou Heilman; Sam Bonacci; Charlotte Gardner; Bob Long; Margie Kleinman; Sue Anello; Dorothy Tucker; Monique McNutt; Rebecca Crandall; Don Guentner; Billie Golden; Roberta Harmon; Mar Gwen Land; Penny Felton; Sherely McPhillips; Margaret Mardis; Allan Caucutt; Tom Convoy; Antony Guadadiello; Barbara Beattie; John Benitez; Charles Bonnett; Barbara List; Debbie Ewing; Mary Howell; Gene Wozniak; Lee Riggs; Marjorie Hughes; and Leven Leatherbury.

We especially appreciate the students from the following schools who contributed the student art reproduced in this book: Lenape Jr. High School, Doylestown, Pa.; Alexandria Jr. High School, Fort Wayne, Ind.; Rancho San Joaquin Middle School, Irvine, Calif.; Benton Central Jr. High School, Oxford, Ind.; Tecumseh Jr. High School, Lafayette, Ind.; Edmonton Art Gallery Classes, Edmonton, Alberta, Canada; Children's Creative and Performing Arts Academy, San Diego, Calif.; Children's Saturday Art Class, Indiana University, Ind.; Azalea Middle School, St. Petersburg, Fla.; Montgomery Jr. High School, San Diego, Calif.; San Diego High School, San Diego, Calif.; Holy Ghost School, Rochester, N.Y.; Maple Dale School, Wisconsin; Lewis Jr. High School, San Diego, Calif.; Tuba City Jr. High School, Tuba City, Ariz.; Spring Hill Middle School, Knoxville, Tenn.; Southside Jr. High School, Columbus, Ind.; Boone Junior/Senior High School, Boone, Iowa; Lewis Cass School, Walton, Ind.; Bedford Jr. High School, Bedford, Ind.; Martin Luther King Jr. High School, Jersey City, N.J.; Shelbyville Jr. High School, Shelbyville, Ind.; Standley Jr. High School, San Diego, Calif.; Whittle Springs Middle School, Knoxville, Tenn.; Ahlya Intermediate School, Khartoum, Sudan; Woodside Middle School, Fort Wayne, Ind.; Northside Jr. High, Columbus, Ind.; St. Joseph Hill Academy, Staten Island, N.Y.; Meridian Middle School, Indianapolis, Ind.; Gompers Secondary School, San Diego, Calif.; Eastwood Jr. High School, Indianapolis, Ind.; Keystone Middle School, Indianapolis, Ind.; Powell Jr. High School, Mesa, Ariz.; Westland Jr. High School, Indianapolis, Ind.; Southport Middle School, Indianapolis, Ind.; Madison High School, San Diego, Calif.; American Fork Jr. High School, American Fork, Utah; Homecroft School, Indianapolis, Ind.; Salem Middle School, Salem, Ind.; Pershing Jr. High School, San Diego, Calif.; Oak Hill Jr. High School, Converse, Ind.; Martinsville East Middle School, Martinsville, Ind.; Christenberry Middle School, Knoxville, Ind.; Muirlands Jr. High School, La Jolla, Calif.; Warsaw Middle School, Warsaw, Ind.; Memorial Jr. High School, Houston, Tex.; Evans School, Evansville, Ind.; Thompkins School, Evansville, Ind.; Calexico High School, Calexico, Calif.; Albert Einstein Jr. High School, San Diego, Calif.; Steven V. Correia Jr. High School, San Diego, Calif. Mowat Junior High School, Lynn Haven, Fla.; C.W. Lon Middle School, Atlanta, Ga.; Jenkins Middle School, Haines City, Fla.; and Correia Special Education Department, San Diego, Calif.